PALM BEACH COUNTY *at* 100

OUR HISTORY, OUR HOME

THE PALM BEACH POST | HISTORICAL SOCIETY OF PALM BEACH COUNTY

Fireworks light the sky along Flagler Drive during the 2005 SunFest in West Palm Beach. The first SunFest was held in 1983.

Greg Lovett
The Palm Beach Post

PALM BEACH COUNTY *at* 100

OUR HISTORY, OUR HOME

JAN TUCKWOOD
EDITOR

REBECCA VAUGHAN
DESIGNER

J.D. VIVIAN
COPY EDITOR

ELIOT KLEINBERG
TIMELINE WRITER

HISTORICAL RESEARCH

DEBI MURRAY
Director of Research and Archives
Historical Society of Palm Beach County

RICHARD A. MARCONI
Curator of Education
Historical Society of Palm Beach County

BRENNAN M. KING   MAPS
RAY GRAHAM   PHOTO COORDINATOR
RANDALL LIEBERMAN   MEMORIES COORDINATOR

James W. Prichard/The Palm Beach Post

PAST, PRESENT, FUTURE: This photograph of the space shuttle Endeavour soaring over the Jupiter Inlet Lighthouse captures two symbols of Palm Beach County's progress. The lighthouse, completed in 1860, is the oldest existing structure in Palm Beach County. The space shuttle lifted off from Kennedy Space Center at 10:06 p.m. on Nov. 30, 2000. Endeavour and its five-member crew delivered solar-energy equipment to the International Space Station. Pratt & Whitney, which has had a plant in Palm Beach County since 1958, produces the turbopumps for the shuttle's three main engines. After launch, the turbopumps deliver liquid fuel to the engines at a rate that would drain a standard residential swimming pool in less than 25 seconds.

Printed in the United States of America

1st printing 2009

Library of Congress Control Number: 2009931255

ISBN: 978-0-578-02541-4

Printed by Ellison Graphics, Jupiter, Florida

SUSTAINABLE
FORESTRY
INITIATIVE

Certified Chain of Custody
Promoting Sustainable
Forest Management

www.sfiprogram.org

The SFI label applies to the dust jacket and text portions of this book

CONTENTS

Paying heed to history

By JAN TUCKWOOD | The Palm Beach Post

History smacks you in the face sometimes — when it arrives with a Cat 3 wind, for example, or hangs by a chad.

Usually, though, history sneaks up on you.

It's like wisdom and wrinkles — it takes time to seep in and settle, and often you don't know you're making history until the passage of years sharpens the view.

"It's like getting old," Judge Marvin U. Mounts Jr. told me years ago, during one of our many discussions about the importance of Palm Beach County's past. "One day, you catch a reflection of yourself, and you think: 'I'm old! How did that happen?'"

History sneaks in like that.

Nobody appreciated local history more than Judge Mounts, whose father, "Red," was the county's first agricultural agent. When Judge Mounts retired from the circuit court in 2002, he had been the longest-sitting elected official in the county and one of the longest-serving judges in Florida.

He was devoted to restoring the county's 1916 courthouse and turning it into a history museum, and he was adamant that *The Palm Beach Post* recognize the county's centennial in a proper way.

So he started calling me — around 2000 — and reminding me: "Don't forget, Jan, Palm Beach County turns 100 in 2009."

It's a big deal, he'd say. Pay attention. Don't let it sneak by.

Then he'd tell a story or two about how history happened here. Like one weekend in the early 1960s, when County Commissioner Lake Lytal removed the signs that said "white" and "colored" from the drinking fountains at the Palm Beach County Courthouse.

"When everyone came to work on Monday, this miraculous change had occurred," Judge Mounts recalled.

But that miracle didn't make the headlines. The larger importance of

JUDGE MARVIN MOUNTS: Like his father, Judge Mounts adored tropical plants and filled his yard in West Palm Beach with them. (Marvin "Red" Mounts Sr. was the county's agricultural extension agent from 1925 to 1965, and Mounts Botanical Garden is named for him.) Judge Mounts died in 2004 at age 71. "He was really the consummate county historian," said Harvey E. Oyer III, former chairman of the Historical Society of Palm Beach County.

Lytal's simple act took time to sink in.

History happened again in 1947, when Reggie Stambaugh graduated from Palm Beach High School. Nobody realized, however, that history had happened — not even Reggie himself — until 1970, when Palm Beach High integrated and the school's name was changed to Twin Lakes.

By then, Reggie had become a prominent local eye doctor, but his gift to history was his own vision: that Palm Beach High School should live on.

Stambaugh and other alumni, including Burt Reynolds' football coach, Bobby Riggs (Class of 1943), gathered up all the school trophies and yearbooks and decided the school needed a museum.

Today the Palm Beach High School Museum is on Flagler Drive in the oldest building in West Palm Beach, a funky little structure with a cone-shaped roof that originally was the Dade County State Bank.

By the early 1990s, when Twin Lakes had closed and school board members wanted to bulldoze the old

EVA BURKHARDT JACKSON: A member of the pioneering Burkhardt family, Eva (center) poses with two friends on Palm Beach, 1914. Her great-granddaughter, Carynn Jackson, re-creates her pose in 2009 (right). Carynn cherishes the fact that she and her great-grandmother attended high school on the same campus. "It means a lot to me," she said. "It seems rare to find families in Palm Beach County who have been here 10 years, let alone more than a century."

DR. REGGIE STAMBAUGH: As a player for the Palm Beach High School Wildcats in 1946 (above) and in later years. Dr. Stambaugh died in 2007 at age 77.

Palm Beach High, Dr. Stambaugh rallied alumni again.

"No," he said. "You're not going to tear down our heritage."

And they didn't. Because Reggie and his classmates paid heed to history.

When *The Palm Beach Post* asked readers for their memories of growing up in Palm Beach County, some wrote about headline-making history, like hurricanes. But most wrote about simple joys: spending carefree days at the beach, saving up six RC bottle caps to get into the "summer fun shows" at local theaters, hanging out at The Hut.

These are the shared memories that bond a community and turn a town into a *hometown*.

"Newcomers think that everybody in Palm Beach County just showed up yesterday," said Reggie, a fifth-generation Floridian. "But some of us have been here a long time."

The Burkhardt family has been here a particularly long time — since 1893. Eva Burkhardt, born in 1895, went to Palm Beach High, soon after it opened on "the hill" in 1908.

Nearly 100 years later, her great-granddaughter, Carynn Jackson, went to class in the very same building, which today is part of the restored and magnificent Dreyfoos School of the Arts.

That building is a tangible link from one generation to the next. So is the

Richard and Pat Johnson Palm Beach County History Museum, housed inside the renovated 1916 courthouse.

This book, too, is a tangible symbol of the intangible and enduring love that Palm Beach Countians have for their history and their home. It is dedicated to the memory of Judge Marvin Mounts and Dr. Reggie Stambaugh — because I promised I wouldn't forget.

And to Carynn Jackson and all the young people of Palm Beach County today and tomorrow — so that they, too, will remember.

Jan Tuckwood has been an editor at The Palm Beach Post since 1986. She is a proud graduate of Lake Worth High School, the oldest continually operating school in Palm Beach County.

The Palm Beach Post

RECORDING HISTORY, MOMENT BY MOMENT

'WERE YOU HERE WHEN …?'

Asking that question is how most of us personally relate to history.

Were you here when the 1928 Hurricane hit?

Or when the freighter Amaryllis beached off Singer Island in 1965?

Were you here when the "missing link" of Interstate 95 finally opened in 1987, and driving from Palm Beach Gardens to Jupiter became a breeze?

The Palm Beach Post has been here.

We began recording the daily history of Palm Beach County in 1916. The forerunner to *The Post* — the weekly *Palm Beach County* — arrived earlier, in 1909, the same year that Palm Beach County was formed.

Our sister newspaper, the *Palm Beach Daily News*, started documenting the world-famous town of Palm Beach even earlier, in 1897.

Newspapers serve a unique role in history. We exist to ensure a better future — to inform residents and to speak for those whose voice would otherwise be muted. But all the news we cover is in the past, and the most comprehensive and detailed record of Palm Beach County's history can be found in only one place: the archives of *The Palm Beach Post*.

That's why *The Post* partnered with the Historical Society of Palm Beach County to produce this one-of-a-kind history book, which has been recognized by Palm Beach County's leaders as the official centennial book.

Palm Beach County at 100: Our History, Our Home recaps the top stories of the past century. It also provides a sentimental journey, and lessons for the future, from those who were there.

Were you here when …?

If so, lucky you, to have spent so much time in Paradise.

If not, read on. It has been an astounding, and exciting, 100 years — and *The Post* will be here, ready to record the milestones of our second century.

ALEX TAYLOR
Publisher, 2009

Here for you,
Yesterday, Today and Tomorrow.

The Palm Beach Post offices on Datura Street in 1927.

Almost as long as hardy souls have been journeying to this paradise, we at The Palm Beach Post have been here to report on it. From monumental world events to the news of your neighborhood, in print and online, we're proud to be the home page of paradise. Every day.

The Palm Beach Post

FLORIDA

Palm Beach County

WHAT IS PALM BEACH COUNTY?

By SCOTT EYMAN | The Palm Beach Post

FLORIDA ALWAYS HAS BEEN A PLACE FOR DREAMERS —

whether they're in pursuit of eternal youth or great fortune, of endless sunshine or good times.

No place has embodied more of these pursuits than Palm Beach County.

From its beginnings, as a glorified gleam in Henry Flagler's eye, it has been a place where money collided with poverty, where the agrarian butted up against the urban.

And let's not forget sheer size.

The county is large — a total land and water area of 2,386 square miles, the third largest county in Florida, both in size and population. As a result, it can encompass every imaginable sort of group without any one parcel of people feeling cornered.

If Chicago is a pretty petticoat on the fringe of an ordinary skirt — the lakeside is stunning, but as you move inland, the terrain gets progressively plainer — then Palm Beach County is as colorful and patterned as a Lilly Pulitzer shift.

If you ask folks in Southampton about Palm Beach County, they'll talk about the Everglades Club or the Bath & Tennis Club. If you ask farmers, they'll say we're all about sugar. And if you ask retirees from New Jersey who live in a condo in Boynton Beach, they'll say Palm Beach County is a nice suburban neighborhood with too many strip malls.

And they'll all be absolutely correct.

Palm Beach County is all these things — and in the extreme.

TO THE EAST IS PALM BEACH, an iconic name known the world over, where almost every household earns $200,000 and up and more Rolls-Royces are found than any other spot in America.

To the west is Belle Glade, where most families make less than $10,000, and many residents struggle to survive, just as they have struggled for 100 years.

This vast divide — of wealth, ethnicity and lifestyle — once prompted West Palm Beach artist Ann Norton

PALM BEACH COUNTY IS ...

Richard Graulich/The Palm Beach Post

FAMOUS

Flagler, Vanderbilt, Phipps, Kennedy ... and Trump! Palm Beach County has been the winter home of business titans since Henry Flagler's first hotel opened in 1894. Donald Trump's Palm Beach address, Mar-a-Lago, is most famous of them all. "There's nothing like it," says Trump, posing in April 2009 in his living room. "It's a masterpiece." Trump bought the estate in March 1986, renovated it and turned it into the private Mar-a-Lago Club.

... and FABULOUS

Marjorie Merriweather Post built Mar-a-Lago in 1927 as her personal party palace, and Donald Trump's additions — ballroom (top of photo), spa and more — have kept the champagne and charity money flowing. "She'd be so happy to see what we've done," says Trump, who adds that Mar-a-Lago was set to be demolished when he bought it. "Of all the homes in Palm Beach, this is the most important for two reasons: Marjorie Merriweather Post and the architecture. By saving it, I think I've done a great service to Palm Beach, to Florida and to the country."

Eliza Gutierrez/The Palm Beach Post

ABUNDANT ...

The rich soil of the Glades has lured farmers for generations. George Wedgworth's parents, Herman and Ruth, arrived in Belle Glade in 1930. Eight years later, they owned a 320-acre vegetable farm, a packing plant and a fertilizer plant. They were building an ice plant when Herman was crushed under an ice machine in 1938. Under Ruth's leadership, Wedgworth Farms grew into 7,300 acres of sugar cane and 10,500 acres of pasture. Son George (left) is founder and president of the Sugar Cane Growers Cooperative of Florida. His children (from left) Katie, Dennis and Keith keep the farming tradition alive.

to sum up Palm Beach County in this simple way: "The Intracoastal Waterway is the widest body of water in the world."

Palm Beach is less than 50 miles from Belle Glade — but it might as well be 50,000 miles.

A book like this could be written about any number of the county's distinct areas — from Palm Beach, Jupiter and Boca Raton, in the east, to Belle Glade, Pahokee and South Bay in the west. That is how colorful and diverse Palm Beach County is.

To take one example at random:

Clewiston, just west of the Palm Beach County line in Hendry County, was the idea of one Alonzo Charles Clewis. He was the great-grandfather of novelist Ted Bell, who lives in Palm Beach.

Clewis, a banker — he founded the Exchange National Bank in Tampa — had the bizarre notion that sugar could be produced in Florida. He sent agricultural specialists to take soil samples. Would it work in the Everglades? The answer was a resounding "yes." Soon afterward, a railroad extended from Tampa to the Everglades.

Sugar became a major Palm Beach County industry — a nod to progress but an eventual challenge to the natural

John J. Lopinot/The Palm Beach Post

After Henry Flagler, the most prominent county developer was the brash and eccentric John D. MacArthur, who founded Palm Beach Gardens in 1959 and was famous for saving trees. Here, he welcomes a 60-foot Norfolk pine to the grounds of his Colonnades Hotel on Singer Island in the early 1970s.

... and BOLD

glory of the Everglades.

It would be contrary to history to pretend that much of the fuel for Florida's growth hasn't come at the expense of some of the rich natural beauty and resources that have drawn people here in the first place. But that's the price of success.

ONE WAY TO DEFINE PALM BEACH COUNTY is by the people who formed it, from the nearly forgotten Alonzo Clewis to the revered Henry Flagler to the quirky John D. MacArthur. MacArthur — who served as the bridge between Flagler and today — has sometimes been ignored by history because, though his achievements were upscale, he was resolutely down-market.

A billionaire thanks to his insurance business, MacArthur worked out of a coffee shop at the Colonnades Hotel, which he owned on Singer Island, and dressed like a beachcomber outfitted in the finest JCPenney. He bought what became Palm Beach Gardens from a bankrupt developer, then went to work.

"I've got a bushel basket full of money," he would tell people. "Dip in and take what you want. But you have to be honest with me." (By "honest," he meant "accountable.")

MacArthur tried to persuade Walt Disney to locate his planned Florida theme park in Palm Beach County. In the 1960s, Disney came down and spent several days with MacArthur. It was midsummer and hot.

MacArthur took Disney to Leyton's, a fishing station on the Intracoastal Waterway right across from where the marina is now in Riviera Beach. It was the end of the day, and although Disney enjoyed

PALM BEACH COUNTY IS ... SPRAWLING ...

By the real-estate boom of 2004, the western suburbs of Wellington lured residents to developments like the vast Olympia. "It's becoming as big as a metro area," says County Commissioner Jess Santamaria, who was a major developer in Wellington and Royal Palm Beach from 1982 to 2002.

Looking for the country life? It's getting hard to find in Palm Beach County, but polo greats such as Nacho Figueras find a horse haven in Wellington, where polo lures stars from around the world each winter.

Greg Lovett/The Palm Beach Post

Bill Ingram/The Palm Beach Post

and SPECTACULAR

a drink now and then, neither he nor MacArthur wanted to be taken advantage of in a business deal. So both were cold sober. They opted for RC Cola.

At that point, MacArthur said, "Do you like to swim?" When Disney said yes, MacArthur took off all his clothes and jumped nude into the Intracoastal. Not to be outdone, Disney took off his clothes and jumped in, too. Two of the richest men in the world, skinny-dipping in the Intracoastal, might cause a rumpus in other places. Palm Beach County? Not so much.

Disney ended up getting a better deal farther north, in Orlando. But MacArthur kept the cards moving around the table, and he prided himself at playing the local game better than the locals played it. His parting shot was always, "You sons of bitches have heard enough from an old man."

To see the things that Flagler and MacArthur saw in scrub and swamp and sand, you had to be a romantic —

with that quality of belief in self and dreams that lies deep in the American grain, no matter how grim the immediate circumstances might be.

Because of those men, whose desires were more elaborate and better-funded than those of most of us who have come here over the decades, Palm Beach County is a microcosm of America. There is no demographic that isn't part of our neighborhoods. We're a sampling for some future Noah's Ark, all organized neatly into subsets.

PALM BEACH COUNTY'S SECOND CENTURY begins at a daunting time: The twin engines that drove Florida for a century — real estate and tourism — are struggling. The state that once attracted countless sunseekers because it was a cheap place to live and visit can't make that claim anymore.

Nevertheless, peeking around the

corner is a fresh batch of dreamers: scientists at the new Scripps Research Institute at Scripps Florida and at other biotech companies. Will biotech become the next commercial engine for Palm Beach County — the way Pratt & Whitney and IBM were in the 20th century?

The odds are good. When former Gov. Jeb Bush lured Scripps President Richard Lerner to Palm Beach County in 2003, Lerner liked what he saw — because what he saw was beautiful. Palm Beach County reminded Lerner of Scripps' headquarters in La Jolla, Calif.: sunny, lovely, warm in every sense of the word.

His dream was big: to use science to help people feel younger, healthier, happier. He picked the very same place that has lured dreamers for 100 years, and he chose wisely.

Palm Beach County has always been a great place to live.

No. The *best* place to live.

Palm Beach County is ...
HOME

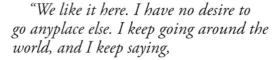

Barbara and Jack Nicklaus

Photo by Jim Mandeville
Provided by the Nicklaus Family

"We like it here. I have no desire to go anyplace else. I keep going around the world, and I keep saying,

'You know, I've seen a lot of places, but I've never seen a better one.'"

— JACK NICKLAUS,
Palm Beach County resident for almost 50 years

Palm Beach County is ...

Where summer spends the winter, and you wish you were here ...

Almost every morning after breakfast, my four brothers (Tommy, Joey, Bobby and Johnny); my cousin Woody; our neighborhood pals (the Salmons, Doyles, Griffins and Riccis); and I would go straight to the beach. It was our playground.

We would surf and skim-board all day long. When we needed to rinse off, we would simply jump into the pool at the Racquet Club, the Rutledge Inn or the Colonnades Hotel. We were unofficial guests.

When we got hungry, we would go home, and my mother would make us peanut-butter-and-jelly sandwiches. We wore no shoes, no shirts and no hats — nothing but our "Birdwell Beach Britches," which were handsewn by Mrs. Butterworth at the Juno Surf Shop.

It was our daily uniform. We were a roving band of surf rats.

We were all as brown as a coffee bean, with peeling noses and shoulders, and heels as hard as leather. In the background was the music of the Beach Boys, Beatles and Rolling Stones. It was a wonderful time to grow up in Palm Beach County. It was truly an endless summer.

— WILLIAM E. JOHNSON

Johnson's grandfather, Archie Raymond Johnson, was one of the early pioneers of West Palm Beach; and his father, Tom Johnson, served as state attorney of Palm Beach County, state senator and circuit court judge. Johnson is an attorney in West Palm Beach, where he practices law with two of his brothers. He is married to Judge Laura Johnson. They have three children and live in Jupiter.

William Johnson grew up across the street from the ocean on Singer Island. "There was no development on the beach back in the 1960s except for a handful of mom-and-pop motels," he recalls. "Riviera Beach was a small fishing village, and the main road of travel in Palm Beach County was U.S. 1. My mother did her grocery shopping at the Piggly Wiggly, and we carefully timed our trips to the mainland because the two-lane drawbridge would rise on the half-hour." Days were spent in the sand and on the water. Above, Bill, 8 (left), and brother Bobby, 7, get neck-deep. Right, Bill (left) and older brother Joey at the Buccaneer Yacht Club in Palm Beach Shores in 1966.

Even in hard times, the good times seem near ...

More than just a pretty face, with all the sun you'll need ...

I was born in South Bay and grew up in Belle Glade at a time of innocence. We drove to the beach for entertainment. That was our big trip — to Lake Worth Beach or Phipps Park. I moved to Wellington in 1980, back when Wellington was like Belle Glade: undeveloped and sports-oriented. My husband and I have traveled all around the world, but wherever we go, we can't wait to come back. Why? Because Palm Beach County is home.

— JEANNETTE BUSS CEARLEY

(At left): "In 1958, I won the Miss Harvest Queen Pageant, which got me interested in pageants. After I graduated from Belle Glade High School, I moved to West Palm Beach and worked for Southern Bell. The guys in the engineering department donated blood to have me entered in the Palm Beach County Blood Bank Pageant. Gloria Swanson came to the Bazaar International shopping plaza to crown me the queen. I ended up winning 11 titles and went to the Miss Florida competition, where I won Miss Photogenic. This photo was taken along the Intracoastal Waterway in West Palm Beach, around where Phillips Point is now."

The center of our social universe in the 1950s was the Sunset Lounge in West Palm Beach. They had a balcony for seating, and the bandstand was upstairs, which made a big dance floor below. It was very nice inside. All the different clubs held their affairs there.

— MARY LOPEZ

(Above): Mary Lopez, now 80, can't recall if she won the Bathing Beauty Pageant in 1949 or '50. But she does remember where the pageant was held: the Sunset Lounge, Eighth Street and Henrietta Avenue, West Palm Beach. The Sunset featured top black entertainers — including Count Basie, Duke Ellington, Buddy Johnson and James Brown — along with pageants, proms and pot-luck dinners.

And if you grew up here, you feel lucky, indeed ...

Palm Beach County is ...

one of the largest and most diverse counties in America.

At the same time, it is both historic and modern ...

... For thousands of years, indigenous peoples occupied what is today Palm Beach County. Yet our major population growth and economic development have occurred only in recent decades.

... Our population includes some of the wealthiest people on Earth, as well as some of the most economically challenged areas in America.

... We are known worldwide for The Breakers, Worth Avenue and the opulent winter homes of our nation's great industrialists. Nevertheless, our western agricultural fields provide much of America's winter vegetables, cut flowers and sugar.

... The rocket engines that allowed the United States to win the space race were developed here; the personal computer was invented here; and our future will likely be linked to bioscience, thanks to Scripps Florida and Max Planck Florida.

In one short century, Palm Beach County has moved from the frontier of civilization to the launching ground of innovations that are leading the advancement of the human race.

— HARVEY OYER III, fifth-generation Palm Beach County native and former chairman of the Historical Society of Palm Beach County (2002-2009)

Official birth date: July 1, 1909
Palm Beach County was carved out of Dade County, which, at that time, stretched from the St. Lucie River to the southern tip of the Florida peninsula.

County population in 1910: 5,577
County population in 2008: 1,294,654 (estimate)

Race

White	73.3%
Hispanic or Latino of any race	16.7%
Black	15.6%
Other	11%

Source: U.S. Census Bureau, 2007 American Community Survey

Religion
Catholic: 300,456 (23.2%)
Jewish: 274,000 (21.2%)
Southern Baptist and other Evangelical Protestant: 103,789 (8%)
United Methodist, Episcopal and other Protestant: 51,270 (4%)
Other or none: 561,373 (43.4%)

Source: Association of Religion Data Archives, North American Jewish Data Bank

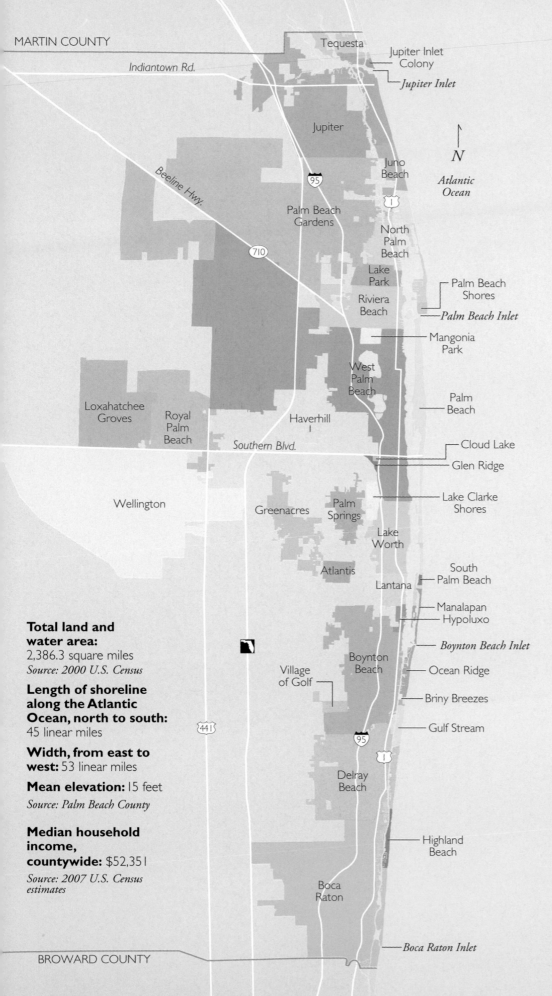

MARTIN COUNTY

Indiantown Rd.

Tequesta

Jupiter Inlet
Colony

Jupiter Inlet

Jupiter

Beeline Hwy.

Juno
Beach

*Atlantic
Ocean*

Palm Beach
Gardens

North
Palm
Beach

Lake
Park

Riviera
Beach

Palm Beach
Shores

Palm Beach Inlet

Mangonia
Park

West
Palm
Beach

Palm
Beach

Loxahatchee
Groves

Royal
Palm
Beach

Haverhill

Southern Blvd.

Cloud Lake

Glen Ridge

Lake Clarke
Shores

Wellington

Greenacres

Palm
Springs

Lake
Worth

Atlantis

Lantana

South
Palm Beach

Manalapan

Hypoluxo

Boynton Beach Inlet

Village
of Golf

Boynton
Beach

Ocean Ridge

Briny Breezes

Gulf Stream

Delray
Beach

Highland
Beach

Boca
Raton

Boca Raton Inlet

BROWARD COUNTY

**Total land and
water area:**
2,386.3 square miles
Source: 2000 U.S. Census

**Length of shoreline
along the Atlantic
Ocean, north to south:**
45 linear miles

**Width, from east to
west:** 53 linear miles

Mean elevation: 15 feet
Source: Palm Beach County

**Median household
income,
countywide:** $52,351
*Source: 2007 U.S. Census
estimates*

Population
Palm Beach County
1,294,654

Atlantis	2,147
Belle Glade	17,141
Boca Raton	85,293
Boynton Beach	66,671
Briny Breezes	417
Cloud Lake	164
Delray Beach	64,220
Glen Ridge	262
Greenacres	32,548
Gulf Stream	716
Haverhill	1,553
Highland Beach	4,164
Hypoluxo	2,448
Juno Beach	3,674
Jupiter	49,783
Jupiter Inlet Colony	370
Lake Clarke Shores	3,427
Lake Park	9,112
Lake Worth	36,725
Lantana	9,850
Loxahatchee Groves	3,232
Manalapan	354
Mangonia Park	2,223
North Palm Beach	12,530
Ocean Ridge	1,630
Pahokee	6,352
Palm Beach	9,797
Palm Beach Gardens	50,282
Palm Beach Shores	1,418
Palm Springs	15,500
Riviera Beach	35,150
Royal Palm Beach	31,567
South Bay	4,702
South Palm Beach	1,522
Tequesta	5,898
Village of Golf	266
Wellington	55,076
West Palm Beach	103,663
Unincorporated	562,807

*Source: 2008 estimates,
University of Florida*

Palm Beach County is …

GOLDEN

As the sun sets, birds fly over Clear Lake in West Palm Beach.

A century ago, Clear Lake defined the western border of West Palm Beach.
Okeechobee Road was unpaved, and the lake ran right up to the road. Today,
most people get their view of Clear Lake while they're driving along a bustling
Okeechobee Boulevard or the Interstate 95 overpass.

Photo by Bill Ingram/The Palm Beach Post

Palm Beach County is …

ETHEREAL

This surreal scene was taken during a stormy day at Boynton Beach Inlet.

'During the photo shoot, the weather was cold and windy,' recalls the photographer. 'My camera was sprayed with salt water from the waves hitting the rocks. It also was cloudy. I could not shoot the sunrise, so I shot the rocks and the ocean.'

Photo by Ruel P. Tafalla, first-place winner of The Palm Beach Post *Nature Photo Contest, 2007*

Palm Beach County is …

SWELL

Surfers take to the water on Jupiter Beach
early one morning during the Jupiter Pro-Am
Fall Classic surfing contest in 2008.

Michael 'Corky' Roche, who grew up on Singer
Island, has surfed the waves off Palm Beach
County since 1966. 'Back then, if a swell snuck
in, you had a chance to surf uncrowded waves.'

Photo by Brandon Krusel/The Palm Beach Post

Palm Beach County is ... TRANQUIL

North of bustling Atlantic Avenue in Delray Beach is peaceful Wakodahatchee Wetlands.

True to its Seminole name — meaning 'Created Waters' — Wakodahatchee is a man-made, 50-acre marsh recharged daily with 2 million gallons of wastewater. This photo was taken in January 2007. 'I took this photo at 6 a.m. and the wetlands had a truly magical quality,' the photographer recalls. 'Fog hovered in the distance, bird calls of all kinds filled the air, and I heard the flutter of wings. It was a moment of exceptional beauty.'

Photo by Roxane F. Karr, who lives in North Palm Beach. She received an honorable mention in The Palm Beach Post *Nature Photo Contest, 2007.*

Palm Beach County is ...

ALLURING

Lake Okeechobee attracts anglers from around the world, including these fishermen, who wait for the lake's bounty just after sunrise.

At 730 square miles, Lake Okeechobee is the second-largest freshwater lake located completely within the continental United States (after Lake Michigan). The most popular game fish in Florida — and at the lake — is the largemouth bass.

Photo by Greg Lovett/The Palm Beach Post

Palm Beach County is ...

PARADISE

Two flamingos perform their courtship dance.
The male is on the left.

The flamingos are part of Flamingo Island at
the Palm Beach Zoo at Dreher Park in West
Palm Beach. The zoo houses more than 1,700
animals within 23 acres of lush tropical habitat.

Photo by Taylor Jones/The Palm Beach Post

Palm Beach County is …

One century old, still changing and young.
Look at this road — that was U.S. 1!

Traffic?
What traffic?
Fran Watson
rides her bike
on "the new
U.S. 1"
in Juno Beach
in 1957.

Ocean Terrace, 1951: The Watson
family shows off the new sign for
their motor lodge.

Bill Watson, 1953

In 1947, Mom and Dad — Jim and Fran Watson — bought about 8 acres of oceanfront land along U.S. 1 (now known as State Road A1A) in Juno Beach and got into the tourism business.

The property had a beautiful beach, and the highway was the main road to Southeast Florida. It also had a 20-foot ridge of yellow Florida sand splitting the property, which provided the name for our motor court: Ocean Terrace.

Juno Beach was remote in the early days. In fact, a trip to the nearest grocery store meant going to Northwood Road near central West Palm Beach — some chore for Mom!

In Jupiter, there was virtually no place to shop because its population was about 200. Center Street was a graded, two-lane shell-rock road from Alternate A1A to almost the current intersection with Indiantown Road.

We lived simply in those days. But then, so did almost everyone.

Two things happened in the late '50s that changed Juno Beach: In 1957, Pratt & Whitney Aircraft announced that it would build a huge research and testing facility in northwestern Palm Beach County. And Florida decided to build a new four-lane highway from Jupiter to the Seminole Country Club.

These events prompted a major expansion of Ocean Terrace. Mom and Dad also built a new Gulf service station with three bays. Plus, by this time, our motel had a swimming pool!

— BILL WATSON

Bill now takes his grandchildren fishing at Juno Pier, which is near the site of the former Ocean Terrace motor lodge. The Watsons sold their oceanfront properties in the 1970s, and Bill became a banker. His mother lives nearby, in The Bluffs, in Jupiter. His father passed away in August 1997 at age 80. His son says, "He will be fondly remembered for living a full life — and for being a Juno Beach pioneer."

Ocean Terrace in the early 1960s.

Back in 1952, everybody knew that on the third Thursday of October, the new car models debuted. This was a big deal — a really big deal! It was such a big deal that people wore coats and ties to come see the new cars, and they would go from dealership to dealership to check out the models. We'd serve sandwiches and Coke. (We'd have to hide the new cars until debut day.)

My dad, F. Earl Wallace Jr., had the Ford dealership at Second Avenue and Atlantic Avenue in Delray Beach. A hundred people or more came to see cars like this 1952 Ford Sunliner convertible on the day when Dad introduced the new cars. I was 4.

I think somebody just came in and said, "Let's put that chubby kid in the car and take a picture." Keep in mind — this was before air conditioning, and people dressed up to see the cars. A new convertible was a particularly big deal. If you drove a convertible in 1952, you had it going on!

— BILL WALLACE

What makes a Wallace smile? A new Ford Sunliner convertible! Bill Wallace, 4, poses with his mom, Janet; and his dad, F. Earl Wallace Jr., in 1952.

Bill owns 11 car dealerships in the Stuart area today. He is a third-generation car dealer. His grandfather, F. Earl Wallace, had a Chevrolet dealership in West Palm Beach (on Dixie Highway, near the site of the Carefree Theatre) in the 1930s. His father, F. Earl Jr., worked at the Chevy dealership until he served during World War II. When General Motors diverted work from cars to the war effort, F. Earl Wallace Sr. got out of the car business — until he was lured back to run the Ford dealership in Delray Beach in 1951.

The scenery has changed, but life's still sublime.
Let's put the top down and drive back in time …

1905

1906

1919

1930s

1920

1930

1950

1966

1968

1992

1978

2000

2009

2004

Watermelon Feast in 1914 on Boynton Beach

Historical Society of Palm Beach County

A patriotic party in Boynton Beach. In 1914, the population was around 700.

PALM BEACH COUNTY AT 100

From the beacon illuminating Jupiter Inlet
to the dawn of the biotechnology age

KEY EVENTS THAT SHAPED OUR HISTORY

<1905: Adelina Miron (right) with her friends, the Chadbourne girls. In 1906, Adelina married boat builder Lincoln Holmes, who came to West Palm Beach in 1895.

1906: Thomas Peppers and his wife, Priscilla, with their four daughters in the Styx, a settlement for workers in Palm Beach. Peppers was one of the first black men in Palm Beach, his daughter, Inez, right in photo, recalled in 1994.

1919: The Yamato School near Boca Raton, where children of Japanese settlers attended grades one through eight with local children.

1920: Dr. T.R. Vickers and his son,

Carle, in West Palm Beach. Vickers was one of the area's first black doctors.

1930: Solomon and Jessica Merner of West Palm Beach take a spin in early Palm Beach's favorite mode of transportation: A wicker wheelchair pedaled by a cyclist. They are the grandparents of retired Circuit Judge C. Pfeiffer Trowbridge.

1930s: Gustine and Fanny Geibel in Lake Worth, in a photo taken by their brother, Mike Geibel, who came to Lake Worth in 1924.

1950: Dorothy Wilson sits on the Ford station wagon she and husband Horace owned. She's

posing at their family farm on Okeechobee Road, where an Arrigo car dealership is today.

1966: Mockup of a Pratt & Whitney engine designed for the Supersonic transport. Pratt & Whitney's arrival changed the face of northern Palm Beach County.

1968: Debi , Jill, Chris and Jeff Johansen on Singer Island. Behind them is the Amaryllis, a ship that ran aground during Hurricane Betsy in 1965.

1978: West Palm Beach commissioner Eva Mack. Mack and Ruby L. Bullock became the first blacks elected to the city commission.

Helen Wilkes was elected the first female mayor the same year.

1992: Kravis Center for the Performing Arts opens in West Palm Beach.

2000: County Commissioner Carol Roberts, Judge Charles Burton and Supervisor of Elections Theresa LePore during Palm Beach County's historic election recount.

2004: Hurricane Frances comes ashore. Four hurricanes hit Florida in 2004.

2009: The spire of The Scripps Research Institute at Scripps Florida in Jupiter.

Photos from the Holmes family, the Ineria Hudnell collection, the Mike Geibel collection. the C. Pfeiffer Trowbridge collection, Historical Society of Palm Beach County, Boca Raton Historical Society and The Palm Beach Post

Before 1860

Land of Indians

Pre-1500s:

Hundreds of thousands of Indians live in what will become Florida.

Jeaga, Hobe and Ais lay claim to what is now Palm Beach County and the Treasure Coast.

By the 1700s, they are gone, wiped out by massacres, battles, the slave trade and European diseases.

Late 1700s-1800s:

Seminoles migrate into Florida from Southern U.S.

Three Seminole wars are fought in Florida. The most infamous is the Second Seminole War — the longest and most expensive the white man wages against Native Americans.

Seminole wars

1818: First Seminole War

Gen. Andrew Jackson chases Seminoles across North Florida.

1835-1842:

"Young Tiger": George W. Potter, who moves to Florida in 1873, draws this sketch of "Young Tiger" in 1874 near Miami.

Second Seminole War

Two key battles are fought along the Loxahatchee River in Palm Beach County in January 1838, with the largest single capture of Seminoles — 538 — at Fort Jupiter in February 1838.

U.S. forces build more than 400 forts during the Second Seminole War and clear about 5,000 roads, including what is now Military Trail, to connect them.

1853-1858:

Third Seminole War

This is the last Indian war east of the Mississippi River.

Earliest records

Sept. 23, 1696:

Jonathan Dickinson's journal

A shipwreck strands Quaker Jonathan Dickinson and his family just north of Jupiter. Jeaga Indians start them on their two-month walk to St. Augustine, the closest European settlement. Dickinson's journal is the first detailed account of the region written in English.

1840-1842:

"Lake Worth Region" lures first settlers

Soldiers discover and name Lake Worth in honor of William Jenkins Worth, leader of U.S. forces in the Second Seminole War.

The Armed Occupation Act of 1842 allots 160 acres to anyone who cares for the land for at least five years. At least 21 settlers use the act to apply to settle the region around Lake Worth.

March 3, 1845:

Florida becomes 27th state

1860-1892

Pioneers in Paradise

FIRST, THERE IS LIGHT: Palm Beach County's modern history begins with the Jupiter Inlet Lighthouse, which first lights the shallow waters off the coast in 1860.

Sturdy pioneers brave mosquito-infested swamps — and malaria — to get here. The nearest civilization is 120 miles away, at Titusville.

Eventually, the hardy newcomers tame the last frontier in the Eastern United States — creating a spot of astonishing beauty.

When Henry Flagler arrives in 1893, he declares the area "a veritable paradise."

Timeline compiled by Eliot Kleinberg, The Palm Beach Post, and Debi Murray, Historical Society of Palm Beach County

Jupiter Lighthouse
(circa 1879)

Jupiter Inlet Lighthouse in 1890. This photo was taken from the dock of the Jupiter and Lake Worth Railway — nicknamed the "Celestial Railroad" — the train that took pioneers from Jupiter to Juno and back.

July 10, 1860 Jupiter Lighthouse begins operations

First families settle around lighthouse

Start timeline

Timeline continues >

1860

Population of Florida, according to the U.S. Census: 140,424 (45 percent black), Dade County: 83.

During the early years, there are no roads to the lighthouse; it is surrounded by mosquito-infested swamps. All supplies arrive by sea and are hauled up a wooden slope using oxen and plenty of elbow grease.

Supplies are intermittent because Jupiter Inlet access is frequently blocked by sandbars or storms. The nearest civilization is 120 miles away, at Titusville.

July 28, 1873

First formal homestead claim in Lake Worth Region

Hiram F. Hammon, an Ohioan, files first. Second homestead claim is filed shortly after by Hannibal Pierce, father of Charles Pierce, one of the Barefoot Mailmen and author of *Pioneer Life in Southeast Florida*. Population of the Lake Worth Region is fewer than a dozen.

1861-1865

Civil War devastates Florida

Florida secedes from the U.S. and suffers among the largest economic declines of the Confederate states.

In 1861, Augustus Oswald Lang, assistant keeper of Jupiter Lighthouse and believed to be the first settler on Lake Worth, seizes lighting mechanism to help Confederate blockade runners.

He hides it until after the war. Jupiter Lighthouse finally is relighted on June 28, 1866.

Photos from the Historical Society of Palm Beach County

From left: Margretta M. Pierce, Hannibal D. Pierce (her husband), Andrew W. Garnett, James "Ed" Hamilton, Lillie E. Pierce and Charles W. Pierce. Hannibal and Margretta held the second homestead on the lake. Their property was on the southern end of Hypoluxo Island. Garnett, Hamilton, and Charles Pierce all walked the Barefoot Mailman route to Miami and back at various times. Hamilton died in the line of duty on one of his trips to Miami.

timeline continued

April 1876

Houses of refuge

The federal government opens first of 10 houses of refuge for mariners along Florida's coast, including Gilbert's Bar on Hutchinson Island and Orange Grove in Delray Beach.

The Orange Grove House of Refuge was built in 1876.

Jan. 9, 1878 Providence from the Providencia

Providencia, a 175-ton brig, wrecks in Palm Beach with its cargo of animal hides, logwood and coconuts. Pioneer Will Lanehart later writes, "There were 20,000 coconuts, and they seemed like a Godsend to the people. For several weeks, everyone was eating coconuts and drinking wine." The pioneers planted the coconuts.

1881 Lake Worth Region gets first doctor

Richard Potter was the first medical doctor to settle in what became Palm Beach County.

Hiram F. Hammon, George Potter, Grace Lainhart (little girl standing behind George), Martha Lainhart, Ellen E. Potter and Dr. Richard Potter. Ellen was George and Richard's sister. The Lainharts and the Potters were close friends, and they spent both work and leisure time together.

May 21, 1880 Lake Worth Region's post office is established.

Timeline continues >

1880

First hotel

Elisha "Cap" Dimick opens Lake Worth Region's first hotel, the Cocoanut Grove House.

Elisha N. "Cap" Dimick was one of the area's most influential pioneers. He opened the first hotel, the Cocoanut Grove House, in 1880 and became Palm Beach's first mayor in 1911. He also helped to found the region's first bank, the Dade County State Bank. Today, a statue of Dimick holding his trademark cap — he was called "Cap" because he liked to wear hats — stands on Royal Palm Way in Palm Beach. He died in 1919.

June 1881

First attempt to drain

Hamilton Disston buys 4 million acres of Central and South Florida and begins the state's first large-scale drainage effort.

'Everything looks so promising, we think we will stay here awhile. There are plenty of boats for free use of guests, there is sea bathing, there are ducks, birds and deer in the everglades, which are just beyond the ridge on the opposite side of the lake.'

— *Emma Gilpin, who comes to the Cocoanut Grove House in Palm Beach as a tourist from Pennsylvania, writes this in 1890.*

Sharpies (fishing boats) line the dock at the Cocoanut Grove House in 1890.

Historical Society of Palm Beach County

*In 1880,
the standard
room rate at the
Cocoanut Grove
House, the area's
first hotel, was $2
per day or $10
for the week.*

COCOANUT GROVE HOUSE
LANDING.

PALM BEACH, FLA.

Historical Society of Palm Beach County

The train had to go backward on the return trip north because there was no place to turn around.

July 4, 1889
The Celestial Railroad

The Jupiter and Lake Worth Railway, the first in South Florida, opens, spanning 7 1/2 miles from Jupiter to Juno. It becomes known as the Celestial Railroad, and intermediate stops between Jupiter and Juno are cleverly named Venus and Mars.

The railroad is never larger than three freight cars; two passenger coaches; and one steam engine, called "Old No. 3." Engineer Blus Rice rents out his hound-dog to riders who want to hunt along the route.

March 1886
First schoolhouse

Dade County's first schoolhouse opens in Palm Beach.

1884-1893
Barefoot Mailmen trek the beach

Rugged pioneers carry the mail 136 miles — 56 in boats, 80 on foot — from Jupiter Lighthouse to Cape Florida (now Key Biscayne). A road to Miami in late 1892 ends the careers of the 20 or so Barefoot Mailmen.

The Palm Beach Post

Michael Bornstein walks barefoot down the beach recreating the journey of the Barefoot Mailman.

Historical Society of Palm Beach County

Hattie Gale, the area's first teacher, in the doorway of the first schoolhouse. This schoolhouse was moved to Phipps Park in Palm Beach in the 1960s.

Jan. 5, 1889

The first church, Bethesda-by-the-Sea, opens in schoolhouse. First church building opens in April.

timeline continued

Across
1884 the water

The Rev. Elbridge Gale builds the first log cabin on west side of Lake Worth. First settlers inhabit what is now the Glades area.

Feb. 18, 1889
Juno made county seat

The Dade County seat, which includes what would become Palm Beach County, moves from Miami to Juno.

Dec. 1892
First road to Biscayne Bay Region opens

It runs from Lantana to North Miami.

Why 'Palm Beach'?

It all started with … one wrecked ship,
two creative pioneers, many glasses
of wine and 20,000 coconuts

The most important party ever held here during the winter season was no black-tie affair: It was a humble, wine-soaked beach bash that started on Jan. 9, 1878, when the Spanish brigantine Providencia wrecked along what is now Palm Beach.

The Providencia — a 175-ton, square-rigged brig bound from Carmen, Mexico, to Cadiz, Spain — carried a cargo of 20,000 coconuts harvested from the island of Trinidad.

Since this area's earliest pioneers depended on shipwrecks for supplies, two settlers — William M. Lanehart and his friend, Hiram F. Hammon — eagerly checked out the wreck.

Lanehart later wrote, "I was greeted by the mate of the vessel, with a bottle of wine and a box of cigars, as a sort of olive branch. There were 20,000 coconuts, and they seemed like a Godsend to the people. For several weeks, everyone was eating coconuts and drinking wine."

Lanehart and Hammon sold the coconuts to other pioneers for 2½ cents each. Soon, lush coconut palms dominated the landscape.

When it was time to establish an additional post office in the area (The "Lake Worth" post office was established in 1880), the pioneers had to come up with a name. They chose "Palm City," but that name already was taken.

So their new post office became "Palm Beach" — a name that would soon be associated with the grandest winter resort in the world.

William M. Lanehart (left) and Hiram F. Hammon (right) were pioneers of Palm Beach County and long-time friends.

Lanehart and Hammon partnered on many business ventures, but the sale and planting of the coconuts from the Providencia most affected Palm Beach County.

Photos from the Historical Society of Palm Beach County

1893-1913

The Flagler Era

PALM BEACH COUNTY'S IDENTITY CAN BE TRACED BACK TO ONE MAN: HENRY FLAGLER.

With speed and vision, the Standard Oil tycoon becomes South Florida's first and most influential developer. His railroad and fancy hotels put the area on the map and on the world stage — transforming a tropical wilderness into America's most famous winter playground for the rich.

Paradise has been found — and fortune-seekers become Florida-bound!

Henry Flagler considered this his best photograph and ordered $3,000 worth of copies from photographer E. W. Histed.

1893

Enter Henry Flagler

Flagler visits Palm Beach. He buys lakefront and ocean-front land for $125,000 and the O.S. Porter and Louis Hillhouse family property on west side of the Intracoastal Waterway for $45,000.

First churches for blacks

Tabernacle Missionary Baptist Church and Payne Chapel African Methodist Episcopal churches are founded for blacks living in "The Styx," a shantytown that houses more than 2,000 hotel construction workers in Palm Beach.

The "Styx" was on County Road north of the Royal Poinciana Hotel.

Start timeline

May 1893

Work begins on Royal Poinciana Hotel in Palm Beach

May 11, 1893

Dade County State Bank, first in region, is established on Palm Beach.

August 1893

Henry Flagler lays out the 48-block townsite of West Palm Beach.

In 1890 according to the U.S. Census, fewer than 1,000 people live in all of Southeast Florida, from the tip of Lake Okeechobee to the Keys. By 1900, that number jumps to nearly 5,000. By 1910, Palm Beach County alone has more than 5,000 residents.

Guests lazing on the piazza of the Royal Poinciana Hotel looking over the docks toward West Palm Beach circa 1900.

February 1894

Flagler's grand Royal Poinciana Hotel opens on Palm Beach.

The Royal Poinciana Hotel around 1897.

March 22, 1894

Flagler's Florida East Coast Railway reaches West Palm Beach.

March 25, 1894

Union Congregational Church, first church in West Palm Beach, is founded at Datura Street and Olive Avenue. The first school in West Palm Beach later operates inside the church, with 19 students.

April 11, 1894

Post office established in West Palm Beach.

September 1894

First school for blacks opens at Tabernacle Missionary Baptist Church, at Clematis Street and Tamarind Avenue in West Palm Beach.

timeline continues >

1894

Otto Weybrecht's hardware store was the first building on Clematis Street. He and his family lived in the tent next door. Billy Bowlegs, the Seminole chief, is in the foreground. Mrs. Weybrecht is holding her baby.

First building on Clematis Street in West Palm Beach opens; houses a hardware store.

■ West Palm Beach's "dry" status is lifted; whiskey comes to town, restricted to Banyan Street in West Palm Beach.

■ A water plant is built at Clear Lake.

The Florida East Coast Railroad Bridge to Palm Beach (above) was the second one to be built to the island. The first crossed Lake Worth where the railroad car is resting on all that remained of the original trestle (far left, foreground) in this 1907 photo.

Nov. 5, 1894

West Palm Beach is incorporated

1895

- West Palm Beach's first power plant begins operation.
- Capt. Thomas Moore Rickards and his family are the first settlers in what will become Boca Raton.

Boca Raton Historical Society
Thomas Rickards (center) settled in 1895.

Nov. 16, 1895

First bridge across the lake –

a railroad bridge from around Banyan Street in downtown West Palm Beach — opens.

timeline continued

1895

Maj. Nathan Smith Boynton, William Seelyn Linton and David Swinton arrive to tour the area looking for land to develop. Boynton was a retired Civil War major and former mayor of Port Huron, Mich.; Linton had been postmaster of Saginaw, Mich.; Swinton was a Saginaw bookstore owner.

Nathan Smith Boynton

Nov. 17, 1894

"Flagler Alerts" volunteer fire department in West Palm Beach is organized.

Oct. 18, 1895

Post office established in Linton; changed to Delray on Nov. 19, 1898.

The large building in the center of the background is the Palm Beach Hotel, which opened in 1902. The building to the far right, just hidden by the trees, is the Beach Club, Edward R. Bradley's famous casino.

Historical Society of Palm Beach County

1896

Maps first use spelling of "Boca Raton."
Original plat recorded for town of Linton; now Delray Beach.

First schools in Delray open:

The Linton School, designated School No. 17, opens in spring 1896 at site of present Old School Square. The Census of Youth that year records 33 white children in town (ages 6 through 21). In 1902, the first civic club is established; and, in 1903, the first white church is established in what is now Delray Beach.

■ First school for Delray's black children, called Delray Colored, No. 4, also opens in 1896. Two black churches and a Masonic lodge are established in what is now Delray Beach, from 1896 through 1898.

The Linton School circa 1900.

timeline continues >

Jan. 16, 1896

Henry Flagler opens the Palm Beach Inn. It is expanded in 1901 and renamed The Breakers.

March 15, 1896

Saint Ann, area's first Catholic Church (right), opens at Datura Street and Rosemary Avenue in West Palm Beach.

1897

Holy Trinity, the first Episcopal Church in West Palm Beach, opens.

April 21, 1896

Railroad is completed to Miami.

1898

E.R. Bradley's casino

Col. Edward Riley Bradley opens his famed casino, which operates with impunity until 1945.

May 10, 1899

Palm Beach County seat is returned to Miami from Juno.

Photos from the Historical Society of Palm Beach County

From 1898 to 1945, Edward Riley 'E.R.' Bradley, a racehorse breeder, owned and operated the nation's longest-running gambling casino in Palm Beach. Bradley's was also a dinner club. Floridians could eat there, but they couldn't gamble. Authorities were suspicious of the place, but generally turned a blind eye.

Free Reading Room at the city dock, 1904. This building originally belonged to the Palm Beach Yacht Club in Palm Beach. Donated in 1895 by Commodore Charles John Clarke, it was delivered by barge to the foot of Clematis Street and converted into the first free-standing library. Residents supplied the books to lure workers away from the saloons on Banyan Street.

Nov. 25, 1900

First library building opens in West Palm Beach

It is housed in a two-story lakefront building on Clematis Street.

timeline continued

July 16, 1899

Post office opens in Boca Raton.

Aug. 24, 1900

Post office opens in Boynton Beach.

1901

New rail and pedestrian bridge, at site of present Flagler Memorial Bridge, replaces earlier railroad spur located four blocks south.

Sept. 1, 1902

City fire department (a professional successor to the volunteer Flagler Alerts) is organized in West Palm Beach.

June 9, 1903

The Breakers burns

The 1896 Palm Beach Inn was renamed The Breakers in 1901. This hotel (above) burned to the ground in 1903, and The Breakers was reopened in 1904. The second Breakers also burned down, in 1925, and was replaced in 1926 with the current twin-towered hotel.

Photos from the Historical Society of Palm Beach County

Joseph Jefferson, matinee idol and mogul

Joseph Jefferson, famed actor of the late 1800s, put the spark into West Palm Beach — literally. He owned the first electric plant. Jefferson quoted from the Bible — "Let there be light!" — when he flipped on the electricity for the first time. The actor also owned six houses, the Jefferson Hotel on Clematis Street, a two-story brick building that housed six stores, a store across the street that housed the Anthony Brothers retailers, and the first ice plant. Propelling Jefferson's "Palm Beach coach" (above) is his man Friday, Carl Kettler. Kettler's son, Carl Jr., would later open the grand Bijou and Kettler theaters on Narcissus Street. Jefferson, whose most famous role was as Rip Van Winkle, died in Palm Beach on Easter Sunday, April 22, 1905.

1904 Carry Nation on a mission: If you wanted whiskey, women or trouble in early West Palm Beach, there was just one place to go: Banyan Street, the East Coast's answer to the Wild West. The Banyan bars were so notorious, the famous anti-alcohol crusader Carry Nation hit the street in 1904.

Late 1904

Yamato Colony is founded near Boca Raton

The colony disbands by the beginning of World War II.

Florida State Archives

George S. Morikami is the only settler who stays and continues to cultivate local crops to become a fruit and vegetable wholesaler. This portrait is from 1915.

timeline continues >

West Palm Beach Fire Department, Central Station, at Datura and Poinsettia, with both an engine-driven fire truck and a horse-powered fire wagon.

Sept. 11, 1903

Hurricane strikes region. Nine drown when British steamer Inchulva sinks off coast of Delray Beach. Wreckage now a popular diving spot.

Hudnut's Perfumes—E. T. Moore's Drug Store.

HARDWARE

5	Lake Worth Mercantile Company.
7	McGinley Bros. Company.
47	C. A. Woodruff
75	J. H. Brophy & Company.

HOTELS

3-F	The Tiffany.
23	The Keystone.
54	The Gables.
57	Palms Hotel.
59	Detroit Hotel.
62	Seminole Hotel.
89	Minaret Cottage.
92	The Holland.
95	The Briggs.
	Royal Poinciana
	The Breakers.
119	Earman House
123	Seagle Hotel
154	Palm Beach Hotel.
163	Hibiscus Hotel.

ICE FACTORY

| 67 | Ariston Ice & Electric Company. |

INSURANCE

1	Currie Investment & Title Guaranty Company.
6	B. A. Maxfield
8-C	W. R. Moses.
29	W. I. Metcalf

1912: A page from West Palm Beach's telephone directory.

timeline continued

1909

Central School (right), now the center building on the Dreyfoos School of the Arts campus, opens. It is considered far out of town at the time, and some parents fear for their children's safety. Central School houses all grades, and, later, a junior high and Palm Beach High School buildings are added to this site. C.C. Chillingworth, who later became a well-respected judge who was murdered at sea in 1955, was in the first high-school graduating class in 1913, as was Stetson Sproul, who later became Palm Beach County tax collector.

Calling George Currie? Dial 1!

George Currie (above) — attorney, poet, land developer, cartographer and sixth mayor of West Palm Beach (1901-1902) — got the first two phone numbers when phone service came to town. His office phone number was "1" and his home telephone number was "2."

1905 Telephones!

Telephone company is set up in West Palm Beach. Service is established by 1907, with 18 phones connected.

1906

First settlers inhabit Singer Island (then called Inlet City).

Oct. 28, 1908

Carl Kettler opens Bijou, West Palm Beach's first theater, in the Jefferson Building on Clematis Street.

This 1923 photo shows the second Bijou Theatre, at Clematis and Narcissus, before it was replaced by the Kettler Theatre.

Jan. 3, 1905

Napoleon Bonaparte Broward becomes governor, elected on a promise to drain the Everglades.

1905

First burials occur in Woodlawn Cemetery in West Palm Beach.

Woodlawn Cemetery is built where 17 acres of pineapples once grew.

Photos from the Historical Society of Palm Beach County

Historical Society of Palm Beach County

James A. McCurdy, in a Curtiss aircraft, flies over the Hotel Royal Poinciana in February 1911. It is the first airplane flight in Palm Beach County.

April 30, 1909

Gov. Albert Gilchrist signs bill creating Palm Beach County,

effective July 1, 1909.

Jan. 22, 1912

Henry Flagler opens railroad link to Key West.

Sept. 4, 1911

Delray Beach is incorporated.

April 17, 1911

Palm Beach is incorporated.

Seminole Indians, who lived in the Everglades, were frequent visitors to the coastal towns. "They would bring fresh venison, honey or buckskin to swap for food," pioneer Charles W. Pierce wrote.

Michael Dubiner collection

Main Street in Boynton Beach, 1910

1912

First bridge across Intracoastal Waterway at Delray Beach opens.

1913

■ Delray Beach's school is razed, and a new two-story building opens.
■ First library in Delray Beach opens.
■ First school in western Palm Beach County opens in Canal Point.

May 20, 1913

Henry Flagler dies in Palm Beach.

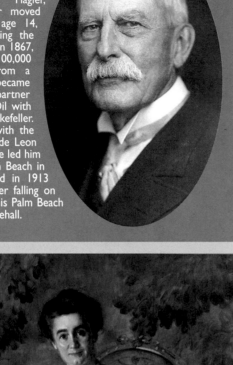

HENRY MORRISON FLAGLER: Born in 1830 in Hopewell, N.Y., to Reverend Isaac and Elizabeth Caldwell Harkness Flagler, Henry Flagler moved to Ohio at age 14, after completing the eighth grade. In 1867, backed by a $100,000 investment from a relative, he became a founding partner in Standard Oil with John D. Rockefeller. His success with the Hotel Ponce de Leon in St. Augustine led him south to Palm Beach in 1893. He died in 1913 at age 83, after falling on the stairs at his Palm Beach mansion, Whitehall.

Photos © Flagler Museum

MARY LILY KENAN FLAGLER: This portrait of Flagler's third wife, which hangs in the Music Room of the Flagler mansion, Whitehall, is notable for her luscious strand of pearls. "She is wearing her (60-inch) opera-length strand of fine Oriental pearls, which Henry Morrison Flagler purchased from Tiffany & Co. for the cool sum of $2 million," said John Loring, design director of Tiffany. He estimates it would be worth almost $40 million today — but it no longer exists as a single strand. It is believed that Mary Lily's heirs divided this strand into several smaller strands after her death in 1917.

THE FLAGLER ERA

THE MAN OF THE CENTURY

By JOHN M. BLADES | The Flagler Museum

Henry Flagler literally invented modern Florida. And, nowhere is Flagler's legacy more evident than in Palm Beach County.

At a time in life when the average man of the late 19th century had reached the end of his life expectancy, Henry Flagler decided to step back from the day-to-day responsibilities of Standard Oil, the company he co-founded. Had he not accomplished another thing for the rest of his life, he certainly would be remembered for his role in what would remain for a century the largest and most profitable corporation in the world. But instead of retiring, Flagler devoted all of his considerable resources and creativity to building Florida.

From St. Augustine to Miami, Henry Flagler built a series of luxury hotels that quickly established tourism as a mainstay of Florida's economy. His Florida East Coast Railway not only connected his hotels but opened the state to growth of all kinds. Through his Model Land Company, Flagler encouraged the agricultural development of millions of acres, thus establishing agriculture as another mainstay of the state's economy. Not content with those accomplishments, Flagler undertook and accomplished the most ambitious engineering feat ever attempted by a private citizen, the building of the Over-Sea Railroad, covering more than 155 miles from Miami to Key West.

Along the way, Henry Flagler fell in love with the Lake Worth area and decided he would build the Hotel Royal Poinciana on the eastern shore of Lake Worth, where a lush grove of coconut palms had grown up following the shipwreck of the Providencia in 1878 with a cargo of 20,000 coconuts. On the western shore of the lake, he established a city he named West Palm Beach, which he hoped would one day become a thriving metropolis larger than Jacksonville. The Hotel Royal Poinciana became the world's largest resort, and Greater West Palm Beach indeed grew into a thriving metropolis

TEA IN THE COCOANUT GROVE: Henry Flagler (in dark suit, center) and his wife, Mary Lily, fourth woman from the left in the white hat, entertain their famous and fabulous friends in the grove of the Hotel Royal Poinciana. The Cocoanut Grove was a hot spot for afternoon refreshments and evening entertainment. *Palm Beach Life* wrote in 1926: "Everyone who is anyone is attending the weekly cakewalks in the Cocoanut Grove. The cakewalks are held every Wednesday evening at nine o'clock and the dancers participating compete in the rigors of the Charleston for an enormous cake of verified delectability."

larger than Jacksonville and the seat of government for one of the largest counties in the Southeast. Around 1900, Henry Flagler decided to build a winter home on the eastern shore of Lake Worth. The home he built was unlike any of his many other homes. It was a home for the Muses, a museum.

Built to evoke an image of a temple to Apollo, Whitehall's public rooms are filled with symbolism related to the Muses of arts and literature. In 1960, Whitehall became a public museum and in 2000, a National Historic Landmark. Today, Whitehall is known around the world as one of America's great historic house museums. But, Flagler's legacy doesn't end there:

■ The park at the east end of Clematis was given to West Palm Beach by Flagler and bears his name as does the drive along the lake.

■ The land the Morikami Museum and Gardens are built on was once farmed by the Yamato Colony, who Henry Flagler attracted to the area through his Model Land Company.

■ The land the Norton Museum is built on was owned by Flagler and later given to West Palm Beach. Likewise, the land the Richard and Pat Johnson Palm Beach County History Museum and the 1916 Courthouse was built on was given to West Palm Beach by Henry Flagler's Model Land Company.

■ The land St. Ann Catholic Church was built on was donated by Henry Flagler. The land the Royal Poinciana Chapel was built on was donated by Henry Flagler.

■ Woodlawn Cemetery was built and given to West Palm Beach by Henry Flagler.

■ The Breakers hotel was established by Henry Flagler. And, the list goes on, and on.

Of all the places Henry Flagler established or nurtured, of all the places

he could have chosen to live and have his greatest impact, he chose the shores of Lake Worth to build the greatest lasting legacy of his amazing life: his winter home and Florida's first museum, the world's largest resort, and a thriving metropolis larger than Jacksonville. And, he gave away thousands of acres for churches, a fire department, a waterworks, a power station, schools, clubs, cemeteries and parks.

While a great many have helped make Palm Beach County the beautiful place that it has become over the last century, the county owes its very existence more to Henry Flagler than to any group of 10 other individuals. More important to Henry Flagler, without a doubt, would be the fact that so many have come to share his love of the place he thought of as "Paradise."

John M. Blades has been executive director of the Flagler Museum since 1995.

Of all the places he could have chosen to live and to have his greatest impact, he chose the shores of Lake Worth to build the greatest lasting legacy of his amazing life: his winter home and Florida's first museum, the world's largest resort, and a thriving metropolis.

THE
GRAND
HALL OF
WHITEHALL

Inside this magnificent mansion, discover the passions of a man

This photo collage captures the Gilded Age glamour of Henry M. Flagler's Palm Beach home, Whitehall, now the Flagler Museum. Photographer John J. Lopinot put together a series of photographs to show the dramatic impact a visitor feels entering into this 5,000-square-foot room topped with its domed ceiling painting of the Oracle of Delphi.

2002 Collage by John J. Lopinot/The Palm Beach

WHITEHALL

© *Flagler Museum*

THEN

Henry Flagler built Whitehall in 1902 as a gift to his wife, Mary Lily. The Grand Hall is spectacular — and larger than any room at George Washington Vanderbilt's Asheville estate, the Biltmore, or any other Gilded Age home.

© *Flagler Museum*

NOW

The scenery has changed in the past century, but Whitehall remains a constant — and a spectacular legacy to the vision of Henry Flagler. It is now the Flagler Museum and one of the most visited and celebrated house museums in America. When Whitehall was built — in an amazing 18 months, for $2.5 million — it was hailed as "more wonderful than any palace in Europe, grander and more magnificent than any other private dwelling in the world." In the past several years, multimillion-dollar renovations have taken the mansion back to the exquisite glamour of Flagler's time — but better. There's now central air-conditioning and a pavilion to protect Flagler's private rail car, which is parked to the south of the mansion. In March 2000, Whitehall was designated a National Historic Landmark.

'Flagler loved technology…

Whitehall had electric lights and a central heating system with controls for each room in 1902. It was modern for its time, with a skeleton of Carnegie Steel…

He was so oriented to the future. This is not a story that's over. It's a story that's just beginning.'

— John M. Blades, executive director of the Flagler Museum, 2002

Photos from the Historical Society of Palm Beach County

Your chariot awaits

See Palm Beach like a tourist (*circa* 1909)

The distinguished folks in the photo above are ready for a big day in Palm Beach. Only a few cars are on the island (and no horse-drawn carriages — the roads are too bad), so many people ride in a "Palm Beach chariot." Mrs. W.K. Vanderbilt (seated) and her husband (far left, holding an alligator) pose with cyclist Lawrence Waterbury and the managers of Flagler's two big hotels — Fred Sterry (far right, manager of the Hotel Royal Poinciana) and Leland Sterry (between the Vanderbilts, manager of The Breakers).

This 1907 Currie Investment Co. map (facing page) and the postcard (below) offer clues as to how people might spend their day.

A day in Palm Beach in 1909 went something like this:

■ By 10 a.m., resort guests — dressed in hat and gloves, coat and tie — head to The Breakers' beach casino to change into bathing attire. Beach rule for ladies: No bare legs. A censor patrols the beach to be sure.

■ By 11 a.m., most guests are out by the ocean, "taking the air."

■ By 1 p.m., they return to the hotel for lunch.

■ Then they rest or hop on a "Palm Beach chariot" — wicker seats atop bicycles, also called "Afromobiles" — and are pedaled down the Jungle Trail. They can visit Alligator Joe's wild-animal farm. Or play tennis at the Hotel Royal Poinciana. Or golf on The Breakers' nine-hole course, even though Flagler thinks golf is "a passing fancy, like ping-pong." Or gamble at E.R. Bradley's Beach Club casino. Or take a ferry over to West Palm Beach.

■ Soon it is time for afternoon tea in the Cocoanut Grove of the Hotel Royal Poinciana. And, then, of course, a lavish dinner and dancing.

Where to Go in a "Palm Beach Chariot"

"Garden of Eden"—three miles—kindly keep to walks while there.
Through the Jungle—five miles. Prettiest, most novel ride in Florida.
Over the long bridge, by chair, to West Palm Beach—two miles.
The Big Maddock and Matthams Pineapple Grove—four miles.
The Famous Everglades and Drainage Trucking Farms.
To the Baseball Grounds. 25 cents.
To the Golf Club House. 25 cents.
To the Gun Club. 50 cents.
To the Bathing Beach, Casino and Swimming Pool, passing en route the Gardens of the Royal Poinciana, Flagler Mansion, the Golf Links and Breakers. 25 cents.
To the Ocean Pier for fishing of all kinds and sharks. 25 cents.
Boat Trip from Palm Beach Hotel to the Inlet, Houseboat and Dr. Munyons' Island. 75 cents.
To the Richard Croker place. To the Spencer "Old Homestead."
To the Alligator Farm and Circus.
To the beautiful McFarlane Avenue to the sea.
To the Palm Beach Farms Company and Everglade Development.
To "Ducks Nest" 35 cents, thence by rowboat across the fresh water lake to the Jungle and Ocean. No charge. Keep to the walk to the left of Cottage.
To the Church. 25 cents.
Last, but not least, ices, tea and sweets "Under the Southern Palms."

Palm Beach Hotel: This hotel ($3 a night) is a more affordable option than Flagler's hotels. (In 1901, a room at The Breakers costs $5, including three meals.)

Hotel Royal Poinciana: Guests take a ferry from these docks in West Palm Beach to Palm Beach.

Lake Trail: Flagler's mansion, Whitehall, is in the background.

Beach Club casino: E.R. Bradley's famous gambling and dining spot is just north of the Hotel Royal Poinciana.

Mule-drawn train car: This car transports guests from The Breakers to the Hotel Royal Poinciana.

MAP ISSU
THE CURRIE INVES
WEST PAL
FLOR
EMIL A. EHMAN
WEST PA

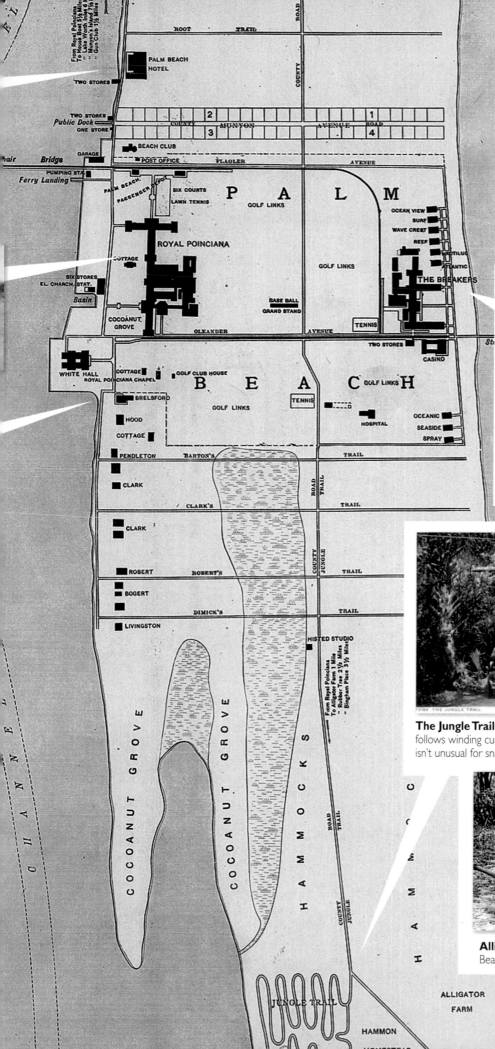

Map labels (Palm Beach):

ROOT TRAIL · ROAD · COUNTY · PALM BEACH HOTEL · TWO STORES · TWO STORES · Public Dock · ONE STORE · 2 · 3 · 1 · 4 · COUNTY · MUNYON · AVENUE · ROAD · BEACH CLUB · POST OFFICE · FLAGLER · AVENUE · GARAGE · Bridge · PUMPING STA. · Ferry Landing · PALM BEACH · PASSENGER · SIX COURTS · LAWN TENNIS · P A L M · GOLF LINKS · OCEAN VIEW · SURF · WAVE CREST · REEF · NAUTILUS · ATLANTIC · ROYAL POINCIANA · COTTAGE · GOLF LINKS · THE BREAKERS · SIX STORES · EL. CHURCH. STAT. · Basin · COCOANUT GROVE · BASE BALL · GRAND STAND · OLEANDER · AVENUE · TENNIS · TWO STORES · Sta. · CASINO · WHITE HALL · COTTAGE · GOLF CLUB HOUSE · B E A C H · GOLF LINKS · ROYAL POINCIANA CHAPEL · BRELSFORD · TENNIS · GOLF LINKS · HOOD · COTTAGE · HOSPITAL · OCEANIC · SEASIDE · SPRAY · PENDLETON · BARTON'S · TRAIL · CLARK · CLARK'S · TRAIL · ROAD · TRAIL · CLARK · ROBERT · ROBERT'S · COUNTY · JUNGLE · TRAIL · BOGERT · DIMICK'S · TRAIL · LIVINGSTON · HISTED STUDIO · From Royal Poinciana To Alligator Farm 1 Mile "Rubber Tree 2½ Miles "Bingham Place 3½ Miles · C O C O A N U T   G R O V E · C O C O A N U T   G R O V E · H A M M O C K S · ROAD · TRAIL · COUNTY · JUNGLE · H A M · JUNGLE TRAIL · ALLIGATOR FARM · HAMMON · HAMMON HOMESTEAD · I N L E T · O C E A N

Garden of Eden: This tropical garden, north of the Palm Beach Hotel, is not on the map.

The Breakers, 1909: Henry Flagler bought the oceanfront Palm Beach Inn in 1896 and renamed it The Breakers. This is the second Breakers hotel. The first burned in 1903. This one burns down in 1925 — and the fire is so furious that sparks blow west and burn down the Palm Beach Hotel, too.

The Jungle Trail: This trail runs alongside County Road and then follows winding curves in an area where Worth Avenue is today. It isn't unusual for snakes or alligators to cross the Jungle Trail.

Alligator Joe: His wild-animal farm is one of Palm Beach's most popular attractions.

Building The Breakers

By ELSIE CLOUGH WEEKS
as told to Randall P. Lieberman

My family arrived in West Palm Beach on Sept. 2, 1925.

Daddy — Waynal Greenleaf Clough — drove a Buick Touring Car down from South Carolina, where Daddy had been a farmer. After boll weevils got into the cotton, Daddy heard there was work in Florida, where The Breakers was being built.

Daddy stopped in Kelsey City, now Lake Park, for gas. The service-station man told Daddy to go over to Arnold Construction Co. and see either J.Y. Arnold or Herman Arnold. The Arnolds put Daddy right to work on The Breakers hotel in Palm Beach.

My mother, Nellie, and my five siblings and I came down by train. Our first Florida home was in a "tent city" at Camp Howard Lake Tent Park at the corner of what is now Okeechobee Road, Parker Avenue and Georgia Avenue. Lots of people looking for work during the Boom stayed there.

We moved to a bigger camp, Bunker's Camp, between Bunker Road and Selkirk Street, at the end of

Singer Island, 1925: Elsie Clough (second from left) with her siblings, two friends and mother Nellie (second from right). They used a lean-to for shelter from the sun. The building in the background is the abandoned Blue Heron Hotel. Paris Singer, heir to the sewing-machine fortune, was building the hotel when the real-estate crash hit.

1926. It was on the west side of Parker Avenue. We had sand floors and picnic tables, and we didn't have beds. I don't know how my mother survived it with six kids and a baby.

Our family moved from Bunker's Camp to 406 Malverne Road in West Palm Beach on March 3, 1928. Rent at that time was "cheap." Mother has a note — "paid on Dec. 15, 1928, $25.00 for rent of December."

We were living on Malverne Road when the 1928 hurricane hit. The roof of our house was blown off and landed in a lot across the street. We never saw my youngest brother, Lloyd, who was only a baby during the hurricane, that whole night. I only recently found out that Mother had tied him with a sheet around my older sister's stomach so he'd be safe.

In the '20s and '30s, money was tight, so we would go to the skating rink on Datura Street, pay 10 cents and watch the skaters. On Saturday afternoon, Daddy (who was known in Palm Beach as W.G.) would take the car to Clematis Street, park, and we would watch the people walking up and down Clematis.

My early memories are fishing, and our picnics on Singer Island and at DuBois Park in Jupiter. A highlight was enjoying the Seminole Sun Dance.

We enjoyed swimming at Gus's Bath and Pier on Palm Beach. There were poles with ropes. You held onto the ropes so that the strong currents didn't take you out into the ocean.

We had fun. We had a good clean life. We didn't have any money, but we thought things were wonderful.

Nellie Clough, Elsie Clough Weeks' mother, at Gus's Baths on Palm Beach, 1926. There was a rope for swimmers to hold while sea bathing.

Clough/Weeks family

The Cloughs' second home in Florida was called Bunker's Camp, between Bunker Road and Selkirk Street on the west side of Parker Avenue, Elsie Clough Weeks recalled. The Clough tent is on the lower right. Many workers lived in tents in the early '20s.

Gertrude Clough, Elsie Clough Weeks' sister, in 1930 in front of The Breakers hotel, which their father, Waynal Greenleaf Clough, helped build.

If Ralph Lauren had photographed
an ad campaign in 1900,
it might have looked like this . . .

beautiful women . . . carefree poses . . .
perfect clothes . . . idyllic scenes

Pretty
IN
PALM BEACH

By JAN TUCKWOOD | The Palm Beach Post

Photos from the Historical Society of Palm Beach County

FUTURE CONGRESSWOMAN, 1899: Frances Payne Bingham first vacationed at Figulus with her parents in winter 1896. She and her husband, Chester Bolton, eventually built a home, Casa Apava, next to Figulus on the family's land. In 1939, Chester died while serving as a Republican congressman from Ohio. Frances finished out his term and then served 14 consecutive terms, until 1969. She was a "formidable woman," recalled Dudley Blossom III, grandson of Frances' sister, Elizabeth.

These photos are the rarest of family snapshots:
Stunning, spontaneous images from the early 20th century.

Making them particularly special are the subjects: The Bingham and Blossom families, who spent winters from 1894 to the 1970s at Figulus, the first privately owned residence built on the ocean in Palm Beach.

George Lainhart — a pioneer carpenter whose business, Lainhart & Potter, is still operating in West Palm Beach — built the wood, shingle-style home for Charles William Bingham and his wife, Mary Payne Bingham. Bingham was a prominent industrialist from Cleveland, who got the idea of wintering in Palm Beach from a business associate, Henry Flagler.

One of the young women pictured here is the daughter of C.W. and Mary: Frances Payne Bolton, who became Ohio's first congresswoman.

Debi Murray is used to rummaging through old family snapshots.

Usually they come to her torn and tattered and piled into shoeboxes.

But when Dudley Blossom III, who winters in Vero Beach, walked into the Historical Society of Palm Beach County, where Murray is director of archives and research, in 2004, he showed her family snapshots of a most amazing kind: Eleven bound albums of spontaneous and stunning images of his ancestors, the Binghams and the Blossoms, hanging out in Palm Beach from 1894 to 1936.

The photos were "lovely, beautiful," Murray said. "The quality was superb, and they've all got names and dates, which never happens."

The photos tell the story of a close-knit family and their friends over a few generations — from girls air-drying their hair on the porch of their Palm Beach home, Figulus, to young fellows boating on the Intracoastal and drinking coconut milk.

C.W. Bingham — patriarch of the clan that spent their first winter in Palm Beach in 1894, the same year Flagler's train arrived — was the brother-in-law of Standard Oil bigwig Oliver Hazard Payne. His daughter, Frances, became the first woman to serve in Congress from Ohio.

Dudley Blossom III's grandmother, Elizabeth, was Frances' sister. Blossom remembers spending idyllic spring breaks at Figulus, which was about a quarter-mile south of Southern Boulevard on the ocean.

"I remember the smells — the jasmine mingling with the orange blossoms and the slightly musty scent of the interior of the house," said Blossom, 68.

When the expenses of upkeep forced his aunt to demolish the house in 1974, Blossom found the transition "very difficult. I recognized that a generation and an old style of life was gone."

To preserve what he could — his family's amazing photographic legacy — he reached out to the Historical Society.

And now the elegance of a grand old age — when ladies played tennis in frilly white gowns and napped on sleeping porches and shook out their long hair to dry — remains alive, captured forever in the pages of 11 perfectly bound albums.

SLEEPING PORCH, 1904: Edith McBride snoozes on a hammock at Figulus, which was about a quarter-mile south of Southern Boulevard on the ocean.

LAZY DAY, 1909: This young woman relaxes in her bathing suit on the porch of Figulus. In the early days, beach censors made sure ladies kept covered while swimming.

FIGULUS, THE ESTATE OF C.W. BINGHAM AND HIS FAMILY IN PALM BEACH, 1894-95: Figulus was a modern marvel in 1894, with large porches, wide overhangs and cross-ventilation to keep the family cool. The wood-frame, shingle-style home was the first private home to be built on the ocean in Palm Beach. Until then, homes were built on the Intracoastal, since most traffic was by water. Fresh water was pumped to Figulus by a windmill northeast of the house, and landscaping was selected by Dr. David Fairchild, namesake of Fairchild Tropical Botanic Garden in Miami.

Winnings at the Beach Club $10.00!

JACKPOT!: A Figulus guest excitedly holds up her winnings from the Beach Club casino: $10. Women gamblers helped make the casino a success.

"OH, HORRORS!": How did young ladies dry their hair in 1905? By shaking it out! This photo shows women identified as "Hettie" and "Julie" drying their hair on the porch of Figulus, the Palm Beach oceanfront home of the Bingham family.

Isn't LIFE GRAND?

Oh, to be a member of society's smart set at the turn of the 20th century!

Palm Beach was the very definition of divine: Ladies "sea bathed" in black stockings, and powerful gents nursed cocktails and cigars at Henry Flagler's hotels.

Everyone was dressed to the nines and corseted to the brink of suffocation — yet their steps seemed light.

At least, that's what one long-ago visitor said in *Palm Beach Life*, the ever-popular journal that has chronicled society hijinks since 1906.

"When one owns a home here, they can smell the delightful odors that come from the trees, the flowers and grasses," the visitor said. "It puts a new vitality into the system, the shoulders are braced a little firmer, and the step is lighter, and the man and woman are again a boy and a girl."

Or perhaps the man and woman indulged in a few too many grapefruit cocktails, known to smart-set sippers as the "forbidden fruit."

Then, as now, *Palm Beach Life* has been there, covering the island's "thrills that are not easily exhausted."

After all, there is just one Palm Beach.

Without it, Palm Beach County would seem dimmer … and definitely less vital.

Society scribes

Back in 1910, the staff of the *Palm Beach Daily News* and *Palm Beach Life* magazine consisted of five people, including Publisher Richard Overend Davies (in the white suit and boater's cap) and Ruby Edna Pierce (center), who joined the paper in 1907 as cashier and then held the position of editor and general manager for more than 40 years. *The Palm Beach Daily News* first began publishing in February 1897, launched by S. Bobo Dean, an Alabama native who had come to Florida in 1892, and his brother Joel. The paper first was called the *Daily Lake Worth News* but by 1899 had been renamed the *Palm Beach Daily News*, then the only daily newspaper between St. Augustine and Key West. In its earliest years, the *Daily News* was a four-page tabloid costing a nickel. The phone number to the paper's offices was 11. The *Daily News* is now owned by Cox Enterprises, the owners of *The Palm Beach Post*.

1908

2008

Good looks are always in fashion. In 1908, *Palm Beach Life's* cover models are "Misses Marion and Evelyn Dean, the Charming Twin Daughters of Mr. and Mrs. John E. Dean of Chicago." In 2008, actor George Hamilton, who went to Palm Beach High School and still has a home here, graces the December cover.

What's a visit to Palm Beach without the *Palm Beach Daily News*? Visitors to Figulus, the oceanfront estate of C.W. Bingham, hold up a copy for the benefit of history. The women in this 1905 photo are identified as (from left): Edith Cook, Betty, Helen Green, Frances and Julia. Frances is Frances Bingham Bolton, who would later become an Ohio congresswoman.

Miss Ruby speaks

Ruby Edna Pierce, the most powerful journalist in Palm Beach from 1907 until the mid-1950s, kept copious records on Palm Beachers, though she never printed a negative word about them. She categorized Palm Beach society this way:

■ Old Guard: They know who they are and don't give a hang if their names never appear in print. They are the ones we prefer to write about, with discretion.

■ The international set.

■ Socialites.

■ The monkey set: They do anything they can to attract attention for they have nothing else to qualify them and, goodness knows, they won't get far with their ridiculous shenanigans.

Miss Ruby had many close Palm Beach friends in high places, but she didn't consider herself a "Palm Beacher." "You're working press, and you better remember it," she reminded herself and her staff. "If Palm Beach wants you, it's because you keep your place."

— *M.M. Cloutier*

From the Jan. 17, 1902, edition of the Daily News, boasting about an expansion of the Hotel Royal Poinciana:

'Even in a metropolis, the opening of the largest hotel in the world would be an important event. At Palm Beach, it marks a red-letter day. This ... has lifted the Hotel Royal Poinciana into the premiership in size among hotels of the world. The Waldorf-Astoria in New York has heretofore held this honor, but never — even during the rush of Horse Show week — has the Waldorf-Astoria accommodated more than 1,400 guests.'

Photos from the Historical Society of Palm Beach County

A shop inside the Hotel Royal Poinciana: The 1902 expansion of the hotel added shops with large windows along the new, north hallway of the hotel, which was so grand the *Daily News* dubbed it the "Broadway of the Hotel Royal Poinciana." Greenleaf & Crosby, Florida's oldest jeweler, had a store inside the hotel and is still in business in Palm Beach.

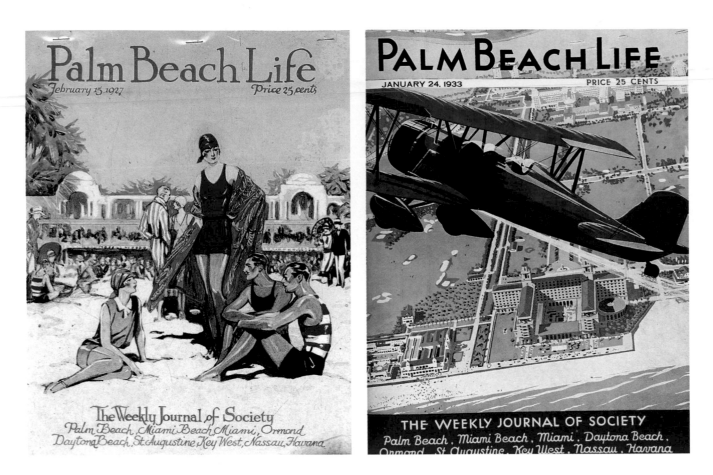

Guardians of good taste

Inside these artful covers from the 1920s and '30s are witty observations such as this, from 1931: 'In Palm Beach, hard times are only make-believe, and when they occur provide just a novelty for the fashionable set in the resort.'

'Thank whatever gods of good taste there may be, formal jewels are now worn only on formal occasions,' reads a society column from 1931. 'We do not find madame chasing the elusive golf ball and wearing pearls of nearly the same size dangling over her panting bosom.'

Louis Burkhardt

Max Sirkin

Richard J. Chillingworth

George O. Butler: In 1963, *The Palm Beach Post* called him the "Father" of Palm Beach County.

J.C. Stowers   Gus Anthony   Marion E. Gruber

By DEBI MURRAY
Historical Society of Palm Beach County
with research by Steve Erdmann

Great change can come out of the simplest conversations.

For example...

When Guy Metcalf, former publisher of the area's first newspaper, *The Tropical Sun*, commented to Louis Burkhardt, West Palm Beach business owner, that he thought Dade County was too big, and that "we ought to have a county of our own," Burkhardt agreed and gathered a group of like-minded men who wanted to whittle a new county from the old.

The group called themselves the County Division Movement, and they elected eight men to oversee the division: Burkhardt, Dr. Henry C. Hood, second medical doctor on the lake; William I. Metcalf, lawyer and father to Guy; Richard J. Chillingworth, former Dade County sheriff and past West Palm Beach mayor; and Max Sirkin, Marion E. Gruber, A.P. Anthony and John C. Stowers, all West Palm Beach business owners. The gentlemen made it clear from the beginning that they were not seeking any public office at the county level (many of them served in city government), nor were they creating a fuss because the south end of the county wanted to stay "dry" on the alcohol issue while the north wanted to stay "wet."

Dr. Henry C. Hood

FATHERS OF A NEW COUNTY

The men who fought to carve Palm Beach County from Dade

The County Division Movement's complaint was that while northern Dade County paid 60 percent of the taxes, it did not receive its fair share of those monies. The northern end of the county was in desperate need of better roads and schools.

The first attempt at separation occurred in April 1907, and while the measure passed in the state senate, it failed in the state house. Since the Florida legislature only met every two years, the County Division Movement had time to prepare for the next meeting in 1909.

Their first job was to find a candidate who would support their petition in the state house of representatives. They found George O. Butler, a man who some would later call the Father of Palm Beach County.

Although he had been born in New Hampshire, Butler grew up in Dade County and had worked as a surveyor and as the county's tax assessor. He had traveled the whole county and agreed it was too big.

During his campaign for state representative from Dade County, he boldly stated that his No. 1 priority if elected was to push for the creation of Palm Beach County. Butler and the newly elected state senator from Dade County, Frederick M. Hudson, worked to push the bill through the Florida legislature. On April 30, 1909, Governor Gilchrist signed the document making Palm Beach County official as of July 1st of that year. George O. Butler ran again successfully for the Florida legislature in 1910 — this time as a representative of Palm Beach County. Then he became Circuit Court Clerk (1913-1920 and again 1933-1940) and helped create the 15th Judicial Circuit. He also served as a West Palm Beach city commissioner from 1927-1933. When he wasn't working for the public, he was an engineer with the firm of Butler, Barnett & Taylor. The company did surveying and grading on road projects such as Conners Highway — the first toll road from West Palm Beach to Okeechobee — the road that eventually became Southern Boulevard.

Why did they want more local control? Tax money.

DAUGHTER OF A NEW FRONTIER

She came to Delray Beach as a child — then saved her city's seaside charm

By JAN TUCKWOOD | The Palm Beach Post

She had a twinkle in her eye in 1908, when this portrait was taken — and that sparkle was just a hint of Ethel Sterling's dynamic demeanor.

Ethel arrived in Delray Beach in 1896, when she was 5. When she and her mother, Mary — a proper woman from Philadelphia — got off the train in the wilderness then called "Linton," Mary began to cry. "She looked at me and said, 'You poor dear. You will never see anything, hear anything or know anything here,'" Ethel recalled in the 1970s. "But my father told her, 'It's up to you whether she ever sees, hears or knows anything here.' My mother dried her eyes, squared her shoulders and never faltered again from that time on."

And, oh, boy — Ethel saw, heard and learned a few things in Delray Beach.

She became a community powerhouse — a commercial property manager, historian and leader who was behind the drive to retain Delray Beach's "village by the sea" charm. Co-founder and first president of the Delray Beach Historical Society, Ethel was "a renaissance woman who wielded a strong fist inside a white glove," says her grandson, Bill Williams, a local attorney.

Anyone who's ever enjoyed a stroll down Delray's charming Atlantic Avenue or walked along the beach there — without the shadow of towering condominiums — owes a debt to Ethel Sterling Williams, who lived to be 95 and never lost that twinkle in her eye.

Photos from Delray Beach Historical Society

ETHEL STERLING, 1908: "She was an independent thinker," recalled her grandson, William Sterling Williams. "A maverick." When a short first marriage failed, she drove a convertible along Biscayne Bay in Miami and tossed her diamond ring into the water, he said. Ethel's second husband, Dr. William C. Williams, was chief of staff at St. Mary's Hospital and on the staff of Pine Ridge Hospital, which served the black community. He was a driving force for the establishment of Bethesda Hospital.

A 20th-century spitfire

"Sometimes, we'd go to out to the railroad tracks, flag down the train and get the rare treat of a glass of ice water ... So much depended on that train. If there was a freeze coming through, a storm or a hurricane approaching, we'd learn about it by having the train whistle signal us."

"Later I went to West Palm Beach for music lessons. The train would go north at 7 a.m. and return south at 11 p.m. and someone would have to wave a lantern at the brakeman so he'd know where to leave me off."

— *Ethel Sterling Williams' oral history quoted in the book "Public Faces —*
Private Lives: Women in South Florida, 1870s-1910" by Karen Davis

Ethel met Henry Flagler when she was a child (shown here in 1895), her grandson, Bill, recalled. He is pictured with his grandmother in 1962 (right). Now an attorney at Lytal, Reiter, Clark, Fountain & Williams in West Palm Beach, he remembers his grandmother telling him: "There's nothing so permanent as change. Be ready to accept it." One change she didn't accept: Rampant development. "She called rows of condos 'filing cabinets,'" her grandson said. "She didn't want the charm of Delray Beach to be taken away like so much of the rest of Florida."

'The Dream City of the Western World':

Addison Mizner wanted to turn Boca Raton into "the Dream City of the Western World," with Venice-like canals and a mixture of "snob appeal and greed appeal." In 1925, vans took prospective land buyers from Worth Avenue (below, right) to Boca Raton, and *The Palm Beach Post* boldly stated: "It is reasonable to suppose that each lot buyer ... should make quick and large profits." Mizner completed some homes, and his grand hotel, the Cloister Inn, now part of the Boca Raton Resort (above) opened in February 1926. Ladies enjoy the loggia of the inn (below, left). But the Bust would soon doom Mizner's dream.

Promotional material emphasized Palm Beach County's elegant lifestyle and potential for growth.

I AM THE RENDEZVOUS
OF THE RICH

EACH PASSING DAY SEES A
NEW ERA IN MY EXISTENCE

I AM THE DREAM
OF A GENIUS

THE MATERIALIZATION
OF A MAGICAL MIRAGE

I AM THE SUN PORCH
OF AMERICA

I AM BOCA RATON IN 1927

— From a Mizner Industries brochure
promoting Addison Mizner's Boom-era
developments in Boca Raton.

1914-1925

Boom Times

HOW HEADY WERE THE BOOM YEARS IN PALM BEACH COUNTY? Look at the numbers: In five years, from 1920 to 1925, West Palm Beach's property value increases five-fold, to $61.7 million.

In Boca Raton, buyers rush to grab the first lots offered for sale there in May 1925 and set a sales record: $2.1 million in one day. Mansions dot the oceanfront from Palm Beach to Manalapan, and sugar farming arrives in the Glades. Life seems too good to be true … and it is.

1916

The weekly *Palm Beach County* becomes the daily *Palm Beach Post*.

Start timeline

1914

Emergency Hospital, forerunner of Good Samaritan, is founded in West Palm Beach.

July 1, 1915

Legislature creates Lake Worth Inlet District, later Port of Palm Beach District.

PINE RIDGE HOSPITAL: This photo from the Collie family shows John Collie's son, Warren (in black suit) and one unidentified gentleman standing in front of the new Pine Ridge Hospital shortly after it opened. This hospital served black patients in five counties until 1956, when St. Mary's Medical Center integrated. In 2008, the property was sold to the Charmettes Inc., an international service organization. Charmettes was founded locally by Frankie Drayton Thomas and Gwendolyn Rodgers, whose husband, Edward Rodgers, was Palm Beach County's first black judge.

Photos from the Historical Society of Palm Beach

JOHN M. COLLIE (left): A prominent businessman in early West Palm Beach, Collie owned a pool room and saloon at 431 N. Rosemary. He also invested in real estate and hired Hazel A. Augustus, the city's first black architect, to build business and residential properties in the Northwest neighborhood. The picture at right shows members of the Collie family and Hazel Augustus on his motorcycle.

April 15, 1916

Pine Ridge Hospital for blacks opens

at Fifth Street and Division Avenue in West Palm Beach. Until well into the 1950s, it is the only hospital open to blacks in five South Florida counties.

John M. Collie is honored by an elaborate funeral procession that transports his casket from St. Patrick's Episcopal Church to Evergreen Cemetery in 1926.

timeline continued

June 1916

Evergreen Cemetery for blacks opens in West Palm Beach; cemeteries will stay segregated for a half-century.

1917

■ Industrial High School for blacks opens in West Palm Beach.

■ March 31: Post office is established at Torry Island; replaced by the Belle Glade Post Office on March 29, 1921.

■ April: New Palm Beach County courthouse opens in West Palm Beach. (In March 2008, the Richard and Pat Johnson Palm Beach County History Museum opens in the restored courthouse.)

Palm Beach County courthouse, 1917.

INDUSTRIAL HIGH SCHOOL'S CHORAL CLASS, 1931: Industrial High for black students opened in West Palm Beach in 1917. By 1931, Industrial's chorus — "the largest Negro High School Choral Class in Florida," said reports of the day — won both the 1931 and 1932 singing contest against Booker T. Washington High School in Miami, according to local historian Ineria Hudnell.

Ineria Hudnell collection

Members of the influential Collie family (below) pose at the Kelsey City gates, 1920s. The back of the photo indicates the woman on the left is "Grandmother Amy Collie."

1918
- Post office opens in Pahokee.
- Post office opens in Canal Point.

1919
- Bridge from Lake Worth to beach opens.
- Post office opens in South Bay.
- Southern Bell buys the West Palm Beach telephone company, which covers area from Delray Beach to Stuart.

1920
- Port of Palm Beach opens.
- Town of Boynton is incorporated; named Boynton Beach in July 1941 after nearby town of Boynton Beach changes name to Ocean Ridge in 1937.
- Post office opens in Belle Glade.

Collie Family collection/Historical Society of Palm Beach County

Harry Kelsey

In 1919, Massachusetts restaurateur Harry Kelsey envisioned his dream town, Kelsey City, as the state's first planned community. At his peak, Kelsey owned 120,000 acres and 14 miles of oceanfront between Miami and Jupiter. The real-estate crash and the 1928 hurricane ruined Kelsey, who left his city in 1931. Eight years later, residents changed its name to Lake Park.

timeline continues >

Jan. 15, 1919
Everglades Club opens in Palm Beach.

Paris Singer

In the 1920s, Paris Singer, part of the sewing machine family empire, and his business partner, architect and developer Addison Mizner, built the Everglades Club on Worth Avenue, intending to use it as a rest home for World War I veterans. They also planned the Blue Heron Hotel, a $4 million resort on what is now Singer Island. Singer died in 1932; the hotel was never finished, and its half-finished hulk stood for 14 years before it was razed during World War II. Blue Heron Boulevard, the road to Singer Island, is named for the hotel that never was.

Historical Society of Palm Beach County

Architect Marion Sims Wyeth designed the first Good Samaritan Hospital

'We went to all the escapist musicals ... shown mostly at the Kettler Theatre . ... If we had 15 cents left over, we stopped at the New York Pastry Shop on Clematis for eclairs! Or at Woolworth's for a banana split!'
— Patricia Ferner Cobb, of West Palm Beach, moved here in 1928 at 8 months old

May 19, 1920

Good Samaritan, area's first permanent hospital, opens

with 35 beds at 12th Street and the lakefront in West Palm Beach.

1921
■ George Washington Carver High School, Delray's first high school for blacks, opens.
■ Lantana is incorporated.

C. Spencer Pompey:
Carver High School icon

This bust of Pompey — who was a teacher, coach and principal at Carver High and other schools for more than 40 years — is inside the Delray Beach City Hall. He was instrumental in getting equal pay for equal work for Palm Beach County's black teachers.

Historical Society of Palm Beach County

1924 Kettler Theater (above) opens at Narcissus and Clematis. The $500,000 facility has 1,400 seats, colored lights, fans, and smoking rooms for men.

1923
■ Town of Delray Beach incorporated.
■ Palm Beach County fair moves to a 56-acre site in Howard Park area.
■ March: First Glades sugar mill opens, in Canal Point.
■ Oct. 27: First synagogue in West Palm Beach, Temple Israel, founded.

Jan. 26, 1924

First city library building in West Palm Beach opens.

timeline continued

1922

■ Post office opens in Clewiston.
■ Pahokee is incorporated.
■ Riviera incorporated; renamed Riviera Beach in 1941.

July 24, 1924 Conners Highway opens

The road, running west along the West Palm Beach Canal from 20-Mile Bend to Lake Okeechobee, then north to the town of Okeechobee, connects West Palm Beach and the Glades community. By linking with existing highways to the west coast, the highway creates the first cross-peninsula route.

(To retrace Conners Highway, take State Road 80 west. Conners Highway began at 20-Mile Bend. Continue on S.R. 80 to U.S. 98 and turn right. Proceed to U.S. 98/441 in Canal Point and head north to Okeechobee.)

Boca Raton Historical Society

1924-1925

Height of real-estate boom in South Florida. Some lots leap in value from $250 to $1,000 to $50,000.

1925

■ First bridge from mainland to Singer Island opens.
■ West Palm Beach property value: $61.7 million — a five-fold increase over 1920.
■ West Palm Beach's two tallest buildings are constructed: the Comeau Building, on Clematis Street; and the Harvey Building, on Datura Street.
■ Jupiter is incorporated.
■ Gulf Stream is incorporated.
■ First regular steamship service begins at Port of Palm Beach.

The Comeau Building, 2009.

Aug. 2, 1924

Town of Boca Ratone incorporated; it begins using "Boca Raton" spelling on May 5, 1925.

timeline continues >

Oct. 14, 1924

High school football game between Palm Beach and Gainesville is first event ever at Municipal Athletic Stadium in West Palm Beach; later called Wright Field and, eventually, Connie Mack Field.

Bang! Bang! It's John Ashley's rifle: The nastiest local gangster of the 1920s was John Ashley, leader of the Ashley gang. Ashley was just 18 in 1911 when he was suspected in the slaying of a Seminole trader. More violence and robberies followed, and the Ashleys operated stills and ran rum from the Bahamas. Ashley's rifle is now on display at the Richard and Pat Johnson Palm Beach County History Museum.

Nov. 1, 1924

Members of the Ashley Gang, which has terrorized South Florida for more than a decade, are ambushed and killed near Sebastian.

John Ashley

Photos from the Historical Society of Palm Beach County

< Guests of the Palm Beach Hotel scramble to escape the flames that will demolish the 23-year-old building. The fire started from sparks generated by The Breakers hotel fire on the other side of Palm Beach. The following February, the Alba Hotel (later known as the Biltmore Hotel) opened on the site.

THE BREAKERS IN FLAMES (above). Marjorie Merriweather Post was talking to actress Billie Burke (wife of Flo Ziegfeld) at the front desk when word came that the south wing of the hotel was ablaze, according to Breakers historian Jim Ponce. Also among those who took to the fire escapes that day: Margaret Tobin Brown of Denver, also known as the "Unsinkable Molly Brown," who had survived the sinking of the Titanic 13 years earlier.

Jan. 25, 1925

Seaboard Coast Line Railway opens to West Palm Beach.

ALL ABOARD, SNOWBIRDS:
Anne and Paul Gilbert wave goodbye to their grandkids in January 1957, as they prepare to board a Seaboard Coast Line Railway train in West Palm Beach for their return trip to New York. "My paternal grandparents used to visit us in Florida every winter," recalled Sherri Gilbert of West Palm Beach. "In their later years, they moved to West Palm Beach, and they have since passed away."

March 18, 1925
The Breakers burns again
The cause: a "new-fangled curling iron."

May 24, 1925

First offering of lots in Boca Raton sells for $2.1 million, a first-day sales record.

1925-1926

West Palm Beach Canal opens from Lake Okeechobee.

timeline continued

OPPOSITE PAGE: Sam Kassatly (center, top photo) with sons Ed (left) and Bob. Today, Ed and Bob run the store (bottom photo).

Parade down Worth Avenue in Palm Beach: American soldiers parade down Worth Avenue, in front of the Venice Lace Shop (now Kassatly's), in this World War II-era photo (right).

'This is God's country!' Sam Kassatly, a traveling linen and lingerie salesman from New Jersey, first saw Palm Beach in 1922 and supposedly shouted, "This is God's country!" In 1923, he and wife Alice founded the business now operated by their sons, Ed and Bob, at 250 Worth Ave. Kassatly's, the longest-operating business on Worth Avenue, has always been a family affair. Sam served as "sidewalk ambassador," standing outside the linen and lingerie shop and chatting with passers-by. Alice designed custom lingerie.

"Worth Avenue's Oldest Shop"
Kassatly's Inc.

Table, Bed & Bath Linens, Lingerie, and Men's Wear
TRADITION SINCE 1923

Kassatly's Inc.

250 Worth Avenue • Palm Beach
(561) 655-5655

1926-1949

Hard Times & Hurricanes

FIRST, THE 1920s REAL-ESTATE BOOM CRASHES HARD, THEN NATURE DEALS AN INCREDIBLE SECOND BLOW: The great hurricane of 1928, which crumbles the dike around Lake Okeechobee, drowning as many as 3,000 people.

Soon the glamorous days of the Flagler Era seem far away — Flagler's great Royal Poinciana Hotel falls to the wrecking ball in the mid-1930s — and the danger of World War II comes vividly close. German subs sink boats right off the coast of Palm Beach County, and residents rally for the war effort.

Hurricane 1928 The Glades

Finding the Dead after

Photo from Sue Day

HORROR BEYOND WORDS: The great storm of 1928 — which drowned as many as 3,000 people in the Glades — is by far Palm Beach County's worst natural disaster. Author Zora Neale Hurston wrote in her novel, *Their Eyes Were Watching God*: "It woke up old Okeechobee, and the monster began to roll in his bed." Only a handful of people died along Palm Beach County's coastline in the storm, even though property was demolished. (Right, downtown West Palm Beach is reduced to rubble, except for sturdier structures such as the courthouse, far right, where many people took shelter.) In the Glades, bodies were everywhere (above). Some bodies were brought to West Palm Beach, some were burned on the spot and some were buried in mass graves — "a layer of bodies, a layer of lime, a layer of bodies, a layer of lime," one old-timer said.

Start timeline

How the bottom dropped ... and crawled back

1929
West Palm Beach's property value at boom high of $89 million.

1930
West Palm Beach property value plummets to $41.6 million.

1935
West Palm Beach's property value hits bottom at $18.2 million.

1949
West Palm Beach property value hits $72.9 million.

1926

Three West Palm Beach banks fail

One is Commercial Bank and Trust; its largest depositor, with $700,000, is the city of West Palm Beach. In June of '26, the closing of Palm Beach Bank and Trust sparks the first run on area banks. By April 1930, 11 Palm Beach County banks have failed.

- Delray Beach High School opens.
- Sept. 17, 1926: Hurricane smashes east coast; heavily damages Miami, killing 392, and hastens South Florida's real estate crash. It also breaks Lake Okeechobee dike and kills 300 to 400 in Moore Haven.

<1920s: The Breakers was rebuilt into the twin-towered masterpiece we know today in 1926, and the fabulous Circle Dining Room was added in 1928. Behind these railings inside the Circle Dining Room is a private Prohibition-era dining area.

The Palm Beach Post

Prominent family

Harry Johnston Sr. and his wife, Frances (below), in 1936, at their home on Monroe Drive in West Palm Beach, with daughter Mary Frances and son Harry Jr. Harry Sr. served in World Wars I and II and, for 35 years, as an attorney in Palm Beach County. He died in 1983. Frances owned a knitting shop during the Great Depression on Flagler Drive. She died in 1978. Their three children were raised in West Palm Beach.

Mary Frances married an attorney and lives in Orlando near her two daughters. Harry Jr., an attorney for 50 years, served in the Florida Senate and in the U.S. House of Representatives. Son Howard, born in 1938, is an attorney in Atlanta.

The Colony Hotel, still a fixture on trendy Atlantic Avenue in Delray Beach, opened in 1926.

1927

- First full-scale sugar-cane operation begins in the Glades.
- Boynton Beach High School opens.
- Addison Mizner's corporation files for voluntary bankruptcy protection.
- Towns of Delray and Delray Beach merge.

Johnston Family photo

Sept. 16, 1928

The great hurricane

Hurricane crumbles dike around Lake Okeechobee, drowning up to 3,000. Second-deadliest disaster in U.S. history.

July 4, 1930

President Herbert Hoover signs bill approving construction of the dike around Lake Okeechobee. The project will cost $286 million, spread over almost 40 years.

Timeline continues >

Orange Blossom Special postcard

1928

- Jan 8: Seaboard Coast Line's Orange Blossom Special makes first stop in West Palm Beach.
- Belle Glade is incorporated

Born in the 1928 hurricane

Gladys Alma Kimbro Smith Jenkins was 4 when she posed for this photo in West Palm Beach. Her mother was eight months pregnant and in labor when the roof blew off their house on Lakewood Road in the '28 storm. "Helpers took her to Good Samaritan Hospital, where my grand entrance was in a bedpan! I was so small, my survival was in question, so my birth certificate reads 'baby girl.'"

1931

■ Town of Boynton Beach, which later becomes Ocean Ridge, splits off from Boynton and incorporates.

■ Manalapan is incorporated.

October 1933 Palm Beach Junior College, first in state, opens.

Saint Mary's Hospital postcard.

Michael Dubiner collection

ST. MARY'S HOSPITAL   WEST PALM BEACH, FLORIDA

1934

Casino magnate E.R. Bradley buys *The Palm Beach Post* and *Palm Beach Times.*

1936

■ Everglades Memorial Hospital opens in Pahokee.

■ July 31, 1936: WJNO-AM 1230, West Palm Beach's first radio station, signs on.

■ Fall 1936: Industrial High School football team in West Palm Beach wins area's first state sports championship.

Grace Morrison

■ Dec. 19, 1936: New West Palm Beach airport is dedicated; named Morrison Field in honor of secretary Grace K. Morrison. Eastern Airlines flies inaugural departure.

March 8, 1939

Saint Mary's Hospital opens in West Palm Beach

■ September 1939: National Guard Armory opens at Howard Park, on Lake Street south of Okeechobee Boulevard in West Palm Beach. It will become an arts center in the 1980s.

The Palm Beach Post
The Robert & Mary Montgomery Armory Art Center, 2007.

Sept. 2, 1935

"Labor Day Storm," most powerful hurricane ever to strike North American mainland, kills up to 600 and destroys Henry Flagler's Overseas Railroad through the Keys.

1937

■ Boynton Beach changes name to Ocean Ridge; adjacent town of Boynton becomes Boynton Beach.

■ Town of Golfview is chartered.

1940

Riviera Beach buys 1,000 feet on Singer Island; it will annex parts of the island in stages over the next several years.

timeline continued

The Palm Beach Post

Feb. 17, 1932

Palm Beach Kennel Club opens.

Greyhounds racing at Palm Beach Kennel Club, 1975.

1938

Belle Glade Memorial Hospital opens.

Ralph Norton, founder of the Norton Gallery of Art

1941

■ Norton Gallery and School of Art opens.

■ South Bay is incorporated.

■ Airport opens in Lantana.

1947

- Publisher John H. Perry buys *The Palm Beach Post*, *Palm Beach Times* and *Palm Beach Daily News*.
- Mangonia Park is incorporated.
- Glen Ridge is incorporated.
- Sept. 17: Hurricane causes storm surges of up to 22 feet around Lake Okeechobee; the dike holds.
- Oct. 12: Second hurricane in a month causes worst flooding on record in South Florida.
- Dec. 17: New terminal opens at Palm Beach International Airport, formerly Morrison Field.

1949

Letter from Seacrest High.

- Seacrest High in Delray Beach, later Atlantic High opens to serve students from Delray Beach, Boynton Beach and Boca Raton.
- Airport opens in Pahokee.
- Estelle Murer is elected West Palm Beach's first female city commissioner. It will be 26 years before the next one, Carol Roberts, is elected in March 1975.
- Highland Beach is incorporated.
- Aug. 26, 1949: Last major hurricane to strike Palm Beach County in the 20th century. Lake dike and flood-control system reduce damage.

June 10, 1949

Controlling the water

Spurred by flooding caused by two hurricanes in 1947, the government acts, forming the Central and Southern Florida Flood Control District, later the South Florida Water Management District.

Battleships off Palm Beach (below): German U-boats were a constant danger to U.S. ships cruising our coast, like these ships in 1942. The U-Boats would spot their prey silhouetted in the lights of the oceanfront hotels that drew tourists to Florida. Palm Beach County residents painted their headlights black, took part in blackouts and drills, patrolled beaches on foot or on horseback. Meanwhile, jumpy authorities rounded up virtually anyone with a German-sounding accent or Asian features.

War off our shore

Key events during World War II

Feb. 28, 1940: Morrison Field is leased to U.S. Army for an air base; it is eventually enlarged to 1,825 acres, with expanded runways and taxiways.

Dec. 7, 1941: Morrison Field Army Air Force Command is activated.

1942-1945: Military bases and personnel fill Florida. Among them: Morrison Field (now PBIA), Boca Raton Army Air Field (now Boca Raton Airport/FAU).

Jan. 11, 1942: Practice blackout throws Palm Beaches into darkness.

Jan. 19, 1942: Air Transport Command begins operations; increases the airport to 2,270 acres. Runways are expanded; a north-south runway is closed. Runways, taxiway lights, a control tower, aprons, ramps, roadways, and water and sewer systems are built by U.S. government.

February-May 1942: German U-boats sink 16 ships between Cape Canaveral and Boca Raton. Local Coast Guard Reserve, headed by Gleason Stambaugh, aids in saving crew members from burning ships.

Oct. 15, 1942: Boca Raton Army Airfield opens.

Dec. 11, 1942: The Breakers hotel is commandeered by Army, becomes Ream General Hospital.

March 1945: Belle Glade prisoner-of-war camp for Germans opens. It closes in December.

June 30, 1947: Morrison Field return to county control; it is renamed Palm Beach International Airport on Aug. 11.

COLLISION OF THE GULFBELLE AND THE GULFLAND OFF PALM BEACH, 1943: This painting depicts the worst sea tragedy of World War II off the Southeast Florida coast. During a blackout, on Oct. 20, 1943, the tanker Gulfbelle, northbound with a full load of gasoline, collided head-on with the empty southbound tanker Gulfland off Palm Beach. As *Palm Beach Post* reporter Bill McGoun later wrote: The sea around the two ships soon was a hell. "We couldn't get too close," said Gleason Stambaugh, the Coast Guard officer in charge of rescue operations. "The intense heat singed our hair and curled paint on the boats." Only 28 of the 116 men aboard the ships survived. Here, the Gulfbelle is in the background and Stambaugh's rescue boat is in front, with Stambaugh standing. The artist, R.W. Lewis, served with Stambaugh in the U.S. Coast Guard Reserve, and the painting was created from his memory of the events of that night.

Fire on the water: THE WAR COMES HOME

By daylight, Palm Beach County residents watched as U.S. ships by the dozens cruised offshore on their way to deliver war supplies.

By night, they waited in darkness and fear.

Gleason N. Stambaugh

German U-boats, determined to disrupt shipping channels, were right offshore and torpedoing ships.

Gleason N. Stambaugh headed the local Coast Guard Reserve in charge of sea rescues.

As his son, Dr. Reginald Stambaugh recalled in 2007: "When World War II came, all the people with boats 30 feet and up joined the Coast Guard Auxiliary. Jack Butler, who used to own Butler Lumber Company, got it started and then Pop took over as commander. When the ships got torpedoed off of the coast, they'd go and look for survivors. And they'd also go out and patrol.

"One night, Pop was out patrolling, and he went out on top of a wave. And he had a spotlight — and the light went right on a German submarine! The only thing he had on the boat was a shotgun, so Pop was delighted that the sub got scared and went down and didn't come back up and finish them off."

Stambaugh organized horse and dog patrols along the beaches, and residents also served as lookouts.

"During the war I saw thousands of lives lost that could have been saved if the Intracoastal Waterway had been completed by then," Gleason Stambaugh told a reporter in 1966.

Off Florida alone, German U-boats sank 24 ships. Sixteen went down in a 150-mile stretch of Florida coastline from Cape Canaveral to Boca Raton between February and May 1942.

'Suddenly, we were jolted by a thunderous boom!'

It was about 5 o'clock in the morning on May 9, 1942. Bill Hankins and I, a couple of Palm Beach County native-born teenagers, were preparing newspapers for delivery in Delray Beach on our bicycles.

Bill, who was born in West Palm Beach, delivered *The Palm Beach Post*. I, a native of Delray Beach, had *The Miami Herald* route.

Our newspapers were brought to us each morning at the Standard Oil gas station at the intersection of U.S. 1 and Atlantic Avenue in Delray Beach.

As we rolled our newspapers and secured them with rubber bands, we compared our papers' front-page headlines about the battles in Europe and the Pacific Ocean at places with strange-sounding names. In the quiet of the morning, the war seemed so far away.

Suddenly, we were jolted by a thunderous boom! That was followed by another boom!, and another.

It all seemed to be coming from the direction of the beach, about a half-mile away. Wide-eyed and curious, we jumped on our bicycles and raced to the beach.

About 3 miles offshore was a large American oil tanker ablaze from stem to stern. It had been torpedoed by a German submarine. As we watched in awe, the explosions continued with flames streaking high into the sky.

We were soon joined by local townspeople, many of whom joined the rescue efforts with their boats.

Later, after Bill and I delivered our newspapers, we returned to the beach to see dozens of crew members covered with crude oil and suffering burns. We learned later that of the 44 crew members, only 31 survived.

Suddenly, the headlines in our newspapers took on a whole new meaning. World War II was no longer being fought just in faraway places with strange-sounding names. No — suddenly, World War II was right here, only about 3 miles east of our little town of Delray Beach.

— ERNEST G. SIMON

Simon, who went on to join the U.S. Navy when he turned 18, later became an attorney. His family has lived in Delray Beach since 1920.

1946

Ernie Simon, center, serving in the U.S. Navy, is shown with brothers Charlie (left, 12) and Sandy (9) in Delray Beach.

Sun, surf and softball

1945

Among Murray Gordon's jobs: Removing all the beautiful furniture from The Biltmore and replacing it with double-deck beds.

I arrived in West Palm Beach in 1945, when I was 18 and newly enlisted in the Navy. An officer pointed to the beautiful Biltmore hotel across Lake Worth and informed us that the Navy was turning the hotel into a naval hospital.

The most memorable experiences of my 365 days at The Biltmore, in Palm Beach, were these: sun and surf, "sea-time" spent going over to West Palm Beach on the ferry for a nickel, and playing softball. We started a hard-pitch-softball league with men from the Boca Raton Army Air Base and Morrison Field.

I went on to become a doctor and practiced for most of my career in the Chicago area. But, like many men who spent the war years here, I eventually came back to Palm Beach County.

— DR. MURRAY R. GORDON

Gordon retired as a surgeon three years ago and lives in Palm Beach Gardens.

From schoolboy to soldier

My parents, Harry and T'Rose Leibovit, moved here from Sanford, Fla., in 1923. I

1944

Art Leibovit

was born in Good Samaritan Hospital on Sept. 28, 1925.

Dad opened a men's clothing store, Roby's Menswear, on the northwest corner of Clematis Street and Dixie Highway.

I graduated from Palm Beach High School in 1943 and spent one semester at the University of Florida before the U.S. Army called me to active duty. This photo was taken on Jan. 30, 1944, at our home at 1500 Florida Ave. in West Palm Beach.

The next day, I went to Camp Blanding in Jacksonville — then on to occupation duty in Japan.

— ART LEIBOVIT, *West Palm Beach*

We're in the Army now!

1. Be a SPAR: The U.S. Coast Guard uses this motto to recruit members for its Women's Reserve (SPAR) units. SPAR is an acronym formed by the Coast Guard motto, "Semper Paratus," and its English translation, "Always Ready." **2. Dear Mother:** A U.S. Army Air Corps pillow sham honoring Mother, sold as a Morrison Field souvenir. **3. Welcome home!** A crowd gathers at the West Palm Beach train station to welcome returning servicemen, 1945. **4. Nancy's rations:** A World War II ration book issued to a Rosarian Academy student, Nancy Emrich, who lived at 231 Bradley Place, Palm Beach. **5. Entertaining the troops:** Members of the U.S. Army Air Corps with an entertainer. **6. Palm Beach canteen:** Exterior of the V for V (Volunteers for Victory) Soldier Canteen, 416 S. County Road, Palm Beach. **7. Socializing:** Interior of the V for V Soldier Canteen. **8. Military parade:** Troops march along Clematis Street in West Palm Beach, circa 1942-1945. **9. Dancing with the SPARs:** A member of the U.S. Coast Guard Women's Reserve (a SPAR) and a member of the U.S. Army Air Corps. His ID badge reads "Morrison Field, West Palm Beach." **10. Refreshing treat:** Members of the Junior Women's Club hand out fresh watermelon to soldiers, 1945. **11. Pedal to the metal:** Testing a Jeep near Morrison Field in West Palm Beach. **12. Music:** A washboard band performs for troops at Morrison Field. **13. Home base to 3,000:** Entrance to Morrison Field (now Palm Beach International Airport), circa 1943. **14. Morrison Field activated:** The U.S. War Department sends this telegram in 1940, stating that an air base will be established in West Palm Beach. **15. Coffee?** Ration stamps. **16. Prancing with the SPARs:** Members of the U.S. Coast Guard Women's Reserve train at boot camp at the Biltmore Hotel, Palm Beach.

Pillow: Pat Crowley collection
Photos: Historical Society of Palm Beach County

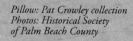

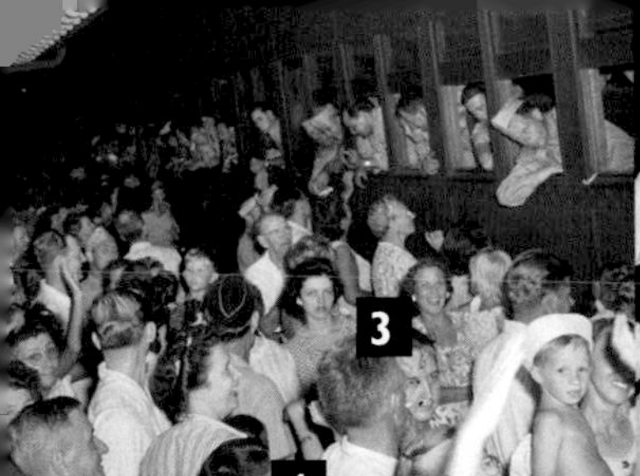

3

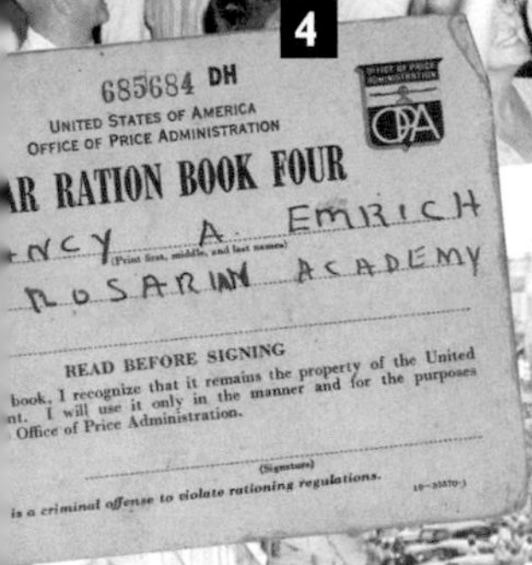

4

685684 DH
UNITED STATES OF AMERICA
OFFICE OF PRICE ADMINISTRATION

AR RATION BOOK FOUR

NCY A. EMRICH
(Print first, middle, and last names)
ROSARIAN ACADEMY

READ BEFORE SIGNING

book, I recognize that it remains the property of the United
nt. I will use it only in the manner and for the purposes
Office of Price Administration.

(Signature)

is a criminal offense to violate rationing regulations.

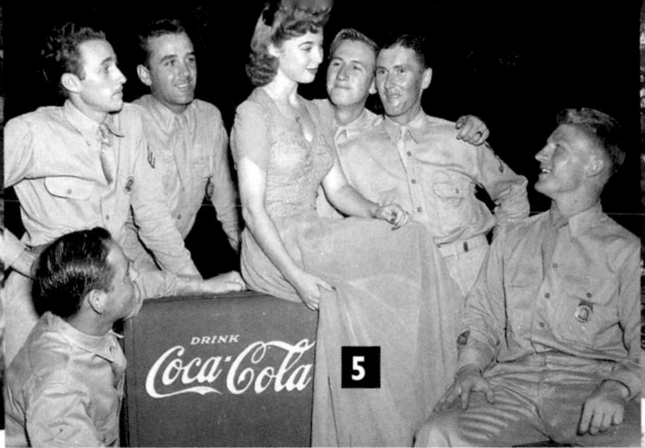
DRINK
Coca-Cola

5

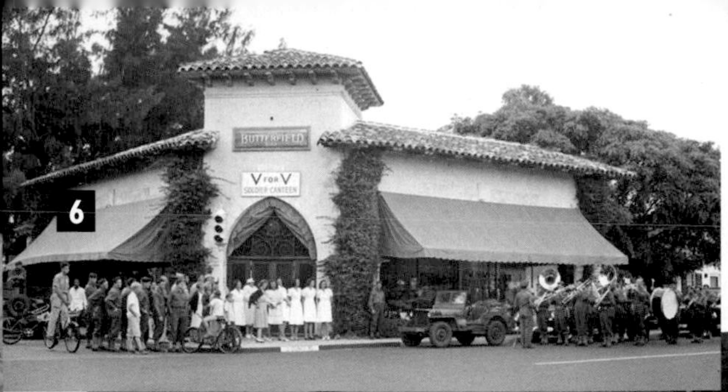
BUTTERFIELD
V FOR V

6

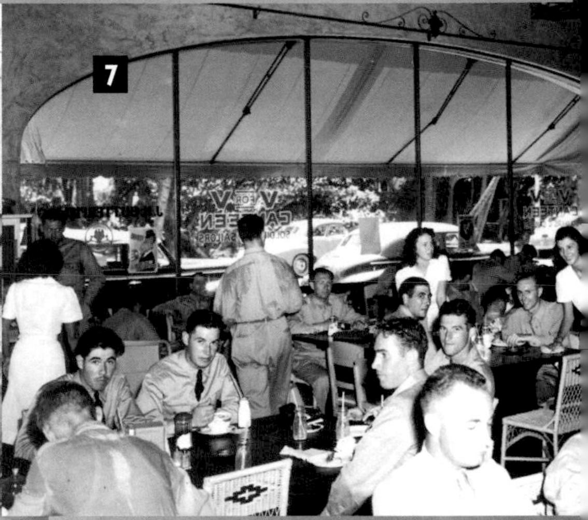

7

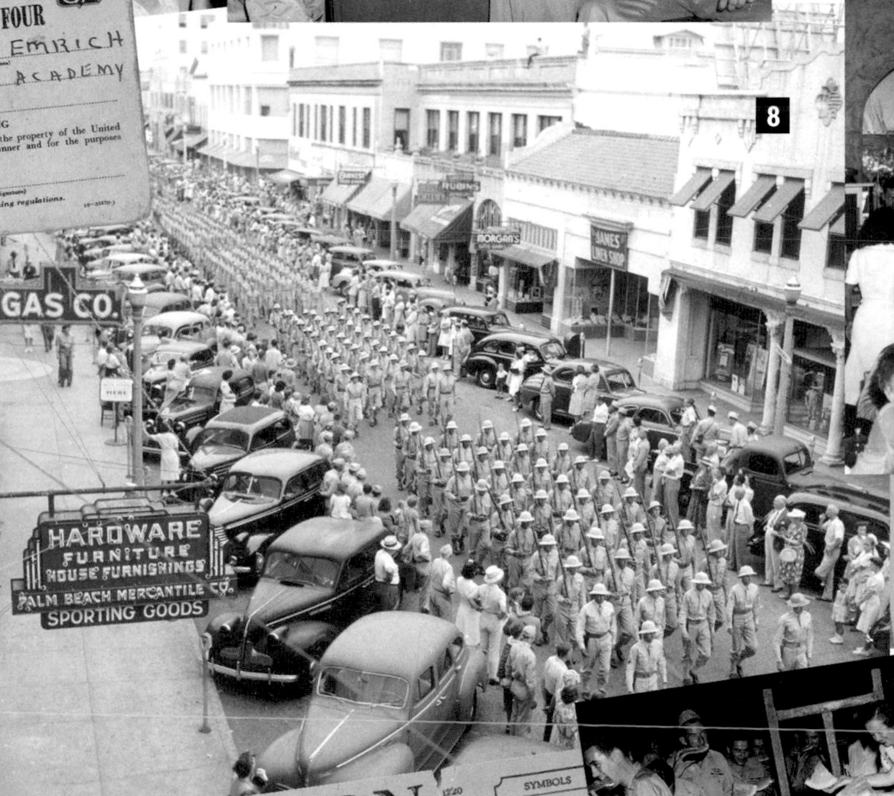
GAS CO.
HARDWARE
FURNITURE
HOUSE FURNISHINGS
PALM BEACH MERCANTILE CO.
SPORTING GOODS
RUBIN'S
MORGAN'S
JAMES'

8

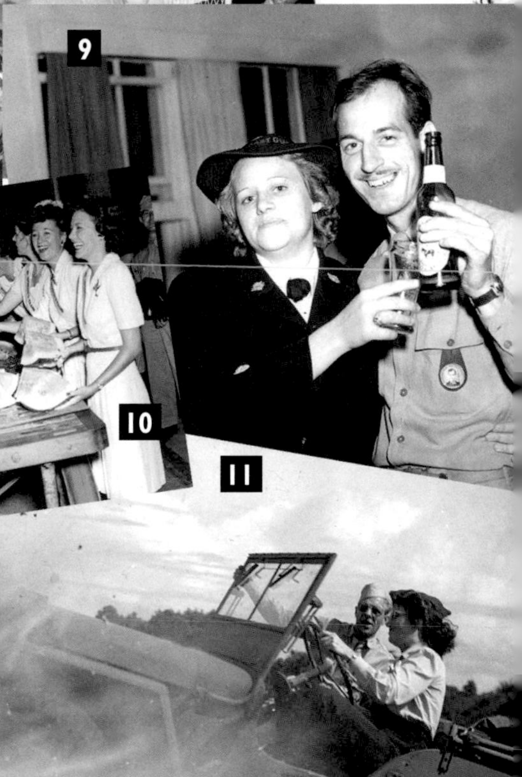

9

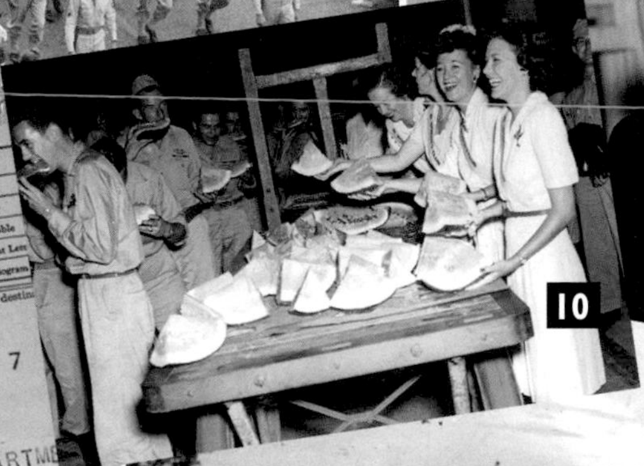

10

11

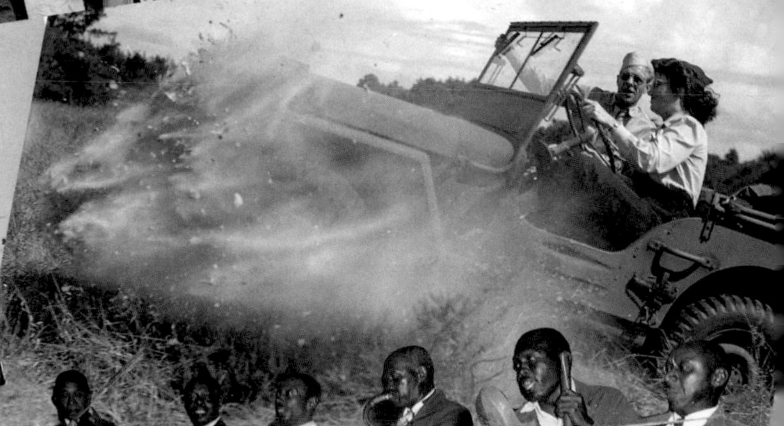

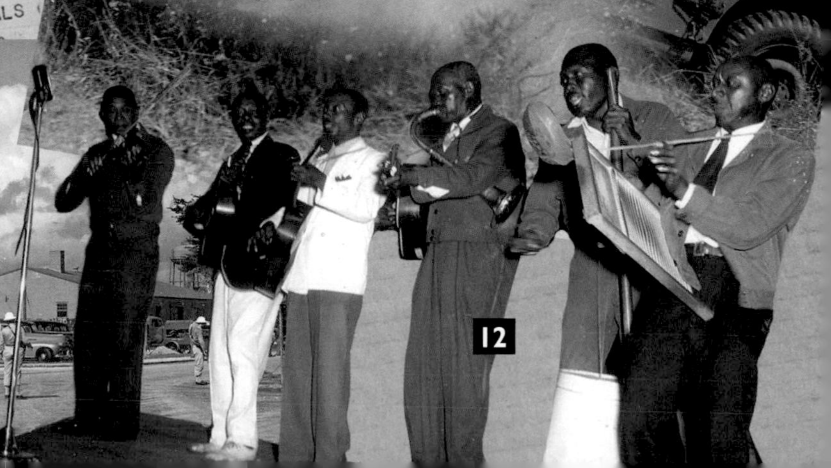

12

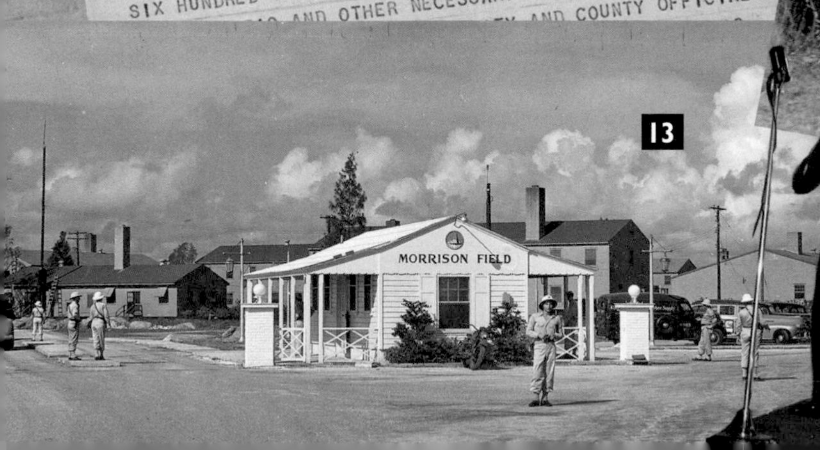
MORRISON FIELD

13

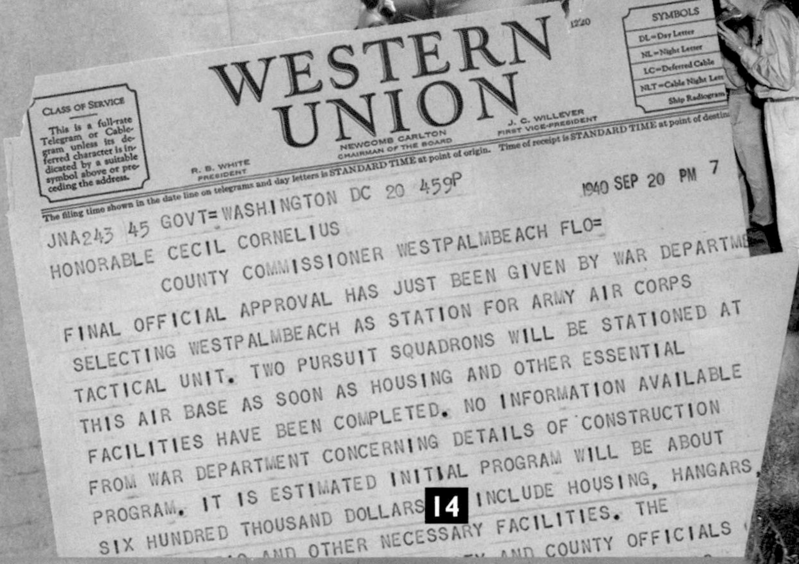

14

WESTERN UNION

CLASS OF SERVICE
This is a full-rate Telegram or Cablegram unless its deferred character is indicated by a suitable symbol above or preceding the address.

R. B. WHITE, PRESIDENT
NEWCOMB CARLTON, CHAIRMAN OF THE BOARD
J. C. WILLEVER, FIRST VICE-PRESIDENT

SYMBOLS
DL=Day Letter
NL=Night Letter
LC=Deferred Cable
NLT=Cable Night Letter
Ship Radiogram

The filing time shown in the date line on telegrams and day letters is STANDARD TIME at point of origin. Time of receipt is STANDARD TIME at point of destination

1940 SEP 20 PM 7

JNA243 45 GOVT=WASHINGTON DC 20 459P
HONORABLE CECIL CORNELIUS
COUNTY COMMISSIONER WESTPALMBEACH FLO=
FINAL OFFICIAL APPROVAL HAS JUST BEEN GIVEN BY WAR DEPARTME
SELECTING WESTPALMBEACH AS STATION FOR ARMY AIR CORPS
TACTICAL UNIT. TWO PURSUIT SQUADRONS WILL BE STATIONED AT
THIS AIR BASE AS SOON AS HOUSING AND OTHER ESSENTIAL
FACILITIES HAVE BEEN COMPLETED. NO INFORMATION AVAILABLE
FROM WAR DEPARTMENT CONCERNING DETAILS OF CONSTRUCTION
PROGRAM. IT IS ESTIMATED INITIAL PROGRAM WILL BE ABOUT
SIX HUNDRED THOUSAND DOLLARS [...] INCLUDE HOUSING, HANGARS,
[...] AND OTHER NECESSARY FACILITIES. THE
[...] AND COUNTY OFFICIALS

1946, Saturday Evening Post

Stambaugh Family

From 1930 through the 1970s, The Hut — complete with "curb girls" and shakes from the local Alfar Creamery — was West Palm Beach's top teen hangout. Between Flagler Drive and Holy Trinity Episcopal Church, The Hut was torn down in the early 1980s when Phillips Point was built.

< "What was life like for teens in the '50s? The Hut, the beach, the pools — Lido Pools across from the Palm Beach Pier, and the Lake Worth Casino — and the soda fountains!"
— CAROLYN STROUPE STAMBAUGH

She became a New York model after growing up here. She was on the cover of Ladies' Home Journal (left) in 1955. In 1956, she became a model on a new TV game show with Bill Cullen: The Price Is Right (far left).

1950-1963

Happy Days

THE WAR IS OVER, PROSPERITY HAS RETURNED, AND IT SEEMS EVERYBODY — YES, EVERYBODY — IS MOVING TO FLORIDA, lured by enticing ads showing folks freezing in one panel and sunning in the next. In the decade, from 1940 to 1950, the state's population jumps by half, from 2 million to 3 million.

Palm Beach County's sleepy coastal towns shoot west like crabgrass. But prominence and progress — and the crime of the century, the Chillingworth murders — begin to overshadow the good life of small-town South Florida.

Gillian Wimbourne Davis

Hey, kids, it's time for *Playhouse Party*: In 1957, dance students from Imperial Studios in Palm Beach entertained the local TV audience on WPTV's *Playhouse Party* show. Their teacher, Gillian Wimbourne Davis, went on to run Miss Gillian's School of Dancing in Boynton Beach from 1958 to 1983.

TV COMES TO TOWN

Sept. 13, 1953

WIRK-TV, Channel 21, area's first television station, signs on. However, frustrated in its effort to move to a lower channel, it closes down Feb. 29, 1956.

Aug. 22, 1954

WJNO-TV, Channel 5, an NBC station, signs on. It becomes WPTV in 1956.

Jan. 1, 1955

WEAT-TV — later WPEC, Channel 12 (ABC) — signs on.

April 1962

WTVX-TV, Channel 34, in Fort Pierce signs on. Four years later, it becomes the Palm Beach County/Treasure Coast CBS affiliate.

The Palm Beach Post

Action news car, mid-1960s: Buck Kinnaird, sportscaster for Channel 5 in the 1960s, recalls when the action news team had one car — "but we put a '4' on it so people thought we had more. We put a phone in the car so people would think we could call different places, but the phone wasn't connected." Here, '60s news anchor Bill Gordon is driving the lone news cruiser.

More TV changes come in the 1980s

■ **July 8, 1982:** Public station WWPF-TV, Channel 42, signs on. It later changes its name to WHRS and becomes WXEL on Jan. 1, 1985.

■ **October 1982:** Independent station WFLX-TV, Channel 29, signs on in West Palm Beach.

■ **Jan. 1, 1989:** As the last fallout of an affiliate swap involving five existing television stations and one new one in the West Palm Beach and Miami markets, WPEC-TV, Channel 12, switches from ABC to CBS; WPBF-TV (ABC), Channel 25, signs on; and former CBS affiliate WTVX-TV, Channel 34, becomes an independent.

1954 'Mr. Mac' makes his mark

John D. MacArthur spends $5.5 million for 2,600 acres in what is now Palm Beach Shores, Lake Park, North Palm Beach and Palm Beach Gardens.

SUBURBS
BEGIN TO SPRAWL

John D. MacArthur, owner of the JDM Country Club, takes a ride in his cart, called "Skipper." MacArthur — founder of Palm Beach Gardens and developer of much of northern Palm Beach County — is second only to Henry Flagler when it comes to the county's development.

1977, The Palm Beach Post

1956
Arvida buys up Boca land

Arthur Vining Davis (in dark suit) and his development corporation, Arvida, buy 850 acres in the Boca Raton area, including the Boca Raton Resort & Club.

Boca Raton Historical Society

Arthur Vining Davis with his secretary, Evelyn Mitchell, and the Oak Brook, Ill., polo team on the polo grounds when they were just south of Camino Real in Boca Raton in 1958.

1959
A wink in Bink's eye: Enter Royal Palm Beach and Wellington

Bink Glisson

Royal Palm Beach is incorporated in 1959. But its roots, and those of Wellington, came earlier — when three savvy investors, including Bink Glisson, buy up swampland.

Sept. 9, 1957

Westward expansion in West Palm Beach

The city sells about 5,500 acres to Westward Developers, Inc., which will develop the sprawling Palm Beach Lakes area.

Historical Society of Palm Beach County

"City within a City": To sell his company's new development, Louis R. Perini Sr. — then also the owner of the Milwaukee (later Atlanta) Braves — built a "paraboloid" to serve as hub of its "Million Dollar Homes Exhibit." This brochure touted the Palm Beach Lakes development as "Tomorrow-ness in action." The star-shaped building, at Okeechobee Road and Florida Mango Road, was gone by the mid-1960s. In 1955, West Palm Beach was just a mile wide and Flagler interests still had control of the city's water supply. A polio outbreak spurred the city to update its sewer system — and the city bought the water plant and nearly 27 square miles of land and marsh west of the city. Perini's Palm Beach Lakes development was on part of that land.

1950

- Haverhill incorporated.
- Cloud Lake incorporated.
- July 16: Southeast Florida State Sanatorium, for tuberculosis, opens in Lantana. It becomes A.G. Holley Hospital on May 7, 1969.
- Fall 1950: Industrial High School, for blacks, in West Palm Beach is absorbed by Roosevelt High School.

1951

- Palm Beach Shores incorporated.
- June 8: Loxahatchee National Wildlife Refuge is established; it is renamed for conservationist Arthur R. Marshall after his death in 1985.

Feb. 2, 1954

WDBF-AM 1420, Delray Beach's first radio station, goes on the air.

1955

- South Palm Beach incorporated.
- Hypoluxo incorporated.

The Palm Beach Post

Pratt & Whitney

Judge C.E. Chillingworth and his wife, Marjorie.

June 14, 1955

Circuit Judge C.E. Chillingworth and wife are murdered at sea.

May 27, 1958

Pratt & Whitney opens plant

Jet and rocket engines are designed and built at the 7,000-acre campus on Beeline Highway in northwest Palm Beach County.

1957

Town incorporations: Village of Golf, Village of Tequesta, Palm Springs, Lake Clarke Shores.

Nov. 1, 1956

Patients of the Pine Ridge Hospital, for blacks, are moved out to the new, blacks-only "north wing" of St. Mary's Hospital.

Aug. 13, 1956

North Palm Beach incorporated.

---

start timeline

timeline continues >

1953

Juno Beach incorporated.

Nov. 30, 1955

West Palm Beach buys water plant from Flagler estate, ending Flagler Water Systems' monopoly on water and sewer dating back to city's incorporation in 1894.

Jan. 25, 1957

The Sunshine State Parkway, now Florida's Turnpike, opens.

1958

- January: Palm Beach County Fair, now the South Florida Fair, moves to current location west of Florida's Turnpike on Southern Boulevard.

- Aug. 13: Beeline Highway opens.

- September: Roosevelt Junior College, for blacks, opens in West Palm Beach.

- Sept. 2: Forest Hill, West Palm Beach's second public high school for whites, opens.

- October: Appeals court rules Palm Beach County schools must integrate.

1959

Suburbs sprout

- Palm Beach Gardens incorporated.
- Atlantis incorporated.
- Royal Palm Beach incorporated.
- University Park, near Boca Raton, incorporated.

timeline continues

Nov. 12, 1959
First mall

Palm Coast Plaza, at southern end of West Palm Beach, opens. It is still open today, with different stores.

Michael Dubiner postcard collection

Nov. 25, 1960

CBS documentary *Harvest of Shame* focuses the nation's attention on what it calls slavery-like conditions among Glades migrant workers.

1960 Bazaar International opens

When the Bazaar International shopping center opened in Riviera Beach, its dramatic "Trylon Tower" — designed by famed architect Alfred Browning Parker — was billed as Florida's tallest tourist attraction. It had an observation deck at the top. Poor retail sales doomed the center, though Siegfried's Bakery celebrated its anniversary with a festive Bazaar-shaped cake (below) in 1961. The tower was demolished in 1998.

The Palm Beach Post

Nancy Blaschke

"Do you remember Bazaar International in Riviera Beach? It was right across from where the Port of Palm Beach is along U.S. 1. Siegfried and Anne Blaschke moved down to Florida from New Jersey in 1960 to open Siegfried's Bakery in the Bazaar International Shopping Center. Unfortunately, the shopping center was a retail disaster, and they moved the bakery to 10th Street in Lake Park after a couple of years and operated it until 1978. Anyone who was around during that time has fond memories of Siegfried's Bakery!"

— NANCY BLASCHKE

Jan. 1, 1959

Cuban Revolution leads to embargo on Cuban sugar. In the 1960s, sugar production in the Glades increases sixfold. Sugar Cane Growers Cooperative is formed in 1960.

Feb. 9, 1959

Bethesda Memorial Hospital in Boynton Beach opens.

Michael Dubiner postcard collection

Bethesda Memorial Hospital opened its doors in 1959 (above) with 70 beds and a medical staff of 32 physicians. Today, 525 physicians staff the hospital and there are more than 400 beds.

1961

- May 24: RCA opens $4 million plant in Palm Beach Gardens.

- September: Africa U.S.A., the county's first major animal attraction, closes after the jungle park in Boca Raton is quarantined by the state. The land is sold to developers for $1 million.

- Oct. 21: The South Florida Science Museum in West Palm Beach opens.

- Jan. 12: Former President Herbert Hoover dedicates the new Herbert Hoover Dike around Lake Okeechobee.

1961, The Palm Beach Post

Jan. 12, 1961: Herbert Hoover, right, and Florida Gov. Farris Bryant at the dike dedication.

Myers Family

1960

Groundbreaking at the South Florida Science Museum: (foreground, from left) Gary Myers, son of Wyckoff and Nancy Myers, and Ellen and Carolyn Downey, daughters of Dan and Doris Downey, dig for buried treasure. The Junior League of the Palm Beaches, founder of the museum, buried toys in the sand for the kids. As Nancy Myers, then-president of the club, writes: "At least 150 kids showed up carrying shovels ... Eventually, we raised enough money to build the first section of the building, which opened in 1961. Then, the Spitz planetarium was built."

April 30, 1962

Library building on the waterfront in West Palm Beach opens. The modern structure will last until 2009, when the city library is moved to West Palm Beach's $154 million City Center.

John Kennedy says goodbye to Sen. Ralph Blank at PBIA as Sen. George Smathers goes ahead to board the presidential plane — the weekend before the president is killed.

Davidoff Studios

Nov. 16-17, 1963

President John F. Kennedy spends the last weekend of his life in Palm Beach. Following his assassination, directors of the planned Lake Worth Hospital vote to change its name to John F. Kennedy Memorial Hospital.

timeline continues >

Sept. 11, 1961

School integration

The first two blacks enrolled in a white public school begin classes at Lake Worth High School, making Palm Beach County the fourth in the state to begin integration. Later that day, Palm Beach Junior College gets its first black student.

1963

- Briny Breezes incorporated.

- March 9: West Palm Beach Municipal Stadium opens with the Milwaukee (later Atlanta) Braves as the first spring-training tenant.

- April 25, 1963: Professional Golfers Association officially moves its national headquarters to Palm Beach Gardens.

Tom Fleming greets President Lyndon B. Johnson at the opening of Florida Atlantic University in Boca Raton. Fleming — who founded two banks in Boca and was a city councilman and mayor — pushed for the college, politically and financially. "Education is our responsibility," he said in 1961, when his bank, First Bank & Trust, became the first in the nation to set aside 1 percent of its profits for higher education. "We can't just sit and gripe about it."

Boca Raton Historical Society

New York World's Fair, 1964: Palm Beach County hostesses (from left) Sandra Swayne, Lyn Vaughn, Linda Juretie, Jacqueline Gans, Sandra Campbell and Regina Riggs. The big thrill at the Palm Beach County exhibit was a "photo-mat ride" that tilted and featured photos of local scenes, says Linda Juretie Hess, who now lives in Boynton Beach.

PALM BEACH COUNTY AT 100

1964-1983

Hello, Suburbia, SunFest — And Snow!

THE THEMES OF THE '60s — from civil rights issues such as school integration to that groovy Age of Aquarius — dramatically change the mood in fast-growing Palm Beach County. So does an incredibly modern innovation: the first personal computer.

PERSONAL COMPUTER, 1987: This is IBM's Personal System/2 Model 50. The first personal computer arrived in 1981, thanks to Philip "Don" Estridge and his team at IBM in Boca Raton. Estridge and his wife, Mary Ann, died in the 1985 crash of a Delta jet hit by wind shear while landing at Dallas-Fort Worth Airport. Today, technology-minded students attend Boca Raton's Don Estridge Middle School.

Don Estridge

Start timeline

Sept. 10, 1964

Florida Atlantic University opens in Boca Raton.

March 7, 1965

Spitz Planetarium opens at South Florida Science Museum.

Sept. 7-8, 1965

Hurricane Betsy's outer edge causes scattered damage to Palm Beach County.

Hurricane Betsy's surprise visitor: The ship Amaryllis, which remained grounded behind the Rutledge Inn on Singer Island until 1968.

Brochure for Lion Country Safari circa 1970s.

Pride of Lions in Lion Country Safari   Photo by Larry Wise

Florida's only drive-through safari, shown here in the early years, now features more than 800 animals.

1967

■ July 15: Boca Raton Community Hospital opens.

■ July 30-Aug.: After a four-hour riot in adjacent Riviera Beach, scattered gangs set fires, smash windows and shoot at police in West Palm Beach.

■ Aug. 20: Lion Country Safari, a 659-acre jungle park, opens 15 miles west of West Palm Beach along Southern Boulevard. It will host about a half-million people a year.

■ September: IBM opens in Boca Raton. In the early 1980s, a "dirty dozen" team of engineers develops the first IBM personal computer. Employment soars to 9,500. In 1988, IBM moves PC assembly lines to North Carolina.

■ September: West Palm Beach Auditorium opens.

■ Oct. 26: The 87-store, $20 million Palm Beach Mall opens, with Gov. Claude Kirk presiding.

West Palm Beach Auditorium

The Palm Beach Mall, height of chic shopping in 1968, featured 87 stores including Jordan Marsh, Richard's and J.C. Penney. In 1979, it gained a new tenant — Burdines, an institution in downtown West Palm Beach for more then 35 years. Sears, then on Dixie Highway, followed in 1980.

timeline continues >

1966

■ Feb. 17: John F. Kennedy Memorial Hospital opens in Atlantis.

■ Oct. 29: Five-building terminal is dedicated at Palm Beach International Airport.

■ Dec. 14: First part of Interstate 95 — a 3.6-mile stretch from Okeechobee Boulevard to 45th Street — opens. Expressway is completed north to Palm Beach Gardens in 1969.

Michael Dubiner postcard collection

Palm Beach International Airport — the height of modern architecture — in 1966. This terminal was replaced 22 years later by the current airport, where 3 million passengers fly in and 3 million fly out every year.

1969

■ July 1: Publisher John H. Perry sells his newspapers, including *The Palm Beach Post* and *Evening Times,* to Cox Enterprises.

■ Nov. 28-30: The Palm Beach International Music and Arts Festival, 31/2 months after Woodstock, draws 40,000 to Palm Beach International Speedway (later Moroso Motorsports Park, now Palm Beach International Raceway) northwest of West Palm Beach. Freezing rain turns site into quagmire. Acts run late; last act, the Rolling Stones, appears near dawn.

Feelin' groovy

The Palm Beach Post devoted most of its front page for three days to the Palm Beach International Music and Arts Festival — our area's own Woodstock. One *Post* story tried to explain the hippie mentality: "The world is an uncomfortable place to the hippie sometimes ... Most of the hippies are warm people when they accept you into their circles ... they claim to be persecuted by those who don't take the time to understand." *The Post* quoted one "hippie" in attendance this way: "I mean, we are really freaking out in Vietnam. Who needs war, man, when you've got love ... It's a real groove here. There's no hassle. The only hangups are the ones you come with." There were a few more hangups: Rain, mud and police. Sheriff William Heidtman, a self-described "tough son of a bitch," later admitted he had men plant red ants at the concert site and lure alligators into canals where people were swimming. "I had to do what I had to do to get them to know they weren't going to run the show — we were," Heidtman said.

1970

■ May 4, 1970: *The Palm Beach Post* wins a Pulitzer Prize in feature photography for its images of the poverty and poor working conditions of farm-workers in the Glades.

■ Fall 1970: Palm Beach High School and Roosevelt High are combined into the integrated Twin Lakes High School. Within two years, a federal judge rules that Palm Beach County schools are integrated.

1971

■ 1971: Palm Beach Junior College (now Palm Beach Community College) opens Boca Raton campus at Florida Atlantic University.

■ July 19, 1971: *National Enquirer* tabloid moves to Lantana.

■ November 1971: Scientists find the first cases on the South Florida mainland of lethal yellowing, a plant disease that nearly wipes out Palm Beach County's namesake coconut palms.

Feb. 17, 1972
Wellington begins

The Palm Beach County Commission approves the first planned unit development for a far-flung 7,400-acre tract that will become Wellington.

1968

■ September: Palm Beach Atlantic College opens in downtown West Palm Beach with 88 students.

■ Oct. 6: Carver Hospital, for blacks, opens in Belle Glade.

■ December: Palm Beach Gardens Medical Center opens.

Jan. 22, 1973

Doctors Hospital, later Palm Beach Regional Hospital, opens in Lake Worth.

July 3, 1976

Interstate 95 is completed between Palm Beach Gardens and Miami.

June 1982

Palm Beach Junior College opens Palm Beach Gardens campus.

The Palm Beach Post

Jan. 19, 1977

SNOW!

The first-ever recorded snow in West Palm Beach. Snowfall is reported at Palm Beach International Airport from 6:10 to 8:40 a.m., with most flakes melting on impact. Accumulations of up to one-quarter-inch reported in sheltered areas from Jupiter to Delray Beach. Snow falls as far south as Miami.

The Palm Beach Post

Gateways to growth

In the late '70s, the Palm Beach International Airport still had a small-town feel (above). Meanwhile, in Lake Park, the old Kelsey City gates (left) — a remnant of Harry Kelsey's 1920s dream of a Boom-era resort named for him — were about to meet the wrecking ball, a victim of highway expansion and changing times.

1978

- January: Palm Beach Junior College campus in Belle Glade opens for classes.
- March 28: After West Palm Beach begins electing commissioners by district rather than at-large, Eva Mack and Ruby L. Bullock are the first blacks ever elected to the City Commission. Helen Wilkes is elected the first female mayor.

1979

- Feb. 14: Palm Beach–Martin County Medical Center opens. Changes name to Jupiter Medical Center in September 1984.
- Sept. 3: Hurricane David slides up Palm Beach County coast.

Oct. 4, 1982

Delray Community Hospital, now Delray Beach Medical Center, opens.

timeline continues >

SunFest 2009: The multi-day music festival now has a $4-million-plus budget and an annual attendance of up to 325,000. It is one of the largest and most prestigious events of its kind in the country.

May 6-15, 1983

The first SunFest

The first SunFest draws about 100,000 to Flagler Drive in West Palm Beach.

Jan. 11, 1991

Mizner Park, Boca Raton's 28-acre shopping and entertainment complex, opens.

Eliza Gutierrez/The Palm Beach Post

1984-2009

One Million and Counting

PALM BEACH COUNTY'S PAST 25 YEARS HAVE BEEN MUCH LIKE THE FIRST 25: Rapid growth and astonishing prosperity, followed by a sobering slowdown. At the dawn of the 21st century, the infamous "ballot bedlam" of Election 2000 turns the eyes of the world upon us; then three hurricanes humble us in 2004 and 2005.

Several political-corruption scandals follow. But 2009 ushers in the promise of a high-tech future — and a major new industry for the county: biotech.

Oct. 24, 1988

New passenger terminal and parking garage open at Palm Beach International Airport; named for World War II flying ace David McCampbell.

1988, The Palm Beach Post

1988

Palm Beach Junior College is renamed Palm Beach Community College.

Start timeline

March 1984

Northwood Institute — later Northwood University — opens in suburban West Palm Beach.

Dec. 19, 1987

I-95 closes the 'missing link'

Thirty-four-mile "missing link" of Interstate 95, from Palm Beach Gardens to Stuart, opens, completing the 1,894-mile expressway from Miami to Maine.

Jan. 9, 1989

The Tri-Rail commuter train, a 70-mile line from West Palm Beach to Miami, begins service with 18 trains and an average of 3,000 riders a day.

1991

■ April: A Jupiter woman, Patricia Bowman, accuses William Kennedy Smith, nephew of President John F. Kennedy, of raping her on March 30 behind the Kennedy Estate in Palm Beach. The trial, in Palm Beach Circuit Court, lures the world press to downtown West Palm Beach. Smith is acquitted on Dec. 11.

The Associated Press

Nov. 19, 1991: William Kennedy Smith, left, walks into Palm Beach County Court with his cousin, John F. Kennedy Jr., for jury selection in Smith's rape trial. Several members of the Kennedy clan showed up to support Smith, who was acquitted.

Christine and Eugene Lynn

■ Sept. 20: The College of Boca Raton becomes Lynn University after insurance magnate Eugene Lynn donates $1.6 million.

Florida's First Lady of Musical Theater: Jan McArt (right) ran Boca Raton's Royal Palm Dinner Theatre for 24 years, throughout the '80s and '90s. In 2004, she was hired to expand the theater arts department at Lynn University.

March 9, 1991

Old School Square in Delray Beach opens.

Sept. 19, 1992

The Raymond G. Kravis Center for the Performing Arts in West Palm Beach opens.

1996

■ April 26: Coral Sky Amphitheater opens west of West Palm Beach.
■ July 4: Meyer Amphitheater opens along the downtown West Palm Beach waterfront.
■ Dec. 31: Wellington is incorporated as Palm Beach County's 37th municipality.

1995

■ April 20: New Palm Beach County Courthouse opens.
■ June 26: Veterans Affairs Medical Center opens in Riviera Beach.
■ August: Palm Beach County's first mosque opens in West Palm Beach.

1997

■ Aug. 20: Former Palm Beach High, vacant for eight years, reopens after $29.5 million renovation as Alexander W. Dreyfoos Jr. School of the Arts.

■ Aug. 31: West Palm Beach Municipal Stadium hosts the Montreal Expos minor-league game; it is the stadium's last league baseball game.

timeline continues >

April 22, 1994

North County Airport in Palm Beach Gardens opens.

Feb. 28, 1998

$28 million Roger Dean Stadium complex opens in Jupiter's new Abacoa neighborhood.

June 2008: Florida Marlins pitcher Josh Johnson warms up before a game at Roger Dean Stadium.

Damon Higgins/The Palm Beach Post

Sept. 1, 1998

The 61-year-old Town of Golfview, bought out for use as Palm Beach International Airport property, goes out of existence.

2000

Brazill   Grunow

■ May 26, 2000: 13-year-old Nathaniel Brazill fatally shoots Lake Worth Middle School teacher Barry Grunow.

■ Oct. 27: The 72-acre CityPlace shopping center opens in West Palm Beach.

Lannis Waters/The Palm Beach Post

Nov. 24, 2000: Surrounded by attorneys for the Democrats and Republicans, the Palm Beach County election canvassing board examines ballots in the county Emergency Operations Center, where a hand count of all Palm Beach County ballots is taking place. Holding ballots (from left): County Commissioner Carol Roberts, Judge Charles Burton, Supervisor of Elections Theresa LePore.

Inside the lighting mechanism of the Jupiter Inlet Lighthouse. One pane, shattered in the 1928 hurricane, is held together with bars.

Oct. 1999

For the first time since the Civil War, the Jupiter Lighthouse shuts down for a $856,000 renovation.

timeline continues >

2001

■ July 1: Tenet Healthcare Corp. buys Good Samaritan and St. Mary's Medical centers for $244 million, turning the nonprofit hospitals into for-profits.

■ Sept. 11: The shock of the terrorist attacks strikes home with the discovery that at least 12 of 19 hijackers had lived in Palm Beach County.

Photo editor Bob Stevens

■ Oct. 5: Bob Stevens, a photo editor at Boca Raton-based tabloid publisher American Media, dies of anthrax exposure from a letter he opens.

Mohamed Atta
The Sept. 11 terrorist was on the Boston flight that crashed into the north tower of the World Trade Center. His last address was in Coral Springs; he had bought a membership at World Gym in Delray Beach in July 2001. He rented planes three times from Palm Beach Flight Training at Lantana airport and was spotted at a bar in Hollywood on Sept. 7, 2001.

March 8, 2003

The Norton Museum of Art opens new three-story, $20 million wing, part of an overall $35 million campaign.

2004

Jan. 10: The $83 million Palm Beach County Convention Center opens.

2005

■ May 12: A 36 percent spike in home prices makes Palm Beach County one of the nation's hottest housing markets. Within two years, however, a housing slump hits.

■ Oct. 24: Hurricane Wilma kills 30 people statewide and knocks out power to 3.2 million homes and businesses — more than any single event in Florida Power & Light Co. history.

ELECTION 2000, Nov. 7, 2000: A close vote and a confusing "butterfly ballot" turn all eyes on Palm Beach County. In the end, George Bush won Florida by 537 votes.

HURRICANE FRANCES, Sept. 5, 2004: Frances becomes the first hurricane in 25 years to strike Palm Beach County and the Treasure Coast.

HURRICANE JEANNE, Sept. 25, 2004: Jeanne becomes the second hurricane to make landfall at St. Lucie Inlet in three weeks — and the fourth to hit Florida in six weeks.

2006

■ Oct. 10: Loxahatchee Groves incorporates as Palm Beach County's 38th municipality.

■ Jan. 11: After spending about $875 million to destroy more than 11 million citrus trees since 1995, Florida officials say they will stop cutting healthy trees in the battle against the spread of canker.

2007

■ July 2: Drought-stricken Lake Okeechobee drops to its lowest level on record, 8.82 feet.

■ July 12: The Phillips Point office complex in downtown West Palm Beach sells for $200 million — the richest property sale in county history.

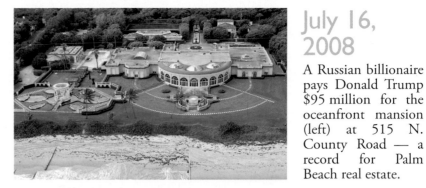

July 16, 2008

A Russian billionaire pays Donald Trump $95 million for the oceanfront mansion (left) at 515 N. County Road — a record for Palm Beach real estate.

2008

■ March 15: Palm Beach County's original courthouse opens as the Richard and Pat Johnson Palm Beach County History Museum.

■ June 24: The state announces a $1.7 billion deal to buy virtually all of U.S. Sugar Corp.'s land in South Florida. The plan: to convert its 187,000 acres into reservoirs and filtering marshes.

■ Aug. 20: Tropical Storm Fay drenches Palm Beach County and the Treasure Coast.

The Associated Press

May 1, 2007: Lake Okeechobee nears a record low because of severe drought. Deep cracks cover the bottom of what should be 5-feet-deep Lake Okeechobee, a backup water source for millions in South Florida and the lifeblood of the Everglades. Two months after this photo was taken, the lake hit a record low: 8.82 feet, down from around 12 feet the year before. The fishing industry around the lake suffered, as Charles L. Corbin Sr. of Belle Glade, owner of Slim's Fish Camp, noted in a letter to *The Palm Beach Post* in September 2007: "There are no customers because you can't put a boat in the water."

Jan. 2009

Time magazine calls Palm Beach County "The new capital of Florida corruption," noting a slew of scandals — the 2000 presidential recount, the sexual scandals of two congressmen, the Ponzi scheme of winter Palm Beach resident Bernard Madoff, and corruption charges against two West Palm Beach city commissioners and three Palm Beach County commissioners.

"Bernie" Madoff was sentenced to 150 years in prison for masterminding the largest Ponzi scheme in history.

Timeline ends

Feb. 26, 2009

The Scripps Research Institute at Scripps Florida holds its grand opening in Jupiter.

RESTORING GLORY

Unwrapping the historic 1916 courthouse

1916

Palm Beach County builds a courthouse of Neoclassical design with three floors and a basement in West Palm Beach, on North Dixie Highway between Second and Third streets. Its single courtroom handles all of the cases for the approximately 18,000 county residents. In addition, the building holds all government offices.

2002

This view shows the 1972 modern structure that "wraps around" the original courthouse. The roofs of the 1916 courthouse and a 1927 addition can be seen jutting through the roof of the "wraparound." In 2002, the Palm Beach County Commission votes to restore the original courthouse.

2004

Hedrick Brothers Construction begins demolishing the 1972 "wraparound" surrounding the original courthouse. Project Manager Robin Lunsford and his team delicately tear down the addition to avoid harming the courthouse, whose windows remain intact. They salvage any parts they can. Then they retrieve the original courthouse columns from nearby Hillcrest Cemetery, where they have been sitting for decades. Stone-carvers and masons analyze each column to see where each one fits, then hoist the massive (as heavy as 3 tons) columns back into place.

2007

Hedrick Brothers turns over the restored courthouse to Palm Beach County on Nov. 12, 2007. Final cost is $18.9 million. Hedrick's team members — including company head Dale Hedrick, Project Manager Robin Lunsford and about 400 others — are ecstatic. Says Lunsford: "We finished on schedule and under budget. I feel great. We are celebrating what we've done here in so many ways. I mean, it could have been a flat park. Instead, Palm Beach County has given back a piece of history to the people." The restored courthouse is now home to the Richard and Pat Johnson Palm Beach County History Museum.

2007 The Royal Park Bridge, looking west toward the skyline of West Palm Beach.

1912 The Royal Park Bridge, looking west toward West Palm Beach. Palm Beachers are so proud of the bridge that they turn it into a postcard. (At the time, this was the southernmost bridge to Palm Beach.)

Entrance to South Bridge from Royal Park,
Palm Beach, Fla.

Historical Society of Palm Beach County

HOW WE GREW

THEN AND NOW: PICTURES OF PROGRESS

Historical Society of Palm Beach County

1925: A train crosses the railroad bridge, heading from Palm Beach to West Palm Beach. At right is the Whitehall Hotel under construction. The hotel addition, built at the back of Henry Flagler's mansion, remains there until 1963.

OUR BRIDGES

By ELIOT KLEINBERG | The Palm Beach Post

The first bridge from the mainland to Henry Flagler's Palm Beach was, of course, created for his clients — not walkers or bikers but wealthy tycoons who needed to get their personal train cars across Lake Worth and directly to the front door of the Royal Poinciana Hotel.

It was a rail spur built in 1895 near present-day Banyan Street in West Palm Beach. (The toll for walkers: a nickel.)

PALM BEACH

Flagler Memorial Bridge (the "north bridge") The first bridge at the site opened in 1901, replacing the earlier railroad spur that was four blocks to the south. (Henry Flagler's wife, Mary Lily, wanted the train and its noise farther away from their mansion, Whitehall.)

The current bridge, which opened in 1938, is the oldest movable bridge over the Intracoastal Waterway between Cape Canaveral and North Miami. It is scheduled for replacement.

Royal Park Bridge (the "middle bridge," at Okeechobee Boulevard): A wooden trestle from Lakeview Avenue to Royal Palm Way opened in 1911. In 1921, a new masonry structure was two days from opening when it collapsed. A temporary wooden structure was built.

Nearly two years would pass before the bridge finally opened on Aug. 11, 1924. The bridge was renovated in 1958 and replaced in 2004.

Southern Boulevard bridge (the "south bridge"): Opened in 1950, the bridge is scheduled for replacement.

Don Jorden

1976: Cars driving east on Blue Heron Boulevard head toward the old bridge to Singer Island (at left side of new bridge) while the current Blue Heron bridge is being built.

RIVIERA BEACH/SINGER ISLAND

Blue Heron Bridge (aka Jerry Thomas Bridge): Opened June 6, 1976. The first bridge from the mainland opened in 1925, to serve Paris Singer's Blue Heron Hotel, which was then under construction. A victim of the real-estate bust, the hotel would never open. A new bridge opened Nov. 12, 1949.

Gary Coronado/The Palm Beach Post

2009: Blue Heron Bridge looking west toward the Riviera Beach mainland. The Marina Grande condominium dominates the view on the right. The bridge has a fixed clearance of 65 feet.

1950: Hundreds attend the grand opening of the Lantana bridge at Ocean Avenue in 1950, including County Commissioner John Prince (right) and 4-year-old twins Lorraine (left) and Lynn Phillips Saunders of Lantana, who have the honor of cutting the ribbon. Newspapers of the day describe "curly-haired Lorraine and Lynn" as "pleased as punch" by the new bridge.

Photos from Lorraine P. Saunders

Boca Raton Historical Society

1927: A strange view toward Boca Raton's bridge. Today sea turtles are protected, but in the early days, pioneers would capture the creatures and butcher them when they came ashore to lay eggs. Early settlers also looked forward to turtle-egg harvests and used the eggs in cooking. In this 1927 photo, Louis Zimmerman pretends to ride on a turtle's back, hurried on by his friend Bill Deyo. The original Palmetto Park Road bridge is visible in the background. It featured a "swing-style" bridge, which was replaced by a drawbridge in 1928.

BOCA RATON

Palmetto Park Road: The city's first bridge across the Intracoastal, at Palmetto Park Road, opened in 1918. The current **Lucas Douglas Memorial Bridge** opened in 1987.

A fixed bridge was built across Boca Raton Inlet in 1928.

LAKE WORTH

Robert A. Harris Bridge (Lake Avenue): The first bridge to the beach opened in 1919. It would serve the beachfront casino and pool, which opened in 1922 to replace the former casino, which had burned down in 1918. A new bridge opened in 1938; the most recent opened on July 11, 1973.

LANTANA

East Ocean Avenue bridge: Opened 1950. Construction on a new bridge is scheduled to start by 2010.

DELRAY BEACH

The city's first bridge across the Intracoastal Waterway opened in 1912. The **Atlantic Avenue bridge** opened on Nov. 10, 1952.

MORE BRIDGES — and most recent openings

JUPITER
- **Jupiter Island bridge:** Opened 1969.
- **Indiantown Road bridge:** Opened 1999.

JUNO BEACH
- **Donald Ross Road bridge:** Opened 1998-1999.

PALM BEACH GARDENS
- **PGA Boulevard bridge:** Opened 1966.

BOYNTON BEACH
- **East Ocean Avenue bridge:** Former span torn down in 1998;

the new one opened in 2001.
- **Southeast 15th Avenue bridge:** Opened 1967.

DELRAY BEACH
- **Northeast Eighth Street/ George Bush Boulevard bridge:** Opened 1949.
- **Jack L. Saunders Bridge** (Linton Boulevard): Opened 1981.

BOCA RATON
- **Theodore Pratt Memorial Bridge** (Spanish River Boulevard): Opened 1971.
- **East Camino Real bridge:** Opened 1939.

OUR INLETS
Created by nature and by man

Aerials by Richard Graulich/The Palm Beach Post

Jupiter Inlet
AT THE MOUTH OF THE LOXAHATCHEE RIVER

This natural inlet dates back at least 1,000 years, according to historians, and might have been visited by explorer Juan Ponce de Leon during his historic first encounter with Florida in 1513. It first appears on maps in 1671.

It originally was very shallow and opened and closed at the whims of nature. It was closed during construction of the Jupiter Lighthouse, which opened in July 1860. During Prohibition, it was open and was a favorite of rum-runners smuggling booze from the Bahamas. A storm closed it in early 1942, enabling horseback patrols watching for German U-boats to cross it.

Since 1947, it has remained open due to regular dredging.

Lake Worth Inlet,
also called 'Palm Beach Inlet'
WIDENED BY MAN

Lake Worth Inlet was first cut naturally, by a storm, in the mid-19th century, opening Lake Worth to the Atlantic Ocean. The unstable inlet opened and closed at times, and even shifted due to the influence of currents. In the summer of 1877, the pioneers dug a new one about a mile north.

In 1918, in yet a different place, the inlet was stabilized at its current location — the result of a federal project involving a variety of agencies.

W hen the first settlers arrived in what would become Palm Beach County, they called their new home the "Lake Worth Region" after the body of water in front of them, Lake Worth. The lake was named for Gen. William J. Worth, who led U.S. forces during the last part of the Second Seminole War. That still is the formal name for the stretch of Intracoastal Waterway between Palm Beach and the mainland.

The Seminoles called the lake "Hypoluxo" — "Water all around, can't get out."

The settlers, who used boats as their main form of transportation, decided they would have to get out.

Today four inlets — two man-made, two natural but "enhanced" — provide access to the open Atlantic.

Looking south from Singer Island at the crews digging Lake Worth Inlet, 1918.   *Historical Society of Palm Beach County*

Boynton Beach Inlet, also called 'Boynton Inlet' and 'South Lake Worth Inlet'

CUT IN THE MID-1920s

Population growth left Lake Worth — "the lake" — choked with pollution, leading to the 1925-1927 creation of this opening. Engineers picked a spot where only 250 feet of land separated the ocean and the Intracoastal Waterway.

Boca Raton Inlet

NATURAL — BUT MANIPULATED BY MAN

Originally a natural waterway, the Boca Raton Inlet has changed locations at least three times during the past 200 years. Around 1930, it was stabilized by the building of jetties.

The inlet was plugged by sand during a Thanksgiving-weekend storm in 1966.

WEST PALM BEACH

THEN 1922

Palm Beach Mercantile (later the Harris building)

City Park

Historical Society of Palm Beach County

C lematis Street, water and Flagler Drive have always played important roles in downtown West Palm Beach.

The one-story Palm Beach Mercantile Co. Building, 206 Clematis St., was constructed around 1900. A series of additions made it a six-story edifice by 1923. That same year, on its east side, the slightly taller Citizens Building was completed.

At the east end of City Park was a dock; residents could board a ferry to take them to Palm Beach.

Of course, no one in 1922 could have envisioned SunFest (at right). (The 1920 population was 8,659.) Nor could anyone have predicted that, 87 years later, the city's residents would number 103,663 — making it, by far, the county's most populous municipality.

The three docks are part of the $19 million City Commons, a downtown- and waterfront-improvement project.

2009 NOW

Harris building

Citizens building

City Park

PALM BEACH

THEN 1934

- Alba Hotel
- Slat House
- Royal Poinciana Hotel
- E.R. Bradley's Beach Club
- Whitehall

Historical Society of Palm Beach County

The Biltmore (formerly the Alba)

The destruction of Henry Flagler's Royal Poinciana Hotel began in 1934 (above). The building, which opened in 1894, was once the largest hotel in the world.

The Slat House — a greenhouse with an octagonal center — was added to the Royal Poinciana when one piece of the hotel was knocked off its foundation during the 1928 Hurricane.

This Slat House is the only piece of the Royal Poinciana that still remains in its original spot. (Pieces of the Royal Poinciana still exist, however. Hundreds of homes were built from wood and bricks salvaged from the massive hotel.)

The Alba Hotel opened in 1926. (The building was converted to a condominium, The Biltmore, in the late 1970s.) When E.R. Bradley's Beach Club casino closed in 1945, Joseph P. Kennedy lamented, "Palm Beach has lost its zipperoo." A wall from Bradley's home — which was next to his casino — is all that remains today. The U.S. Census of 1930 put the population of Palm Beach at 1,707. The 2008 estimate was 9,797.

2009 NOW

Richard Graulich/The Palm Beach Post

THEN 1938

LAKE WORTH

Lake Worth Casino

Gulfstream Hotel

Mike Geibel/Lake Worth Historical Society

S hot from the top of the Gulfstream Hotel, the 1938 photo above shows the newly opened Lake Worth bridge and, in the distance, the Lake Worth Casino. It also shows the junction of Lake Avenue (eastbound) and Lucerne Avenue.

Lake Worth's first census, in 1912, counted 308 residents, 125 houses, 10 wagons, seven automobiles, 36 bicycles and 876 fowls. Today an estimated 36,725 people live within the city limits.

The first Casino was built in 1913 using 1,700 feet of lumber and 17,000 shingles. That building burned down in 1918. A new, expanded complex, the Lake Worth Casino and Baths, opened in 1922 and boasted domed towers and arched columns.

After the 1947 Hurricane tore off the roof, the Lake Worth Casino was rebuilt, featuring its current shoebox-with-windows look.

The historic Gulfstream Hotel, built in the 1920s, has changed ownership many times over the years. A portion of the old bridge, just north of the current one, is visible.

2009 NOW

Lake Worth Casino

The old bridge

Richard Graulich/The Palm Beach Post

BOCA RATON

THEN 1955

Palmetto Park Road

Beach pavilion

Historical Society of Palm Beach County

When architect Addison Mizner arrived in Boca Raton in 1925, the area was still a farming village of just a few hundred hardy souls. By the time Florida's Land Boom started collapsing a year later — Mizner along with it — the city was one of the best-known in Florida.

"Boca to me is the proverbial Florida boom town: wonderful plans, amazing hype, a grandiose concept for the world's most beautiful resort — and, ultimately, not enough money to see it quite through," said Sue Gillis, curator of the Boca Raton Historical Society.

Eventually, the money came back to Boca. In 1956, Arthur Vining Davis, chairman of the Alcoa aluminum company, paid $22.5 million for the Boca Raton Resort & Club and surrounding land. It was the largest land deal in Florida at the time — and led to today's bustling Boca Raton.

The photos show the public beach at the east end of Palmetto Park Road. The 29-square-mile city has 4 miles of public beachfront.

The 1950 U.S. Census counted 992 residents; a special study in 1955 showed 2,762. Boca Raton today has a population of some 85,293 and is Palm Beach County's second most populous municipality.

2009 NOW

Palmetto Park Road

South Beach
Park Pavilion

Richard Graulich/The Palm Beach Post

How South Florida grew

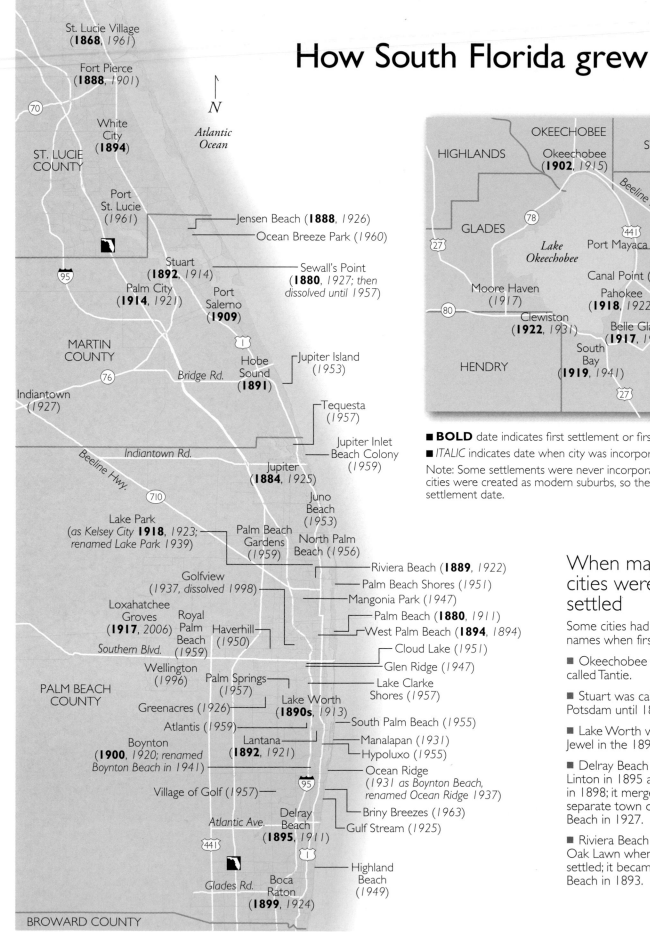

St. Lucie Village
(**1868**, *1961*)

Fort Pierce
(**1888**, *1901*)

⑦⓪

White
City
(**1894**)

ST. LUCIE
COUNTY

↑
N

*Atlantic
Ocean*

Port
St. Lucie
(*1961*)

⑨⑤

Jensen Beach (**1888**, *1926*)
Ocean Breeze Park (*1960*)

Stuart
(**1892**, *1914*)
Palm City
(**1914**, *1921*)

Port
Salerno
(**1909**)

Sewall's Point
(**1880**, *1927; then
dissolved until 1957*)

MARTIN
COUNTY

⑦⑥

Bridge Rd.

Hobe
Sound
(**1891**)

Jupiter Island
(*1953*)

Indiantown
(*1927*)

Tequesta
(*1957*)

Indiantown Rd.

Jupiter Inlet
Beach Colony
(*1959*)

Jupiter
(**1884**, *1925*)

Beeline Hwy.

⑦①⓪

Juno
Beach
(*1953*)

Lake Park
(*as Kelsey City* **1918**, *1923;
renamed Lake Park 1939*)

Palm Beach
Gardens
(*1959*)

North Palm
Beach (*1956*)

Golfview
(*1937, dissolved 1998*)

Riviera Beach (**1889**, *1922*)
Palm Beach Shores (*1951*)
Mangonia Park (*1947*)

Loxahatchee
Groves
(**1917**, *2006*)

Royal
Palm
Beach
(*1959*)

Haverhill
(*1950*)

Palm Beach (**1880**, *1911*)
West Palm Beach (**1894**, *1894*)

Southern Blvd.

Cloud Lake (*1951*)
Glen Ridge (*1947*)

PALM BEACH
COUNTY

Wellington
(*1996*)

Palm Springs
(*1957*)

Lake Clarke
Shores (*1957*)

Greenacres (*1926*)

Lake Worth
(**1890s**, *1913*)

Atlantis (*1959*)

South Palm Beach (*1955*)

Boynton
(**1900**, *1920; renamed
Boynton Beach in 1941*)

Lantana
(**1892**, *1921*)

Manalapan (*1931*)
Hypoluxo (*1955*)

⑨⑤

Ocean Ridge
(*1931 as Boynton Beach,
renamed Ocean Ridge 1937*)

Village of Golf (*1957*)

Briny Breezes (*1963*)

Atlantic Ave.

Delray
Beach
(**1895**, *1911*)

Gulf Stream (*1925*)

④④①

①

Highland
Beach
(*1949*)

Glades Rd.

Boca
Raton
(**1899**, *1924*)

BROWARD COUNTY

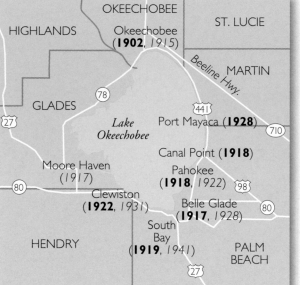

HIGHLANDS

OKEECHOBEE

Okeechobee
(**1902**, *1915*)

ST. LUCIE

MARTIN

Beeline Hwy.

GLADES

⑦⑧

④④①

Port Mayaca (**1928**)

②⑦

*Lake
Okeechobee*

⑦①⓪

Moore Haven
(*1917*)

⑧⓪

Clewiston
(**1922**, *1931*)

Canal Point (**1918**)

Pahokee
(**1918**, *1922*)

⑨⑧

Belle Glade
(**1917**, *1928*)

⑧⓪

HENDRY

South
Bay
(**1919**, *1941*)

PALM
BEACH

②⑦

■ **BOLD** date indicates first settlement or first post office.

■ *ITALIC* indicates date when city was incorporated.

Note: Some settlements were never incorporated. Some cities were created as modern suburbs, so there is no settlement date.

When major cities were settled

Some cities had different names when first settled.

■ Okeechobee was first called Tantie.

■ Stuart was called Potsdam until 1895.

■ Lake Worth was called Jewel in the 1890s.

■ Delray Beach was called Linton in 1895 and Delray in 1898; it merged with separate town of Delray Beach in 1927.

■ Riviera Beach was called Oak Lawn when first settled; it became Riviera Beach in 1893.

POPULATION

1830
Florida	34,730
Southern peninsula	517

1880
Florida	269,493
Dade County	257

1910
Florida	752,619
Palm Beach County	5,577
Boynton Beach	671
Delray	250
Jupiter	398
West Palm Beach	1,743

1940
Florida	1,897,414
Palm Beach County	79,989
Boca Raton	723
Boynton Beach	1,326
Delray Beach	3,661
Greenacres	873
Jupiter	832
Lake Worth	7,408
Lantana	713
Riviera Beach	1,981
West Palm Beach	33,693

1970
Florida	6,791,418
Palm Beach County	348,993
Boca Raton	28,506
Boynton Beach	18,115
Delray Beach	19,366
Greenacres	1,731
Jupiter	3,136
Lake Worth	23,714
Lantana	7,126
Riviera Beach	21,401
Royal Palm Beach	475
West Palm Beach	57,375

2000
Florida	15,982,378
Palm Beach County	1,131,184
Boca Raton	74,764
Boynton Beach	60,389
Delray Beach	60,020
Greenacres	27,569
Jupiter	39,328
Lake Worth	35,133
Lantana	9,437
Riviera Beach	29,884
Royal Palm Beach	21,523
West Palm Beach	82,103

U.S. Census data

How counties changed

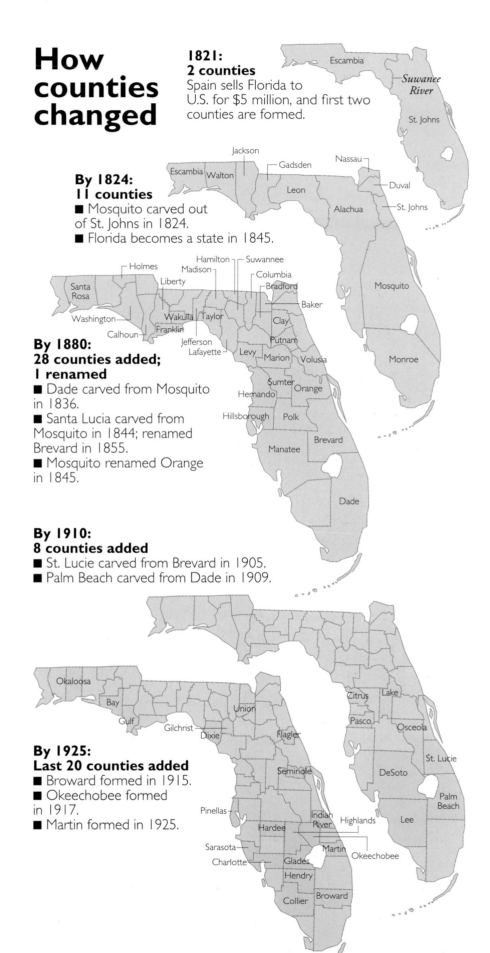

**1821:
2 counties**
Spain sells Florida to U.S. for $5 million, and first two counties are formed.

**By 1824:
11 counties**
- Mosquito carved out of St. Johns in 1824.
- Florida becomes a state in 1845.

**By 1880:
28 counties added;
1 renamed**
- Dade carved from Mosquito in 1836.
- Santa Lucia carved from Mosquito in 1844; renamed Brevard in 1855.
- Mosquito renamed Orange in 1845.

**By 1910:
8 counties added**
- St. Lucie carved from Brevard in 1905.
- Palm Beach carved from Dade in 1909.

**By 1925:
Last 20 counties added**
- Broward formed in 1915.
- Okeechobee formed in 1917.
- Martin formed in 1925.

Greg Lovett/The Palm Beach Post

After back-to-back 1947 hurricanes pushed the level of Lake Okeechobee to 18.77 feet — and flooded much of South Florida — the government took action. From 1950 to 1971, 1,400 miles of canals were built. In the 1960s, a canal "straightened" the Kissimmee River (above). However, the alteration changed the natural flow of water running south into Lake Okeechobee, eliminating marshes that had formerly filtered out pollution and slowed flooding.

TOP 5 EVENTS THAT SHAPED PALM BEACH COUNTY

Eliot Kleinberg of *The Palm Beach Post* asked several state and local historians — including former *Post* staff writer Bill McGoun, author of *Southeast Florida Pioneers* — to name the five biggest events in the county's history.

Here are their selections:

1. Henry Flagler comes to Palm Beach: 1893
With his hotels and railroad, Flagler opened a tropical wilderness to tourism and development.

2. Land Boom: mid-1920s
In a frenzy of capitalism, opportunists bought and sold properties like pieces of a Monopoly game. The thrill was gone by 1927 — but Palm Beach County had sealed its legacy as a "paradise."

3. World War II — and subsequent population boom
Thousands of soldiers who trained in Palm Beach County stayed or came back — boosting Florida's population from 2 million to 3 million from 1940 to 1950.

4. 1947 hurricanes prompt water control
After two hurricanes and a tropical storm hit within five weeks, water covered 3 million acres from Kissimmee to Florida Bay for six months. "Everything from Orlando south was under water except the small drainage districts around Lake Okeechobee,"

recalled Fritz Stein, a third-generation Glades farmer. As a result, Florida created a flood-control agency that later became the South Florida Water Management District, which controls not just where the water is going but also whether there is enough for people to drink.

5. Everglades drainage leads to development of sugar industry: 1900s to 1920s
In 1905, Napoleon Bonaparte Broward was elected governor based on his promise to drain the Everglades. By 1927, a network of canals accounted for 440 miles of levees and 16 locks and dams. As dry areas emerged, farmers and homesteaders poured in — boosting agriculture but harming the natural water systems.

Crime of the century

The murders of Judge Chillingworth and his wife

By ELIOT KLEINBERG | The Palm Beach Post

Was it really the 'crime of the century'?

To understand the magnitude of the June 1955 murders of Judge Curtis Chillingworth and his wife, Marjorie, is to understand how small West Palm Beach was at the time — and how big Chillingworth was.

Even now, the facts of the murders are astonishing:

■ Chillingworth, an iconic local judge, had been targeted by a fellow judge.

■ Goons abducted the judge and Mrs. Chillingworth from Manalapan, a sparsely settled beachfront.

■ The murderers weighed down these pillars of society with lead belts and dumped them in the Atlantic Ocean ("Ladies first," one killer said while pushing Marjorie overboard. The judge told his wife, "Honey, remember, I love you." She replied, "I love you, too.")

■ The murderers, to give the code that the job was done, interrupted crooked Judge Joseph Peel's viewing of *The $64,000 Question* with a four-word phone call: "The motor is fixed."

■ The loose lips by one of the bad guys led to arrests and trials that were so sensational, they prompted two books, led to the founding of the Florida Department of Law Enforcement (FDLE), and ended with what is believed to be Florida's first-ever murder conviction without a corpse.

Now consider that all this happened in a West Palm Beach with about 50,000 residents — less than half what it has now.

And consider that Chillingworth — grandson of a man who served as a West Palm Beach mayor and a Dade County sheriff, son of a city attorney and developer — had been on the bench for three decades and was one of Florida's top judges.

Chillingworth had grown suspicious of Joseph Peel, the city's only municipal judge.

Peel had been protecting bolita (illegal lottery) operators and moonshiners. But it was his mishandling of a divorce that raised the ire of Chillingworth, his superior. Peel feared that he might be suspended, or worse.

So Peel hired, as assassins, two bolita partners who stood to go out of business if they lost Peel's protection: Floyd "Lucky" Holzapfel, a World War II veteran, handyman and Cub Scout leader; and Bobby Lincoln, a moonshiner.

Four years after the judge and his wife vanished, when it appeared that the mystery never would be solved, Holzapfel told a friend, "Man, there's a hole out there in that ocean nobody's found the bottom of."

The friend told Peel, who paid him $8,000 to bump off the big-mouthed Holzapfel. Instead, the man went to the Florida Sheriff's Bureau (forerunner of the FDLE).

Holzapfel was set up: Lured to a Melbourne hotel and loaded with booze, he told everything. In another room, a police officer recorded it all on 30 reels of tape.

The now-fingered Judge Peel fled, but a friend set him up and cops nabbed him in Chattanooga.

Bobby Lincoln was already in prison on a 1958 moonshine conviction when State Attorney Phil O'Connell Sr. offered him immunity for the murders if he would testify. (Since no bodies were recovered, O'Connell needed an eyewitness to prove murder.)

Faced with that, Holzapfel decided not to fight. During a November 1960 hearing, in a crowded courtroom, a sobbing Holzapfel confessed everything, adding that Peel had even ordered him to kill prosecutor O'Connell.

"People like us," Holzapfel said, "should be stamped out like cockroaches because they aren't fit to live with decent people."

The victims
JUDGE C.E. CHILLINGWORTH and his wife, MARJORIE

The murderers

FLOYD "LUCKY" HOLZAPFEL (above, left)
When Holzapfel was sentenced to life for the murder of Judge Chillingworth and his wife, the sentencing judge said, "It was not just a man's life that was taken. It was Judge Chillingworth." Holzapfel suffered a stroke in prison and died in 2006, three years before his parole date.

BOBBY LINCOLN (above, right)
He finished his federal prison term in 1962, moved to Chicago, converted to Islam and changed his name to David Karrim. He died at 80 in Riviera Beach in 2004.

Lucky Holzapfel and Bobby Lincoln woke up the Chillingworths in their Manalapan beach house, bound and gagged them, and led them to a boat. When Mrs. Chillingworth loosened her gag and screamed, Holzapfel struck her with his pistol, drawing blood. The murderers weighed the couple down and pushed them overboard. At Peel's trial, Holzapfel testified, "We did it for Joe."

The mastermind
JOSEPH PEEL
Sentenced to life in 1961, Peel was paroled in 1982 because he had terminal cancer. He died nine days later, refusing to confess even on his deathbed.

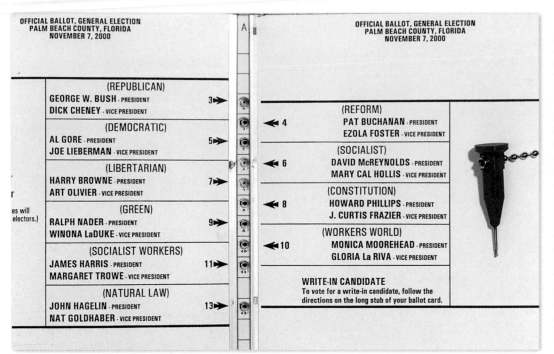

OFFICIAL BALLOT, GENERAL ELECTION
PALM BEACH COUNTY, FLORIDA
NOVEMBER 7, 2000

(REPUBLICAN)
GEORGE W. BUSH · PRESIDENT
DICK CHENEY · VICE PRESIDENT   3➡

(DEMOCRATIC)
AL GORE · PRESIDENT
JOE LIEBERMAN · VICE PRESIDENT   5➡

(LIBERTARIAN)
HARRY BROWNE · PRESIDENT
ART OLIVIER · VICE PRESIDENT   7➡

(GREEN)
RALPH NADER · PRESIDENT
WINONA LaDUKE · VICE PRESIDENT   9➡

(SOCIALIST WORKERS)
JAMES HARRIS · PRESIDENT
MARGARET TROWE · VICE PRESIDENT   11➡

(NATURAL LAW)
JOHN HAGELIN · PRESIDENT
NAT GOLDHABER · VICE PRESIDENT   13➡

OFFICIAL BALLOT, GENERAL ELECTION
PALM BEACH COUNTY, FLORIDA
NOVEMBER 7, 2000

⬅4   **(REFORM)**
PAT BUCHANAN · PRESIDENT
EZOLA FOSTER · VICE PRESIDENT

⬅6   **(SOCIALIST)**
DAVID McREYNOLDS · PRESIDENT
MARY CAL HOLLIS · VICE PRESIDENT

⬅8   **(CONSTITUTION)**
HOWARD PHILLIPS · PRESIDENT
J. CURTIS FRAZIER · VICE PRESIDENT

⬅10   **(WORKERS WORLD)**
MONICA MOOREHEAD · PRESIDENT
GLORIA La RIVA · VICE PRESIDENT

WRITE-IN CANDIDATE
To vote for a write-in candidate, follow the
directions on the long stub of your ballot card.

Nothing symbolizes America's close and crazy Election 2000 quite like Palm Beach County's "butterfly ballot." Palm Beach County Elections Supervisor Theresa LePore had good intentions: She worried about senior voters being able to read a list of 10 presidential candidates. So she approved a design that spread the candidates across two facing pages, with a single column of punch holes in the middle. Many voters who intended to vote for Al Gore said they were confused and marked their ballots for Pat Buchanan. The made-for-TV image of irate retirees and the seemingly endless examination of "hanging chads" put Palm Beach County in the world's spotlight.

Notoriety ripples 'round the world

By GEORGE BENNETT | The Palm Beach Post

For decades, Palm Beach County's political reputation was as a playground for the Kennedys and a national cash cow for candidates.

Then, with the arrival of the 21st century, it suddenly became a hothouse for controversy, corruption and confused voters.

The world's perception of Palm Beach County began to change on Election Day 2000, when a trickle — then a torrent — of Democratic voters said they were baffled by the design of the county's presidential ballot.

When Florida ended up deciding the presidency for Republican George W. Bush by a mere 537 votes, Palm Beach County's "butterfly ballot" became a symbol of international infamy.

Then came a dizzying series of scandals that, in less than three years, drove two congressmen from office in shame and led five local elected officials to resign and to plead guilty to federal corruption charges.

When Mary McCarty left her county commission seat in January 2009, *Time* magazine branded Palm Beach County "The New Capital of Florida Corruption."

The county's image problem was particularly bewildering to those who came of age during a more tranquil period of local politics.

"Unfortunately, it all happened within one decade here," marveled Harry Johnston, who served as state senator from West Palm Beach from 1974 to 1986 and as a member of

Congress from 1989 to 1997.

Even in Nigeria — where Johnston was part of a team of election observers in 2007 — "every one of them knew Palm Beach County," he noted.

Phil Lewis, a presence in the county's real-estate and political circles for more than 60 years, saw the scandals as an unfortunate by-product of the county's growth.

As the county grew, so did the egos of some politicians, he said: "They began to think they were all-powerful."

More than two years after he left office, Mark Foley spoke ruefully of his own contribution to the county's legacy. "That's what lives with me daily — I think that the county that I love so much, I made them suffer through this."

J. Gwendolynne Berry/The Palm Beach Post

Congressman Tim Mahoney answers questions about his "multiple" affairs during an interview at PGA National on Oct. 17, 2008.

THREE YEARS, SEVEN SCANDALS

FALLING FROM GRACE

Mark Foley and Tim Mahoney

Mark Foley was a local boy who made good, a Lake Worth native who rose from city commissioner to election to Congress in 1994 at age 40. In 2006, Foley appeared headed toward a seventh term when it was revealed that he had sent sexually charged Internet messages to teenage boys who had worked in the congressional-page program.

Mark Foley

Foley resigned abruptly on Sept. 29, 2006. Democrat Tim Mahoney, who had campaigned as a champion of "faith, family and personal responsibility," was narrowly elected to Foley's seat.

Two years later, Mahoney was a few weeks away from re-election when it was revealed that he had been carrying on an extramarital affair with a woman he had put on his congressional and campaign payrolls.

When the woman threatened a sexual-harassment lawsuit, Mahoney paid a $121,903 settlement to try to keep the matter silent.

After the affair and hush money became public, Mahoney admitted to "multiple" affairs while in office. He lost his seat to Republican Tom Rooney.

DISHEARTENING DISHONESTY

Five elected officials, five cases of misuse of power

Garden-variety greed torpedoed the careers of five elected officials in less than three years.

RAY LIBERTI, West Palm Beach city commissioner: The former state House member took $66,000 in cash and a $2,000 watch as part of a scheme to force the owners of a massage parlor and a nightclub to sell their properties. He resigned in May 2006, pleaded guilty to mail fraud and witness tampering, and served 18 months in federal prison.

TONY MASILOTTI, Palm Beach County commissioner: He used his office to secretly earn millions off land deals and took $50,000 to pressure the Diocese of Palm Beach to sell land to his associates. He resigned in October 2006, pleaded guilty to honest-services fraud, and was sentenced in 2007 to five years in prison.

JAMES EXLINE, West Palm Beach city commissioner: He took $50,000 from developer John Sansbury without disclosing it, then funneled the money through a jewelry store to try to hide it from the Internal Revenue Service. He resigned in January 2007, pleaded guilty to willfully failing to report income, and served 10 months in federal prison.

WARREN NEWELL, Palm Beach County commissioner: He pushed the county's $14 million purchase of a marina, without revealing that he owed its owners $48,092; used his public office to increase the value of a property, without disclosing that he was a former partner in the company that owned it; and received secret profits from a $217 million state reservoir project, after voting to spend county money to study the proposal. Newell resigned in July 2007, pleaded guilty to honest-services fraud, and was sentenced to five years in prison. In 2009, a judge lopped two years off Newell's sentence after he provided information that helped prosecutors nail County Commissioner Mary McCarty on corruption charges.

MARY McCARTY, Palm Beach County commissioner: She steered county business to her husband's bond-underwriting firms, and didn't disclose that she had accepted free and deeply discounted luxury hotel rooms from a developer — while supporting the developer's bid to build a hotel at the county convention center. She resigned in January 2009, pleaded guilty to honest-services fraud, and was sentenced to 3½ years in prison. "What disheartens me, perhaps as much as the shame I have brought down upon myself, is the continuation of scrutiny that I have brought to the Palm Beach County Commission," McCarty wrote in her resignation letter.

Palm Beach County
BY THE NUMBERS

101 Record high temperature,
set July 21, 1942

24 Record low temperature,
set Dec. 29, 1894

$95 million

Most expensive residential transaction

Sale of mansion at 515 N. County Road, Palm Beach
By Donald Trump to Russian fertilizer billionaire Dmitry Rybolovlev
July 2008

$200 million

Most expensive commercial transaction

Sale of Phillips Point, 777 Flagler Drive, West Palm Beach
July 2007
(The waterfront, two-building complex had last sold in late 2003 for $138 million)

42 stories (390 feet)

Tallest building: Tiara condominium

3000 N. Ocean Drive, Singer Island, Riviera Beach

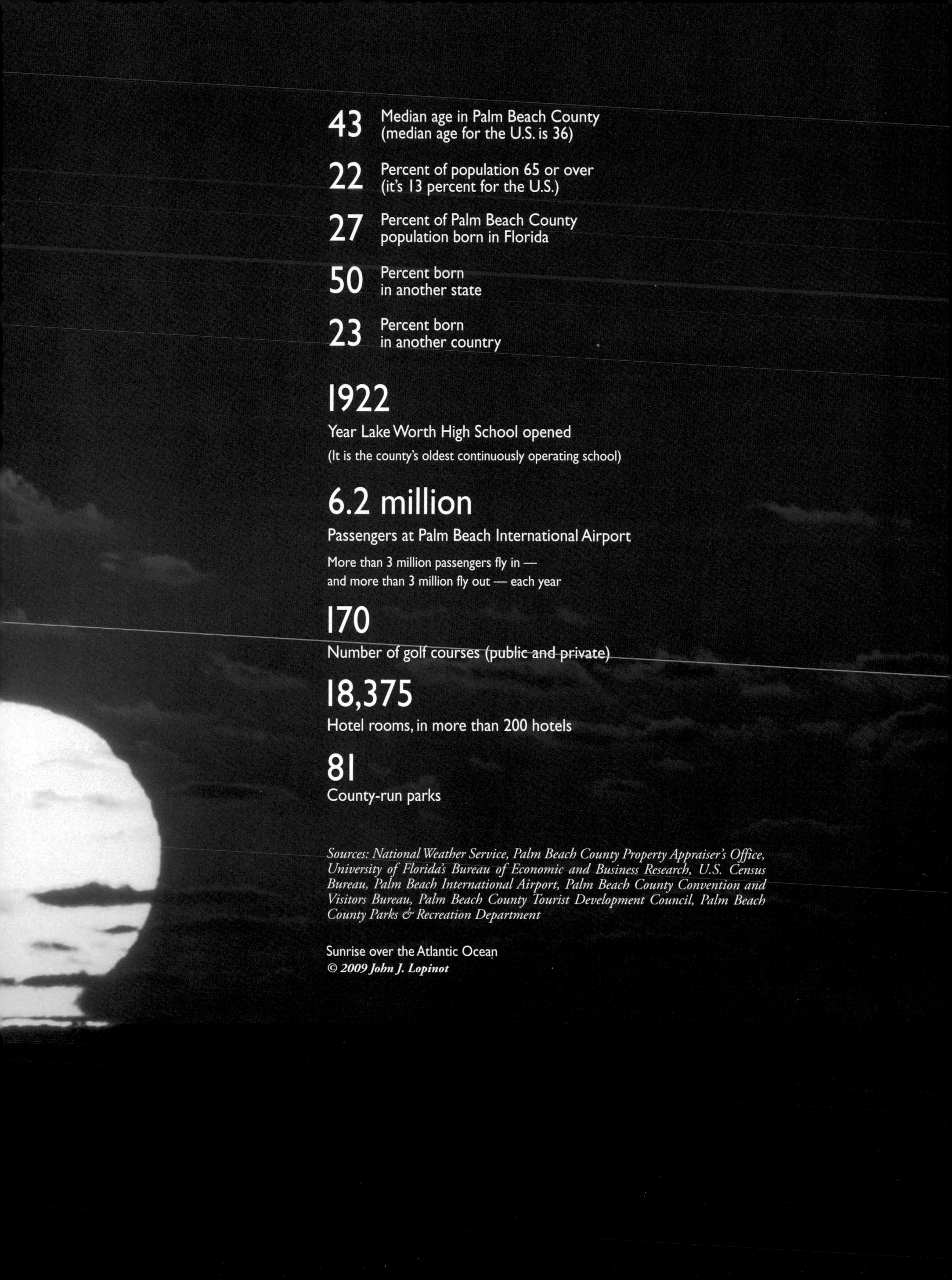

43 Median age in Palm Beach County
(median age for the U.S. is 36)

22 Percent of population 65 or over
(it's 13 percent for the U.S.)

27 Percent of Palm Beach County
population born in Florida

50 Percent born
in another state

23 Percent born
in another country

1922

Year Lake Worth High School opened

(It is the county's oldest continuously operating school)

6.2 million

Passengers at Palm Beach International Airport

More than 3 million passengers fly in —
and more than 3 million fly out — each year

170

Number of golf courses (public and private)

18,375

Hotel rooms, in more than 200 hotels

81

County-run parks

Sources: National Weather Service, Palm Beach County Property Appraiser's Office, University of Florida's Bureau of Economic and Business Research, U.S. Census Bureau, Palm Beach International Airport, Palm Beach County Convention and Visitors Bureau, Palm Beach County Tourist Development Council, Palm Beach County Parks & Recreation Department

Sunrise over the Atlantic Ocean
© 2009 John J. Lopinot

LIDO POOLS, PALM BEACH, FLORIDA

COMMUNITY BLOOD BANK

KNOLL

HYA - GRAPEFRUIT - 6/52 WP

ATHLETICS

FOREST HILL HIGH
"FALCONS"
VS
BELLE GLADE
"GOLDEN RAMS"

NEXT HOME GAME
SEPTEMBER 29
CARDINAL NEWMAN

FOREST HILL ATHLETIC FIELD
SEPTEMBER 22, 19 - 8:15 P. M.
WEST PALM BEACH

TV

William Glenn Mize of Delray Beach rides a stuffed buffalo at Africa U.S.A., a Boca Raton tourist attraction of the 1950s and early '60s that made the cover of *Life*. His grandparents arrived in Palm Beach County in 1925. His maternal grandfather, William Alonzo Gill Sr., built the house on Southwest Second Avenue in Delray Beach that Mize still lives in.

HOW WE PLAY

FUN AND SUN BEYOND COMPARE — AND WATER, WATER, EVERYWHERE!

1. In the 1940s, Worth Avenue extended out over the ocean, thanks to the Palm Beach Pier. On the pier were a coffee shop and a place to rent rods and reels. "In the evening, the jukebox played as we danced on the pier under the stars," recalls Carolyn Stroupe Stambaugh of West Palm Beach.

2. Connie Mack, manager of the Philadelphia Athletics, gets congratulations on his 50th year in baseball from Jerry Browning, 7, in 1946. The A's trained in West Palm Beach from 1945 to 1962.

3. The Sunset Cocktail Lounge in West Palm Beach was the "Cotton Club of the South" in the 1950s. Ella Fitzgerald, Count Basie and Duke Ellington were among the performers at the Sunset, owned by Dennis and Thelma Starks. Mrs. Starks, who died in 2008 at 91, recalled, "We had music in those days."

4. Jeannette Buss Cearley (center) is named Miss Community Blood Bank at the Bazaar International in Riviera Beach, just before its opening in 1960. At left is Chris Noel, who was dubbed "the next Marilyn Monroe"

when she starred in movies such as *Girl Happy* with Elvis Presley. She now runs the Vetsville Cease Fire House, a Boynton Beach center for homeless veterans. At right is actress Gloria Swanson, who presented Jeannette with the blood-bank title.

5. A smiling orange decorates the tour buggy at Knollwood Groves in Boynton Beach in 2005.

6. Mary Diana Obst picks grapefruit at her West Palm Beach home, 1952.

7. Karen Pentzke (front) and Ileana Pentzke of Wellington slide through the Tubin' Tornadoes water slide at the Rapids Water Park in 2007. The Rapids turns 30 in 2009.

8. Lido Pools in Palm Beach was a summer hot spot in the 1950s.

9. Martin Twofeathers holds Houdini, a gator he says he raised from an egg, during a presentation to schoolchildren at Knollwood Groves in Boynton Beach in 1999.

10. Charlie Finley's first day at spring-training camp after he bought the Kansas City Athletics, 1961. Finley (left) welcomes Haywood Sullivan, Hank Bauer and Dick Howser. Hows-

er, a 1954 Palm Beach High graduate, had a stellar major-league career and managed the New York Yankees and the Kansas City Royals. He died at 51 of brain cancer in 1987.

11. A 1950s high school football program.

12. Riding with the Kennedys: President Kennedy, Jackie and Caroline (front seat) take their friends (in back seat, from left, Anita and Paul Fay and their daughters, Sally and Katherine) for a ride to the Lilly Pulitzer store during Easter vacation, 1963.

Kathy Fay now lives in Delray Beach and recalls this trip to the Kennedy Estate in Palm Beach as "like a dream in an ocean full of incredible memories." Paul "Red" Fay was one of the president's best friends. Kathy says, "What stands out in my mind is the intimacy of the entire experience. Everyone, including the president and Jackie, would saunter around in bathing suits, having fun in the pool or sunning on the chaise lounges. At one point, I saw Jackie snuggling up playfully with the president and, at other times, wading in the pool with

Caroline while John-John taunted his father or begged my dad to throw him up and down. Then, spontaneously, we decided to make a quick trip to 'the Lilly shop' on Worth Avenue in the Lincoln convertible, with the president driving."

13. High school friends, preparing to leave West Palm Beach for Florida State College for Women, 1940: (from left) Mary Chalker, Suzanne Goddard (Slaton), Kitty Carr (Mollenberg), Sara Borden (Hawkins), Eleanor Ernst (Robinson) and Pat Watkins (North). Pat is the daughter of Howell Watkins, superintendent of Palm Beach County schools from 1948 to 1964.

14. Savanna Cary at the St. Patrick's Day Parade on Atlantic Avenue in Delray Beach, 2004.

15. 1956: Robert Holt gets a real .22-caliber rifle for winning a safety-patrol award. It is presented by West Palm Beach Chief of Police Robert W. Milburn, with WPTV personality "Cowboy Bob" at left. Holt writes, "I am a native of West Palm Beach and still live in the only home I have lived in since 1945, on Murray Road."

Photos from The Palm Beach Post, Ineria Hudnell Collection, Jeannette Buss Cearley, Emily Obst, Katherine Fay, Sandy Oakley, Robert Holt, Historical Society of Palm Beach County

A TOUR: THE KENNEDYS' PALM BEACH

Where they stayed, where they played – and why it still matters

By THOM SMITH | The Palm Beach Post

Lannis Waters/The Palm Beach Post

FROM THE ROAD: All that tourists can see of the Kennedys' onetime "Beach House" now is the famous wooden door, a hedge and garage.

1. The Kennedy Estate 1095 N. Ocean Blvd.

Designed and built in 1923 by Addison Mizner (and renovated in 1935 by Maurice Fatio), the center of the Kennedys' Palm Beach universe was this 8,500-square-foot home built on 2 acres with a 176-foot beach. Joe Kennedy paid $120,000 for it in 1933. Known as the "Winter White House" during JFK's 1,000 days in office, it had direct telephone lines to the White House in Washington. JFK wrote much of *Profiles in Courage* and his inaugural address there. The family's third generation called the place the "Beach House," and Rose ruled the roost, determining who would visit and when. John and Marianne Castle bought the estate in 1995 for $4.9 million and restored it. Castle, a Republican, made a wise investment; today the estate is appraised at $14.8 million.

The Palm Beach Post

LATE 1930s: Rose Kennedy enjoys a dip in the pool at her estate, while her oldest son, Joe, clowns around.

More on the Kennedy Estate, pages 230-231

JFK

2. Palm Beach Country Club
760 N. Ocean Blvd.

Known as the "Jewish Country Club," it was designed by Donald Ross and built in 1917. An iron-shot away from the Kennedy home, the club runs from ocean to lake, though it's separated from the beach by Ocean Boulevard. The president's golf bag from the club is in the Kennedy Library with a tag that reads: "Palm Beach Country Club for Pres. JF Kennedy, Rack number 1."

3. St. Edward Church

144 N. County Road

Established in 1926, the church was the most prominent address for the Kennedys in Palm Beach, aside from their home. The family would fill a pew (denoted by a small plaque) every Sunday, and Rose seldom missed a daily Mass. JFK last attended the church on Easter Sunday in 1963. The Kennedys also worshiped occasionally at St. Ann Church in West Palm Beach, which JFK visited on the last weekend of his life.

Davidoff Studios

MARCH 1973: Jackie, Rose and John Jr. attend Mass at St. Edward Church. Rose usually went to Mass daily while wintering in Palm Beach.

< 4. Green's Pharmacy

151 N. County Road

An island institution since 1938, Green's lunch counter often hosted Kennedy adults and kids, who came for the legendary burgers and coffee milkshakes.

Davidoff Studios

GREEN'S PHARMACY (background): Rose heads to Mass. Behind her is Green's, where Kennedys could often be spotted at the lunch counter.

5. The old E.R. Bradley's

290 Sunset Ave.

(Now Coco; E.R. Bradley's has moved to Clematis Street in West Palm Beach.)

Another popular watering hole for Kennedy family members, this bar was on the site of the casino that E.R. Bradley ran until 1945. When the casino closed, Joe Kennedy lamented, "Palm Beach has lost its zipperoo."

Davidoff Studios

FEBRUARY 1967: Joan, Ted and Rose Kennedy draw a crowd as they head to St. Edward Church.

THE KENNEDYS' PALM BEACH MOMENTS

'Life isn't a matter of milestones but of moments.'
— ROSE KENNEDY

WINTER 1919

Rose's parents vacation at the Royal Poinciana Hotel

"Father was an extrovert," Rose Fitzgerald Kennedy said of her father, known as "Honey Fitz." "Mother was innately rather shy." The Fitzgeralds often escaped Boston winters by vacationing in Palm Beach. At left, John and Mary Fitzgerald pose on the grounds of the Royal Poinciana Hotel, which was on the Intracoastal Waterway, just north of Henry Flagler's home.

Kennedy Family

6. Marshall Grant's nightclub 265 Royal Poinciana Way (Now the offices of the *Palm Beach Daily News*)
Run by a popular society band leader, Marshall Grant's was occasionally visited by members of the Kennedy family.

7. Chuck & Harold's

207 Royal Poinciana Way

(Now Nick & Johnnie's)

Always a popular restaurant and watering hole through numerous incarnations, including Peter Dinkel's (before), later Grotto, and now Nick & Johnnie's. Frequented by second- and third-generation Kennedy family members. Teddy went to Chuck & Harold's after Easter Mass in 1991, the weekend his nephew, William Kennedy Smith, was accused of raping a woman on the beach behind the Kennedy home.

Lannis Waters/The Palm Beach Post

HOT SPOT, NO MATTER THE NAME: The restaurant/bar on this corner has always attracted notables. Now it's Nick & Johnnie's. But when it was Peter Dinkel's and, later, Chuck & Harold's, Kennedys loved to brunch and imbibe there.

Loren G. Hosack/The Palm Beach Post

1991: The infamous Au Bar, where William Kennedy Smith partied with Uncle Ted and cousin Patrick.

8. Au Bar

536 Royal Poinciana Way

(Now Palm Beach Grille)

On Good Friday in 1991, this one-time "in" spot attracted Ted Kennedy, his son Patrick and his nephew William Kennedy Smith (left). The younger men picked up two women and took them back to the Kennedy house, where events led to a rape charge against Smith. He was later acquitted. After several reincarnations, the bar is now the popular Palm Beach Grill, a spinoff from the Houston's chain.

Lannis Waters/The Palm Beach Post

NOW: Palm Beach Grill is a popular dining spot.

THE KENNEDYS' PALM BEACH MOMENTS

The Palm Beach Post

LATE 1930s

Teddy and his big brother Joe

Ted was just a baby when his father bought the "Beach House" in Palm Beach, but the senator has often talked about the family's happy days there, enjoying the ocean. "They actually lived a private life in Palm Beach," Kennedy author Laurence Leamer says. At left, Ted and his big brother Joe Jr. lounge by the sea. Joe Jr. was the first of the Kennedy boys to die tragically: He perished Aug. 12, 1944, when the plane he was piloting blew up during a risky mission in World War II.

AROUND 1940

The 'baby,' Teddy, with parents Joe and Rose

Dressed up to attend an event, they pose behind their oceanfront compound.

The Palm Beach Post

9. Royal Poinciana Playhouse

70 Royal Poinciana Plaza

The playhouse opened in 1958, and Kennedy family members often attracted the attention of crowds, who would gather to see celebrities on opening night. "They had good seats up front," the late society photographer Bob Davidoff once said, recalling one night when Sargent and Eunice Shriver escorted Rose to the theater. "Jack Benny was performing, and he said he'd like to introduce someone in the audience. He pointed to them, and they stood up, a little embarrassed, and took a bow. It was nice. They mingled with everybody, because they didn't think their faces were as recognizable." In 1964, the playhouse was the site of a concert tribute to JFK by Eddie Fisher. JFK's likeness also was represented in a mural of famous faces on the ceiling of the main room at the adjacent Poinciana Club.

Davidoff Studios

The Duchess of Windsor, Winston Guest and Rose Kennedy in the Celebrity Room at Frank J. Hale's Royal Poinciana Playhouse. "You couldn't help but respect her," photographer Bob Davidoff said of Rose Kennedy. She was "a spunky woman with a very youthful air."

Lannis Waters/The Palm Beach Post

IMPORTANT LOCATION: The Palm Beach Towers condo is on land where the Royal Poinciana Hotel once stood, from 1894 until the mid-1930s.

10. Palm Beach Towers

44 Cocoanut Row

Now a quiet condominium, in late 1960 it was ground zero for the president-elect. Many decisions on appointments to the Cabinet and other positions were made there. Press Secretary Pierre Salinger held press conferences there, and speechwriter Ted Sorenson crafted much of the inaugural address at poolside.

11. The Breakers   1 S. County Road

One of Teddy Kennedy's most vivid childhood memories, he told *Post* editors in the early 1990s, was driving his grandfather John Fitzgerald (known as "Honey Fitz") to The Breakers for his daily scotch (or two). Honey Fitz died in 1950 at 87. His daughter, Rose, matriarch of the Kennedy clan, died in 1995 at 104.

12. Royal Park Bridge

In December 1960, Richard Paul Pavlick, 73, a retired postal worker, stalked and attempted to assassinate JFK. Pavlick had planned to crash his dynamite-laden car into the president-elect's car as he drove to church but aborted the attempt when he saw Jackie and the kids. Four days later, Pavlick was arrested and sent to a federal mental hospital in St. Louis.

13. Athletic fields at Palm Beach Day/Palm Beach Public schools

On Royal Palm Way, just east of Cocoanut Row

A favorite spot for football, soccer and other games, especially among younger Kennedy family members.

Ray Howard

LATE 1950s

Jackie and Joe at the train station

On the back of this photo is the photographer's credit: "Ray Howard, Candid Photos, Palm Beach, Florida." Jackie is identified as "Mrs. John Kennedy," since JFK had not yet been elected president. Jackie married JFK in 1953, when she was 24.

The Associated Press

JANUARY 1961

Happy Jackie waves goodbye

The future first lady waves to the crowd as she heads toward JFK's private plane, the Caroline, at the airport in West Palm Beach. She is returning to Washington for her husband's inaugural celebration.

14. The Brazilian Court

301 Australian Ave.

A popular boutique hotel that spans from Brazilian to Australian avenues, the Brazilian Court was not quite as fashionable as it is today when David Kennedy died there. On April 25, 1984, David, 28, fourth child of Robert Kennedy, died in Room 107 from an overdose of cocaine, Demerol and Mellaril. "He died on the floor of a sh— hotel room in Florida, crammed between the wall and his bed, alone with the pain of knowing that he had disappointed the family that meant everything to him, but he could not be a part of," cousin Christopher Lawford wrote in his memoir, *Symptoms of Withdrawal*. "He was finally free."

David Kennedy

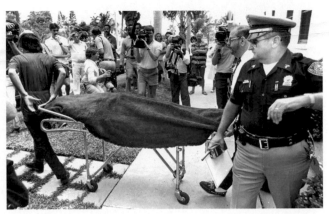

The Palm Beach Post

David Kennedy's overdose death brought media throngs to the Brazilian Court (top). His room was in disarray. Cousin Christopher Lawford wrote that David's painful life and death "was the gift to me that led me to get sober 18 months later." The Brazilian Court has dramatically changed since 1984, and it's now a beautiful boutique hotel.

15. Worth Avenue

The Kennedys loved to shop on the avenue. Before he became president, JFK and Jackie were often seen strolling among the vias dressed very much as Palm Beachers dress today. (Jackie popularized the two-tone "Palm Beach Classic" sandal made famous by Stephen Bonanno and Jack Rogers.) Jack wore penny loafers with, of course, no socks.

Davidoff Studios

Ted Kennedy shops on Worth Avenue, 1968.

WORTH AVENUE LANDMARK: Ta-boó has been a popular spot for nearly 70

*Lannis Waters
The Palm Beach Post*

16. Ta-boó   221 Worth Ave.

Opened in 1941, this watering hole was a favorite of the Duke and Duchess of Windsor. Rumors abound that Joe Kennedy locked himself for a romp in the ladies' room with film star Gloria Swanson — but their affair had ended before Ta-boó opened. JFK did eat there on occasion, but owner Franklyn DeMarco says he can't confirm gossip that, as president, Kennedy would drive to Ta-boó and then duck out the back door to escape his Secret Service detachment for unfettered, and unreported, fun.

THE KENNEDYS' PALM BEACH MOMENTS

Davidoff Studios

DECEMBER 1961

Christmas holiday turns somber

It was JFK's first Christmas as president, and the family gathered to celebrate at the Kennedy home in Palm Beach. But on Dec. 19, patriarch Joe Kennedy suffered a disabling stroke and was rushed to St. Mary's Hospital. In this photo (taken by Bob Davidoff, who chronicled the family's activities in Palm Beach), JFK and Jackie are obviously distraught as they head to the hospital.

Visiting her sick father-in-law

Jackie Kennedy leaves St. Mary's Hospital on Dec. 27, 1961, a week after her father-in-law Joe Kennedy suffered a stroke. The elder Kennedy was confined to a wheelchair thereafter but lived eight more years.

17. Everglades Club

356 Worth Ave.

Although some members of the exclusive club prefer not to acknowledge it, Joe Kennedy was a member. But he resigned after JFK was elected president, in order to avoid awkward questions about belonging to a restricted club. JFK and Mrs. Kennedy attended functions at the club before he was elected president.

MOST PRIVATE ADDRESS: The Everglades Club, considered Palm Beach's snootiest private club, originally did not admit Joe Kennedy because he was Catholic. So he joined the Palm Beach Country Club. Eventually, the Everglades Club admitted Joe.

Lannis Waters
The Palm Beach Post

18. The Colony   155 Hammon Ave.

Another Palm Beach boutique hotel and popular watering hole, The Colony's Annex was rented for President Kennedy's staff and the Secret Service when he visited Palm Beach. Telephone lines would be connected to the White House switchboard, and room service often would take orders for coffee directly from Washington. The day of the president's inaugural, actress Judy Garland, who was staying at The Colony, left her blue sequined dress behind, in her suite. A jet from Homestead Air Force Base was dispatched to Palm Beach International Airport to collect the dress and deliver it to Washington.

Davidoff Studios
Carolyn Bessette Kennedy and John F. Kennedy Jr. at The Mar-a-Lago Club, 1996.

19. Mar-a-Lago

1100 S. Ocean Blvd.

Built by Marjorie Merriweather Post, Mar-a-Lago is now Donald Trump's home and private club. A young Anthony Shriver reportedly did "doughnuts" in the lawn with his Jeep when he was once denied entry.

More on Mar-a-Lago, pages 238-240

'I remember Ted saying how he loved to play this game and swim in every pool down to the center of town, jump from place to place.

The Kennedy family really developed in two places – Hyannisport and Palm Beach. Those were the places where the family came together. The social sense of the Kennedys developed in Palm Beach. When Teddy became an adult, Palm Beach was his playground.'

— LAURENCE LEAMER, *author of "The Kennedy Men" and "The Kennedy Women," and a Palm Beach resident*

The Associated Press

EASTER 1963

Classic style

Jackie wears a lace mantilla and a pink sheath dress. Society photographer Bob Davidoff's famous family shot of the Kennedys from this Easter Sunday is on page 230. Sen. Edward M. Kennedy wrote the foreword to the 2008 book of Davidoff's photographs, *The Kennedy Family Album*, by Linda Corley. Kennedy wrote,"His remarkable personality and charming sense of humor had us all smiling whenever he aimed his camera our way." Davidoff died in 2004.

EASTER 1976

Kennedy women

Rose and her granddaughter Caroline attend a private party in Palm Beach.

Davidoff Studios

Boynton Beach City Library Archives

Waite Bird Farm, Boynton Beach

James and Angela Waite founded this breeding operation, attraction, zoo and shop in 1947. In its prime, Waite's was considered Florida's largest breeder of exotic birds — with some 10,000 parakeets, cockatiels, love birds and more. The farm, with its bright-yellow building at 2626 N. Federal Highway, was gone by 1978.

WHO SAYS MICE ARE THE CAT'S MEOW?
Way before Mickey and Minnie, we had ...

MARTIN TWOFEATHERS! TANZINIKI! AND TRAPPER NELSON!

Treasure hunter Art McKee's son, Mick, posing on a cannon at the Ancient America museum in Boca Raton.

Florida Photographic Collection

Florida Photographic Collection

Ancient America, Boca Raton

This 24-acre attraction operated only from around 1953 to 1958. Esmond Gerrard Barnhill displayed the dug-up bones of indigenous Floridians at the site of an ancient burial mound along U.S. 1 near Yamato Road in northern Boca Raton.

Barnhill had tunneled into the 20-foot-high mound and then installed glass walls so that visitors could see the contents. In the mid-1970s, The Sanctuary neighborhood was built. A 25-acre preserve between the homes and the Intracoastal Waterway includes what is left of the mound, which is now closed to the public.

Autorama, Hypoluxo

Metropolitan Opera star James Melton assembled a collection of vintage cars and created Autorama, a "million-dollar museum of motor memories," in 1953. Autorama also featured the cyclorama "America the Beautiful," depicting the history of our nation. Melton died in 1961; Autorama folded soon afterward.

Florida Photographic Collection

FAMILY FUN IN THE 1950s: Stampeding ostriches and frightening "warriors" at Africa U.S.A. One of the characters at the attraction was "Machakas the Masai warrior" — who was actually a preacher from Delray Beach, explained Shirley Pedersen Schneider. Her father, John Pedersen, founded Africa U.S.A. in Boca Raton. She worked at the attraction, which was along U.S. 1. "Machakas would pretend to speak in an African language, but he knew Japanese and was actually speaking that." Celebrity visitors included *Tonight Show* host Jack Paar, TV announcer Hugh Downs and actor Lloyd Bridges.

Africa U.S.A., Boca Raton

Opened in 1953 and built on 300 acres, Africa U.S.A. — with its wild animals, the Watusi Geyser and the 30-foot-high Zambezi Falls waterfall — drew as many as 2,000 tourists a day. Visitors paid to ride trams for a 6-mile, one-hour tour of Tanziniki, the "country" that founder John D. "Pete" Pedersen invented. At Jungle Town, visitors were greeted by "Masai warriors," most of whom commuted from nearby Pompano Beach. Africa U.S.A. closed in 1961.

The Palm Beach Post

Boynton Beach City Library Archives

Knollwood Groves attracts a crowd in the 1960s. The highlights: homemade fudge, freshly squeezed orange juice, Key-lime pie, alligator wrestling and a tram tour.

The Carefree Center: 'The Playhouse of the Palm Beaches'

Bowling, pinball, pool — and movies! From the 1940s to the '70s, the Carefree Center in West Palm Beach had it all. As C. Debra Welch and Robert Shalhoub recall: "The Carefree Center was the brainchild of our uncle, Elias Chalhub, who in 1939, at 23, established the one-of-a-kind entertainment center on the corner of Dixie Highway and Flamingo Drive. Elias operated the Carefree with his brothers, Leon and George Chalhub. The Carefree boasted 'the largest lobby in the world' — where we'd promote upcoming movies. When *Oklahoma* premiered, our dad, John Welch — with the help of the Riddle family — filled the 75-foot-long lobby with wagon wheels, saddles, horseshoes and other western memorabilia."

The Palm Beach Post

Knollwood Groves, Boynton Beach

For almost 75 years, Knollwood Groves was a little oasis of Old Florida. It was originally 120 acres — bought and planted in 1930 by Freeman Gosden and Charles Correll, who had the most popular show on radio in those days: *Amos 'n' Andy.* Gosden and Correll sold the groves in 1936.

Knollwood Groves — with its kitschy tram tour, delicious orange juice and Key-lime pie — lasted until 2005, when it closed to make way for a housing development. (Knollwood's resident alligator wrestler, Martin Twofeathers, had departed a couple of years earlier because of high insurance costs.)

Remembering the wild man of the Loxahatchee

To entertain guests at the Ocean Terrace Motel in Juno Beach, we rented rowboats with outboard motors from Gus's Fish Camp (now Smilin Jack's Marina) in Jupiter on the creek.

The trip took several hours up the Loxahatchee River to Trapper Nelson's on the far reaches of the main fork of the Loxahatchee River.

Trapper (whose real name was Victor Nostokovich) was a large man with huge hands, and he could eat several sandwiches at a picnic sitting. He once ate an entire cake that Mom had baked for the guests.

Most of the time, he ate off of the 800 acres of land he had obtained for next to nothing. To support himself, he trapped wild animals and sold some of them to zoos in the United States.

In the late 1940s, he opened his property to tourists to help support himself. He displayed alligators, raccoons, possum, fox, wildcats and the like. In the '50s, a long, slender excursion boat, carrying paying passengers, made trips from the docks in downtown West Palm Beach to his zoo.

On arrival, Trapper would provide a tour and talk about his business and animals. From a huge cypress tree at the edge of the water hung a large rope, and we would swing out over the river and drop from a distance into the water. I don't know why, but despite all the alligators in the area, I never saw one around the rope swing.

Trapper was ultimately forced to close his zoo in the '60s when wildlife officials declared it unsafe and cruel to animals.

He was found dead several years later, in July 1968, from a gunshot wound. Stories said that it was self-inflicted because he was suffering from stomach cancer. Others who knew him well believe he was murdered.

— BILL WATSON,
who grew up in Juno Beach at his parents' motor lodge, the Ocean Terrace.

Historical Society of Palm Beach County

At 6-feet-2 and 240 pounds, Trapper Nelson was a big man with a checkered past. He had served time in Mexico for gun-running, then caught a freight train east when he got out of jail. He landed in Jupiter, where he built an isolated homestead and makeshift zoo. Heavyweight boxing champion Gene Tunney once remarked that Nelson's burly hands made his own look feminine.

Guests at the Ocean Terrace Motel wave to the camera as they prepare to row their way up the Loxahatchee River to visit Trapper Nelson's camp. On some days, hundreds of tourists visit — including the Kennedys.

Watson Family

Michael Dubiner postcard collection

Giant banyan tree and Alfar Creamery

How big was that tree on Lakeview Avenue in West Palm Beach (where Esperante is now)? So big that it was a tourist attraction: 60 feet around the trunk, with limbs that spanned 200 feet. Alfar Creamery, advertised on top of the soda shop, was a special spot, too. The dairy, along the railroad tracks west of Dixie Highway between Flamingo and Claremore drives, was owned by native Swede Alf R. Nielson. It opened in 1931. Soon its Dixie Cups were famous: They featured pictures of the latest movie stars under the lids.

Boca Raton Historical Society

Welcome, Shriners!

Dixie Highway (U.S. 1) once was the main route along the East Coast. When a Shriners convention in Miami attracts members from all over the United States, Boca Raton city fathers decide to erect this camel, a Shrine symbol, as a special welcome. The sign suggests a visit to the new "Town Hall" and "rest rooms for the ladies and gentlemen." Today this is the site of Dixie Highway at Boca Raton Road, looking north. The "Town Hall" referred to is the original Boca Raton Town Hall, built in 1927 and, today, home to the Boca Raton Historical Society. The motorcycle policeman is one of two men on the police force.

Historical Society of Palm Beach County

All aboard!

Jane Ann Hadley Caruso remembers early forms of entertainment: "There was a mule-drawn trolley car that carried hotel guests staying at the Royal Poinciana and The Breakers hotels back and forth. The stables for the mules were located where Testa's restaurant is today. On Saturday afternoons, my friends and I would ride the ferry across Lake Worth to West Palm Beach (we got off near where the West Palm Beach Marina is now). The trip cost 5 cents. We went to the Kettler Theatre, where the movie ticket cost 10 cents and a candy bar was 5 cents. After the movie, we took the ferry back to Palm Beach. A great afternoon — all for 25 cents!"

TAKING US FOR A SPIN: The South Florida Fair lights up the
sky along Southern Boulevard, 2009.

Our fair tradition began in 1912 with the first Palm Beach
County Fair, held in a tent in downtown West Palm Beach.
Today nearly 600,000 people attend the annual South Florida Fair.

Allen Eyestone/The Palm Beach Post

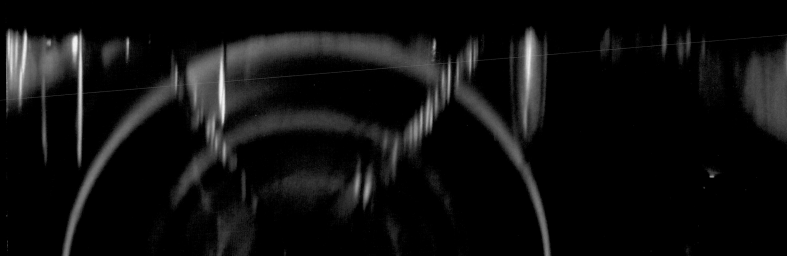

HOW WE PLAY: WHEELS

WHAT A RIDE! A photo salute to cars, carts, cycles and speed

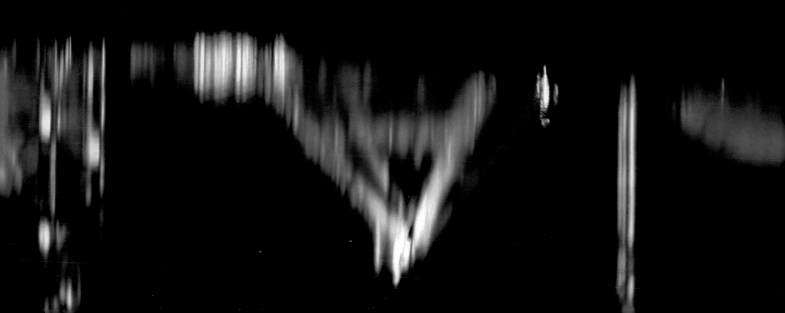

1926: J.B. Wilson in front of Whitehall. He was the sales manager at the Ford garage on Banyan Street in West Palm Beach and clearly admired fine automobiles. J.B.'s brother, Horace, moved to Florida in 1922 and worked as a mechanic on David McCullough's flying boat, a Curtiss Seagull.

Weeks Family

CARS, CARS, CARS!

Boca Raton Historical Society

1950S GLAMOUR: Convertibles and beauty queens promote the Boca Raton Sports Car Races. Until the mid-1920s, it was hard to drive on many Palm Beach County roads, let alone race on them. But, "By 1926, the roads were in good shape for sustained travel," recalls Edward J. Maas, who grew up in West Palm Beach. "I remember a driver who bragged about making it from Jacksonville in one day."

Gilmore Family

1919: Bert Gilmore navigates unpaved roads to drive his Model T Ford from Michigan to Boynton Beach. His son, Harold, recalls that his parents spent the second half of the 1928 Hurricane in this car; his sister, Maxine, was sleeping in the back seat. They had ventured out to check on a friend when the eye of the storm was passing, thinking the storm had ended.

Baker/Cobb Family

SHERIFF BEHIND THE WHEEL: Robert C. Baker succeeded his father George as sheriff of Palm Beach County. Robert Baker became well-known in the 1920s for his pursuit of the Ashley Gang.

Gertrude McElhenney, mother of Honey Duncan, in a parade on Clematis Street, around 1927-28.

Richard Graulich/The Palm Beach Post

Mark (left) and Robert Simpson, co-owners of Palm Beach Motor Cars, drive an Aston Martin DB9 Volante convertible down Worth Avenue in Palm Beach. Palm Beach Motor Cars was founded by Norman and Sonia Gregersen and Bob Simpson in 1979.

Archie and Irene Carswell, longtime Boca Raton residents, pose proudly in front of their car.

CRACKER JOHNSON: One of the black community's most influential residents in the 1920s was James J. Johnson, who was called "Cracker" because he could pass as white. Johnson is shown here parked on Banyan Street between Rosemary Avenue and the railroad tracks, in West Palm Beach's black business district. He owned real estate, opened the Florida Bar and helped found a club for "colored gentlemen." He also reportedly smuggled liquor during Prohibition and was wildly successful running the "bolita" numbers game. He was shot and killed while trying to stop a brawl behind his bar in 1946.

In the 1930s, Jane Ann Hadley (Caruso) takes another kind of spin — a ride with her grandfather, William F. Fremd, in a "Palm Beach wheelchair." "My grandfather, William F. Fremd, was a horticulturist who worked for Henry Flagler and helped choose the plant names for the streets in West Palm Beach: Banyan, Clematis, Datura, Evernia, Fern, Gardenia, Hibiscus, Iris, Jasmine," Caruso recalls.

1913: Percy and Anna Hadley and one of the first automobiles in the area. Hadley owned a car dealership in West Palm Beach in the 1920s.

Reginald "Reggie" Stambaugh was interested in history all his life. No wonder: He made history when he was born — the first baby born in Palm Beach County in 1930. As a result of his timely debut, First National Bank gave him a bank account, and Alfar Creamery donated free milk for a year. The highlight of his boyhood was winning the Soap Box Derby for 1942 and 1943, sponsored by the Boy Scouts and the American Legion. He grew up to become a prominent local eye doctor who rallied his classmates to save Palm Beach High School, which later became Dreyfoos School of the Arts.

Children go for a ride in front of Palm Gardens Sundries, at Third Street and Rosemary Avenue, in 1918. The store was owned by Robert Saunders, who built the Sunset Cocktail Lounge on Eighth Street in West Palm Beach in 1933. Saunders was shot to death at the Sunset in 1936 by an employee whom Saunders had confronted about money missing from a cash register. More than 5,000 people — blacks as well as whites — attended his funeral, held at the Sunset. In 1947, when Robert's widow, Susie, died, she left the property to her nephew Dennis Starks.

WHAT'S UP WITH THE FARM ANIMALS AND THE WAGON, KIDS? C. Pfeiffer Trowbridge, pictured in 1932 at left, says a traveling photographer came around the neighborhood and took photos of the kids. Trowbridge, who became a circuit judge, wintered every year with his grandfather in West Palm Beach. At right is James Lee Shirley Sr., who was 2 when this photo was shot in West Palm Beach.

Driving in style

The Rev. Randolph Washington and his wife, Phyllis, moved to West Palm Beach in 1902. He came to pastor at Tabernacle Baptist Church. He had four children who grew up here in West Palm Beach and lived here all of their lives, including my mother, Daisy Washington Thomas. I still live here in West Palm Beach in my grandparents' home at 517 Division Ave. The home was built in 1926 and remodeled in 1970.

My favorite memories of growing up in West Palm Beach include being able to go anywhere in the city and not worry about being harmed; also, climbing trees for the fruit that grew everywhere (mangoes, tamarinds, sapodillas, mulberries, cherries and many others).

The beach was a great place to picnic. When I was a child, we went to Singer Island and Crocus Beach, which was north of Singer Island.

We had everything we needed in our community. We had so many local businesses. They (whites) came here to go to restaurants, but we couldn't go to their restaurants and get seated.

I became a teacher and taught elementary school for more than 30 years before retiring. I worked at Palmview Elementary and Roosevelt Elementary in West Palm Beach and, after integration, at Highland Elementary in Lake Worth.

— JACQUELINE MORRISON,
West Palm Beach

Photos from the Morrison Family

Phyllis Story, granddaughter of the Rev. Randolph Washington, takes her tricycle for a ride in West Palm Beach. She lived from 1920 to 1925, when she died at age 5 from appendicitis. Her grandfather was a pastor of Tabernacle Missionary Baptist Church, which began in 1893 and was the site of the first public school for "colored" children in Palm Beach County.

Missouri Washington, aunt of Jacqueline Morrison, in front of the car, *circa* 1937-1938.

Ray Graham/The Palm Beach Post

Division Avenue — a main thoroughfare in West Palm Beach's black community — 'was full of businesses,' Jacqueline Morrison says. 'Everything you needed was right here. You name it, we had it. We had a grocery store, doctors' offices, a dry cleaners, a seamstress, a tailor, a music instructor and some of your bigger churches.'

Jacqueline Morrison (above) still lives in the Division Avenue home that her grandparents built in 1926. She is holding the photo, shown at right, with Willard Washington (her uncle), Daisy Washington Thomas (her mother) and Phyllis Washington (her grandmother) in front of the Division Avenue house in the 1930s.

HOW WE PLAY: LIFE ON THE WATER

WHAT A VIEW! Our enduring love affair with the ocean

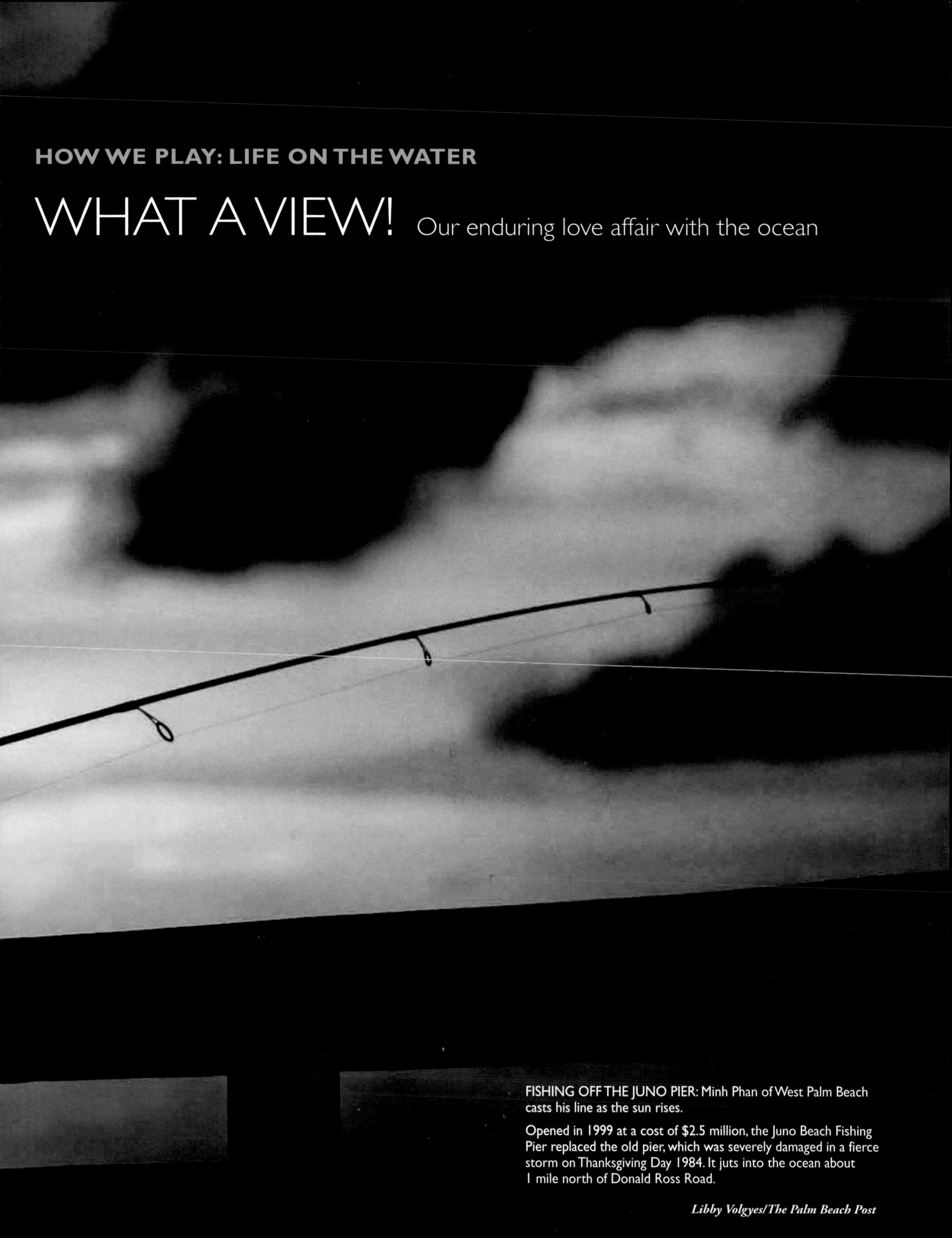

FISHING OFF THE JUNO PIER: Minh Phan of West Palm Beach casts his line as the sun rises.

Opened in 1999 at a cost of $2.5 million, the Juno Beach Fishing Pier replaced the old pier, which was severely damaged in a fierce storm on Thanksgiving Day 1984. It juts into the ocean about 1 mile north of Donald Ross Road.

Libby Volgyes/The Palm Beach Post

1946: This is me! Buried in the sand!

Palm Beach County was a paradise for us kids growing up in the 1940s and '50s. There were no dangers from humans — we seldom locked our doors — but there were rattlesnakes, coral snakes and water moccasins; long, hot summers without air-conditioning; and canals everywhere.

We would go out and play in the morning and not go home until dinner, yet our parents never worried about us. We played in the woods, caught minnows in the canals and made forts in clearings. We climbed on the thick vines in the jungle areas, which were everywhere then.

I remember at least three times when my mother killed a huge rattlesnake in our back yard with a quick whack from a shovel to the back of its head.

During the summer, we spent most of our time at the beach, or at Lido Pools in Palm Beach and the Lake Worth Casino pool.

— SUE VAN DYKE BAILEY
*She grew up in West Palm Beach
and now lives in Palm Beach Gardens.*

Thomas Cordy/The Palm Beach Post

ONE BURIED BOOGER: Booger, an 8-year-old English bulldog, cools off in a pit of damp sand prepared by his owner, Matt Cameron of Palm Beach Gardens. Earlier, the two had been playing in the surf near Juno Beach Pier, in early 2007.

Mark Lee

ON LAKE WORTH BEACH IN THE MID-1930s, with the Lake Worth Casino and Baths in the background, are (from left, top row) Gustine Geibel, Denny Humphry, Lenore Geibel, Mae Geibel; (bottom) Delmas Gish and wife Bobbi Gish; the other three, who were friends of Mae Geibel, are unidentified. Mae Geibel was Denny Humphry's sister and Lenore's mother; Lenore is the mother of Mark Lee.

Historical Society of Palm Beach County/Collie Collection

The Collie Family of West Palm Beach

(left) Laurita Collie Sharpp remembers segregated beaches: "There were a couple of Palm Beach County beaches open to blacks. One was on Singer Island, where this photo was shot (she is not pictured). "There wasn't a bridge then."

Her grandfather, John Collie, settled in West Palm Beach in 1896 and ran several businesses. His son, Warren, born the same year, became one of the area's first black dentists.

Dr. Warren Collie, Laurita's father, was an amateur photographer and chronicled his family's history — and the area's — through photos such as this. This shot, taken in the 1920s on Singer Island, contains no information about who is pictured.

The Simon Family of Delray Beach

(lower left) Linda Zaine Simon, 18, and Alexander Simon, 23, on the beach in Delray Beach on Christmas Day 1925.

Alexander emigrated from Lebanon to Delray Beach in 1920 to be near his father, who had arrived in the city in 1912. Alexander married Linda on Aug. 10, 1924, in Ohio, where she lived. The couple then moved to Delray Beach during the sweltering summer. When Linda realized that Atlantic Avenue, a dirt road, was the main street through town, she began crying and didn't stop for two years — she thought she had made a big mistake.

Linda and Alexander Simon left behind them three generations of children, grandchildren and great-grandchildren who still live in Delray Beach.

The Dalton Family of Palm Beach

(left) Mary Breed and James Dalton in Palm Beach, 1916. (The angler is unidentified.) The couple soon married, on Feb. 28, 1916, at the original Episcopal Church of Bethesda-by-the-Sea in Palm Beach. The Daltons had three daughters — Helen, Laura and Eileen — and lived in Palm Beach.

Writes Eileen Dalton Wozneski: "Many happy hours were spent at the beach, a short walk from our home. We 'rode' the waves; dived off jetties; and combed the shoreline for seashells, 'lucky beans' and coral. Sometimes, Daddy built a bonfire, and we roasted marshmallows while singing songs."

In 1908, James Dalton had left Ireland and arrived through Ellis Island in New York. He settled in Palm Beach, working as a painter at The Breakers and the Royal Poinciana Hotel. Mary Breed, a native of England, was employed by J.S. Phipps of Palm Beach.

Alexander A. "Sandy" Simon Jr.

Eileen Dalton Wozneski

OUR BEACH HANGOUTS

Piers play a big part in the county's fishing history

The Palm Beach Pier at the east end of Worth Avenue, built by Gus Jordahn in 1924, was a wooden structure first known as the Rainbo Pier. The Palm Beach Pier stood for more than 40 years and was battered several times by hurricanes. After two storms in the 1960s, the pier fell into disrepair. The Town of Palm Beach ordered its demolition in 1969.

Jim Barry, retired environmental director for Palm Beach County, practically lived on the Palm Beach Pier as a boy and recalls the fatherly advice he heard from older pier patrons.

"I had 50 fathers out on that pier," Barry said. "They told me to go to school and get an education."

A member of the Palm Beach Pier Sharker's Club, Barry remembers grabbing a rifle that hung on nails in the bait shop and running down the pier to shoot big sharks back when the prevailing attitude was that sharks were man-eaters that should be exterminated. Police officers often would join in, shooting at the sharks with their service revolvers.

Historical Society of Palm Beach County

"COWBOY OF THE SEA": Gus Jordahn, who owned Gus's Baths, a swimming complex near Worth Avenue in Palm Beach, was famous for capturing and riding loggerhead turtles. On his 50th birthday, he swam across Lake Worth and back.

OLD LAKE WORTH PIER: Anglers crowd the pier in the 1960s.

Lake Worth City Museum

< The old Juno Beach Pier, opened in 1950 and torn apart by a Thanksgiving storm in 1984, brings back fond memories for Pete Schulz, co-owner of Fishing Headquarters in Jupiter. Schulz worked at the pier for owner Penny Sheltz while attending Palm Beach Gardens High School in the mid-1970s.

Anglers caught big spinner sharks and bruiser jacks from the pier with topwater plugs, and fall mullet runs often attracted swarms of bluefish. Outstanding pier catches included Mike Freehauf's 53-pound kingfish.

"I remember unbelievable snook runs off that pier," Schulz said. "I'm glad I was part of it."

The new Juno Beach Pier opened in 1999, a few miles north of the old pier.

This 1977 postcard shows (from top) an aerial view of the old Juno Beach Pier; the pier entrance; Walter Sheltz with a snook; pier managers Evelyn and Joe Poole in their pier apartment; and Lisa, Penny and Wally Sheltz walking on the beach with a friend. Wally and Penny Sheltz owned the old Juno Beach Pier — the only ocean pier between Lake Worth and Cape Canaveral.

Richard Graulich/The Palm Beach Post

It took 15 months and $3.4 million (most of the money came from FEMA) to rebuild the Lake Worth Pier after the hurricanes of 2004 broke it into pieces. The seaward half of the 960-foot platform was constructed 5 feet higher than the rest of the pier, like the new Juno Beach Pier, which didn't buckle under the hurricanes. Regulars say the pier always has been notable for its big jacks and bluefish during fall mullet runs, for its summer snook and permit, its winter mackerel, and as a place where ocean fish such as sailfish and kingfish, usually found in deeper water, have been caught.

The Lake Worth Pier was built in 1959 as a working platform for a sewage outfall pipe. It opened as a fishing pier in 1960 to a throng of enthusiastic anglers.

Now named for the late Piermaster William O. Lockhart, the pier at Lake Worth Beach has been rebuilt three times by Murphy Construction Co. following damage from storms, including Hurricanes Frances and Jeanne in 2004.

Anglers have taken sailfish and countless snook, bluefish and jacks from the Lake Worth Pier. But the pier is probably best known for producing two all-tackle world-record permit: a 51.5-pounder caught by William Kennedy in 1978, and Roy Brooker's 53.25-pounder taken in 1994.

Among Lake Worth's most colorful anglers was Herb Goodman, known as the "Shark Man." Goodman owned a tackle and locksmith shop at 805 Lake Ave. and spent his Sundays fishing for sharks from beaches and inlets. When he retired from shark fishing in 1978, Goodman boasted 177 sharks more than 6 feet long, all taken from shore.

Goodman stumped panelists on the television program *To Tell the Truth* in the 1960s by stating that he had caught 30 sharks with one hook at one time. He had beached a big hammerhead carrying 29 pups.

Museum of the City of Lake Worth

LAKE WORTH CASINO AND BATHS, 1922: Built in the style of Addison Mizner, the 35,000-square-foot casino housed a game parlor, saltwater pools and a grand ballroom that, at one point, served as a roller rink. In the early years, pools at the Lido Pools in Palm Beach and the Lake Worth Casino were saltwater, and thousands of Palm Beach County kids have memories of taking swimming lessons in salty water. Both bathhouses also had tunnels that led from the buildings to the beach (note tunnel entrance at left of photo). In 1947, a hurricane damaged the casino, which was rebuilt with a more modern façade. Some community leaders are now lobbying to restore the casino to its 1920s grandeur.

West Palm Beach Fishing Club

75 years of tight lines — and the Silver Sailfish Derby

By WILLIE HOWARD | The Palm Beach Post

The West Palm Beach Fishing Club's Silver Sailfish Derby — started in 1935 — is the oldest continually running billfish tournament in the world.

Sailfish "grudge matches" between famous anglers drew national attention to the Derby during the post-war years. In 1956, golfer Sam Snead, a fishing novice, beat baseball legend and devoted angler Ted Williams. Derby-trophy sponsors included Ernest Hemingway.

For most of its history, the tournament was a weeks-long event in which anyone could participate without paying an entry fee, as long as they fished from a Derby-registered charter boat. In the early years, boat captains would hang dead sailfish at the docks in hopes of booking future charters.

Noting that valuable sailfish were being killed needlessly, the West Palm Beach Fishing Club instituted the use of red "release" pennants in 1938 to allow captains to boast — without bringing in dead fish.

However, big sailfish were still taken in to the docks in hopes of winning a gold button — awarded for sailfish more than 8 feet in total length — or winning the Mrs. Henry R. Rea Trophy for the longest sailfish.

The Silver Sailfish Derby eventually evolved into a three-day tournament with an entry fee and an all-release format. Nowadays, the Rea Trophy is awarded to the angler who releases the most sailfish.

The West Palm Beach Fishing Club, founded in 1934, built its wooden headquarters at Fifth Street and Flagler Drive in 1941. Today it has more than 1,400 members.

West Palm Beach Fishing Club Archives

These colorful posters were for the annual Silver Sailfish Derby, a weeks-long sailfish tournament established in 1935 to boost tourism during the Great Depression. Billed as the longest continually running billfish tournament in the world, the Derby has been held every year except for a hiatus during World War II. The Derby is now a three-day tournament held in January.

West Palm Beach Fishing Club Archives

Golfer Sam Snead (in boat at left) and baseball legend Ted Williams (at left in boat on right) compete in an offshore fishing "grudge match" in 1956 as a promotion for the Silver Sailfish Derby. Snead, a fishing novice, beat Williams, a seasoned angler.

Raborn Family

Captain Kenny Lyman (standing) poses with the day's catch "around 50 years ago." With him are (from left) an unidentified deckhand, Fred Benson, Allan Hall, Dr. Robert Raborn with Richard, and Dr. Donald Hunter with Donald.

Tuppen Family

GREAT FISHING: Sherman "Bud" Tuppen Jr. and his father, *circa* early 1950s, after a great day's catch. In 1956, Sherman Sr. and his sons, Ron and Bud, started Tuppen's, a boat business, in Lake Worth.

Eliza Gutierrez/The Palm Beach Post

Tom Twyford is president of the West Palm Beach Fishing Club. The club, founded in 1934, is hoping to have the building put on the National Register of Historic Places.

Phyllis and George Bass with a sailfish (right). The Basses were well-known, active anglers in Palm Beach County. Phyllis held 24 International Game Fish Association world records.

West Palm Beach Fishing Club Archives

SURFIN' THE AMARYLLIS: John Sennett rides a wave while Pat Angelicchio (far left), Fred Salmon (foreground) and Eddie Scozzari (right) paddle toward the ship.

Gidget who? In the '60s, Singer Island surfers had eyes for just one lady:

A big, bruisin' gal named AMARYLLIS

Living on Singer Island, we felt the beach was always a part of our lives. In the '60s, that meant surfing.

I got my first real surfboard Christmas of 1963 — a 9-foot-6-inch black "Malibu Spoon" from Gunn's Patio Shoppe on Singer Island. Surfing in those days was still a "gentleman's sport."

As a newcomer — paddling into the lineup with my brand-new board under my knees — I remember hearing the senior member of that group say, "Well, you're new. Take your place at the end of the line. When everyone has taken his turn, it's your turn. After you ride, paddle back out and take your same spot."

As new people joined the lineup, you moved up the pecking order. Sometimes, when an extra-nice wave was coming, someone would yell "Party wave!" — and everyone was allowed to take off on the same wave, taking care not to run into each other.

Surfers had nicknames — Animal, Stingray, Toothie, Pudge, Wire, Bongo, Cosmo, Big Dee, Hot Curl, Skinny, Meatball, Tiger, Chummer, Ghost. Once you got a name, you were stuck with it. In April '64, on the eve of having my tonsils out, I blew out my left eye with a firecracker. I joined the pantheon of nicknames; to this day, I'm known as Deadeye.

When the good ship Amaryllis blew

Surf photographer M.E. Gruber came from a pioneer family.

M.E. Gruber Collection/surfhistoryproject.org

ashore thanks to Hurricane Betsy — Sept. 8, 1965 — surfing changed on Singer Island. Fifteen degrees off perpendicular to the beach, the ship was wedged atop an outcropping of reef and would not be moved by man, tide, weather or machine for three years.

It provided a windbreak and a point for the waves to break perfectly. Surfers around the state flocked to surf there. One day, I counted 250 boards just at the ship.

Surf clubs sprang up by the dozens all around Palm Beach County. Local breaks were dominated by their respective clubs. Hunter Joslin and I started Sandy Shores Surf Club in 1967.

M.E. Gruber, a U.S. postman from a local pioneer family, began taking photos just before the Amaryllis arrived. He liked to shoot on the sand dunes in front of the ship, and with his telephoto lens clicking away, he captured many young lives on film during our happiest and most thrilling moments.

He also captured our wipeouts. He shot beach scenes from Lake Worth to Jacksonville from 1965 to 1972. He put together a slide show of the local talents and rented California surf movies to show at the same time.

I stayed close to M.E. — always "Mr. Gruber" to us surfers — over the decades, and I told him I wanted to preserve his treasure trove of surf photos.

He told me, "Well, maybe I'll put you in my will."

Then, in the fall of 2007, I saw Mr. Gruber's obituary in the paper. He had passed on in Fort Worth, Texas, and it listed a sister there. I contacted her; we agreed that his legacy should be saved.

The result: the Surf History Project of Palm Beach County.

Along with fellow surfers Michael "Corky" Roche, Tom Warnke, Bill Keeton and Mike Spellman, we incorporated into a nonprofit and started a Web site: surfhistoryproject.org.

Mr. Gruber's sister, Charlotte Brown, appointed me curator of 5,000 images of those golden years.

With Mr. Gruber's photos as a base, we're documenting surfing in Palm Beach County, from the '30s and '40s to the present day — surf clubs, surfboards, shops, surfers, events, culture.

And the memory of the perfect party wave.

— FRED "DEADEYE" SALMON

'I began surfing in 1966, one year after the Greek freighter Amaryllis beached behind the house I grew up in on Singer Island. I still surf as much as possible. Then, as now, local experience is the key to finding the right spot. One thing that has never changed and never will: the fun of riding good waves with friends.'

— MICHAEL "CORKY" ROCHE,
who took this photo of the Amaryllis from his back patio in 1966

Damon Higgins/The Palm Beach Post

(From left, sitting) Bill Keeton, Mike Spellman, "Corky" Roche, (standing) Tom Warnke and Fred Salmon have started a surf project on the history of surfing in Palm Beach County.

'The main thing I want people to know and remember is that we grew up here when "here" was literally paradise. We would hitchhike to the beach when we were 10 years old, without a care in the world. I thank the Lord that He put me in this place during that time and allowed me to experience the life that I did.'

— BILL KEETON,
a surfer who grew up in Riviera Beach

1997, Cox New Service

The Atlanta Braves work out at West Palm Beach Municipal Stadium in 1997. In March of that year, the Braves did their last spring training in West Palm Beach. On Aug. 31, 1997, the last game was played at the 35-year-old stadium.

Taylor Jones/The Palm Beach Post

Logan (left) and Dallas Robinson, identical twins from Royal Palm Beach, gesture and yell for a player to throw them the ball during a Cardinals-vs.-Marlins spring-training game in March 2009 at Roger Dean Stadium in Jupiter.

THE BOYS OF SUMMER
(and spring)

Richard Graulich/The Palm Beach Post

Roger Dean Stadium, in the Abacoa community in Jupiter, is the spring-training home of the major-league Florida Marlins and St. Louis Cardinals. In addition, two Florida State League teams — the Palm Beach Cardinals and Jupiter Hammerheads — play their home games in the 7,000-seat stadium.

By DAVE GEORGE | The Palm Beach Post

Palm Beach County is a year-round training ground for great athletes. After all, it has sunshine to bless the area's signature connection with golf. It also has a feeder system of top coaches and facilities to make the most of any kid who wants to follow neighborhood legends like Anquan Boldin to the National Football League or Derek Harper to the National Basketball Association.

Baseball is the sport, however, with the deepest roots and the most consistent collection of headline events, and spring training at the heart of it all.

There were "baseball grounds" at Palm Beach's Royal Poinciana Hotel, a ritzy 2,000-guest palace built by Henry Morrison Flagler in 1894. Babe Ruth and the Yankees played an exhibition against the Cincinnati Reds there on March 17, 1920.

When the Philadelphia Athletics came to West Palm Beach to train at Wright Field in 1946, the players and their manager, Connie Mack, stayed at the downtown George Washington Hotel. This was near the end of the grand old man's career as a manager, which ended in 1950 after 53 years.

Mack enjoyed visiting around the community. That's where he met Robert Corbitt, age 8, in 1952. Mack stopped by Phipps Park on South Dixie Highway in West Palm Beach to encourage a group of adults and children who were working to complete the first Little League field in the area.

"They were looking for somebody to take a picture with him, and they picked me," Corbitt said years later, when he was grown up and working in the area as an electrician. "That inspired me to be a catcher — the day I met him — and I went on to play high school baseball at Forest Hill."

In 1955, the Philadelphia Athletics moved to Kansas City, but West Palm Beach's stadium, by then known as Connie Mack Field, remained the team's spring headquarters.

The stadium was a monster by today's standards. The center-field wall was 460 feet from home plate, and massive Frank Howard was one of the few ever to hit a home run straightaway. He hit two as a Los Angeles Dodgers rookie in town to play an exhibition against Kansas City.

Dick Howser and Ken Johnson, a pair of West Palm Beach stars, trained at Connie Mack Field with the Kansas City A's. Herb Score, a Lake Worth legend, pitched in exhibition games there. So did Sandy Koufax.

Others players included Roberto Clemente, Harmon Killebrew, Maury Wills, Al Kaline, Duke Snider, Yogi Berra and Whitey Ford.

Unfortunately, a large segment of the population had no way at all to relate to Major League Baseball until Jackie Robinson broke the color barrier with the Dodgers in 1947. One of his first games in the Brooklyn lineup was an exhibition against the Athletics at Connie Mack Field.

By the time the Athletics left for Bradenton, Fla., in 1962, West Palm Beach already was deep into negotiations to bring the Milwaukee Braves to town.

The Braves, with Hank Aaron and Eddie Mathews, were big news in 1963 as they descended on West Palm Beach and Municipal Stadium, a ballpark that was in the final stages of construction when the team arrived.

West Palm Beach was attractive to Braves owner Lou Perini because he was developing 6,000 acres west of downtown. Where the Palm Beach Mall now stands was a sea of sand.

Perini believed that the Boston Red Sox would eventually join the Braves here. That never happened. But the Expos, Canada's first major-league team, made their National League debut at Municipal Stadium in 1969 on practice diamonds beyond the center-field fence.

The ballpark served the teams well for two decades, until the Braves started talking about wanting a new facility of their own. They eventually left for Disney World in 1998, leaving the Expos and Cardinals to negotiate for spots at Roger Dean Stadium, a new facility built by the county with tourist-tax money and named for a West Palm Beach Chevrolet dealer who put up $1 million for the honor.

That partnership lasted until 2003, when the Marlins transferred down to Jupiter from Melbourne and took the Expos' place. The Marlins and St. Louis Cardinals keep Roger Dean busy just about all year long these days, with a pair of Florida State League teams — the Jupiter Hammerheads and the Palm Beach Cardinals — that play their home games there.

The old Connie Mack Field is buried today under the Kravis Center parking garage. Municipal Stadium's former site is occupied by a Home Depot.

Baseball always has a home in Palm Beach County, however.

It's as stubborn as a tobacco stain and as irresistible as the first taste of springtime to all the Northern transplants who grew up with the game.

Foster Family

In 1952, during construction of the baseball diamond at Phipps Park, the legendary Connie Mack, retired owner and manager of the Philadelphia Athletics, pays a visit. Facing down the right-field line are (from left, standing) Tommy Corbitt, Pud Lytal, Dennis Laracy, Hayes Barbier, Mickey Foster, Johnny Jacobs, unknown, Davis Little, unknown, Billy Shetron, (seated) Mack, Robert Corbitt, unknown. Phipps Park, in West Palm Beach, was the first Little League facility in Palm Beach County.

Little League finds a home

My dad, Mel Foster, laid the groundwork in 1951 for the first Little League in West Palm Beach. During the first year, games were played at Currie Park and Howard Park.

Then, in 1952, my dad and many other volunteers, including Lake Lytal, longtime county commissioner, built the ballpark.

On non-game days, I would go to the field and mow and water the grass. On game days, I would drag and line the field, have dinner across the street at Howley's Restaurant (it's still there) and then play ball. Because my dad was the first president of the Little League, I guess you could say that I was the first grounds-keeper.

I loved every minute of it — even if that darn lawn mower was bigger than I was and just dragged me along for the ride.

— MICKEY FOSTER

At Phipps Park, Mel Foster (left), Lil Roberts and Lake Lytal Sr. measure a bat to ensure that it complies with Little League rules, 1952. The bat has to fit inside the ring. Lake Lytal was the longest-serving Palm Beach County commissioner: 32 years.

Hometown champions

"When I was 11 or 12, the average summer day would be going to Wells or Tate Recreation Center (in Riviera Beach), playing basketball, playing baseball and swimming in the pool."

— FORMER SUNCOAST HIGH SCHOOL STAR ANTHONY CARTER,

whose greatest fame eventually came in football. The first county athlete to be inducted into the College Football Hall of Fame, he ranks second all-time at Michigan for touchdown catches and was a Pro Bowl receiver with the Minnesota Vikings.

"We moved down here in 1968 and bought a condo on the ocean in Palm Beach, and I also have a golf condo at Palm Beach National (west of Lake Worth). Back in my early playing days, we drove a travel trailer to the tournaments. Once we got back home, we'd park it down here at one of the trailer parks right off Lake Worth Road, or up in Jupiter at the inlet."

— LPGA HALL-OF-FAMER JOANNE CARNER,

who originally came to Palm Beach County from the Pacific Northwest because her late husband Don liked to winter here. They were married 36 years and always sought recreation away from the golf course. Fishing, swimming and motorcycle riding were their South Florida favorites.

"I grew up on Seventh Street in West Palm Beach. We ate off paper plates in my neighborhood, not like the fine china over in Palm Beach. The one thing that sticks out to me is how genuine West Palm is. When you think of New York and L.A. and all these big major cities where I have lived, those places are almost untouchable. West Palm Beach — it's a city and yet it's touchable.

"Every time I come home, I drive over by that old North Shore High School neighborhood. I go there on purpose. My rental car gets off the highway and goes right through the projects where I lived, right by Roosevelt Elementary and Roosevelt Middle School and right down Tamarind (Avenue). With all that's changed, it's still fun to revisit your life and all your experiences growing up. It's your platform."

— FORMER NBA STAR AND DALLAS TV PERSONALITY DEREK HARPER,

who bought his mother a new home off Belvedere Road with money from one of his first NBA contracts. For 15 years, he sponsored and put his name on a top holiday high school basketball tournament at Palm Beach Lakes High School.

"I was blessed to have great support from great people, and not only the people who played for me but people in the community besides the Catholic community.

"The closest I ever came to leaving Palm Beach County through all these years was in 1975 or 1976, when I was up for a final interview to join Gary Moeller's football staff at the University of Illinois. I was packed and had everything ready to go, but — wouldn't you know it? — O'Hare (airport) was frozen in.

"They wanted to fly me into Indianapolis, but I just kind of got spooked about the whole thing and said no. I'm originally from the Chicago area, you see, and I told my wife it was not meant to be, because O'Hare was never frozen in."

— SAM BUDNYK,

who retired in 2008 after 44 years as football coach at Cardinal Newman High School in West Palm Beach. He also served as athletic director from the day the school opened in 1961. He is the winningest coach in Palm Beach County football history, with 278 victories during 44 years at Cardinal Newman High and St. Ann Catholic School. Four former players reached the National Football League. He also won two state girls' softball titles while at Newman.

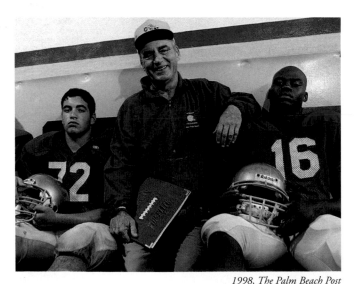

1998, The Palm Beach Post

Cardinal Newman High School football player Nick Rojo (left), Head Coach Sam Budnyk and teammate and Abram Elam.

Along the shores of Lake Okeechobee in 1998, Pahokee High School quarterback Anquan Boldin strikes a pose. At the time, he was one of the best prep quarterbacks in the country. He is now a wide receiver for the Arizona Cardinals.

"I'll take my son to a high school game in Arizona on a Friday night, and it's a completely different atmosphere and a completely different feeling from what they have in Pahokee. The talent is exceptional down there. I've never seen a place so small produce so many football players.

"I spend as much time as I can in Palm Beach County in the off-season. I bought my mom a home in West Palm Beach, and I stay closely tied to the Pahokee football program. I want to see those kids be successful."

— ARIZONA CARDINALS
WIDE RECEIVER ANQUAN BOLDIN,

who has made significant donations to buy football uniforms for Pahokee High School, his alma mater; and to send promising players to football camps.

"I was coaching at Lake Shore High School (in Belle Glade) and working at the elementary school there. A friend and I decided to go to West Palm Beach and look for mangoes, and I said, 'You know, maybe while we're over there, we ought to run down to Carver (High School in Delray Beach) and see if they need any coaches.' And we did just that.

"The schools were not integrated then, and there were some problems — scheduling and stuff like that — but I didn't let them affect me. One of the greatest things was my relationship with Coach Randy Cooper over at Seacrest. Anytime I needed to use his field once we got into the playoffs, he was more than happy to accommodate me because our little stadium couldn't hold all those people. That friendliness is what I miss the most. I love that county."

— ROGER COFFEY,

whose Carver High teams won Class B state titles in 1968 and 1969, the first high school football state championships in county history. Coffey remembers Cardinal Newman High School Coach Sam Budnyk lending him two boxes of new jerseys so that his team would look good for the playoffs.

WHAT A SHOW! Palm Beach County's cultural gems

SERENITY NOW: Since its opening in 1977, the Morikami Museum and Japanese Gardens in Delray Beach has been a center for Japanese arts and culture in South Florida, with rotating exhibitions in its galleries, tea ceremonies and Japanese traditional festivals. This is a 2007 view of the grounds, as the sun burns off fog in the morning.

Taylor Jones / The Palm Beach Post

Palm Beach County has always been a showplace for the arts.

Long before there was a Kravis Center, there was the Paramount Theatre, a Palm Beach venue that played host to Al Jolson and Eddie Cantor, among others.

Long before there was a Palm Beach Opera, the Romanies, a Gypsy-themed chorus, accompanied many a visiting Metropolitan Opera singer. And long before that, there was Henry Flagler — who entertained his Palm Beach guests with top artists.

Here are seven arts institutions that have shaped Palm Beach County over the past century:

Cruzan Amphitheatre

SUBURBAN WEST PALM BEACH

Year opened: 1996

Key details: With a capacity of up to 20,000 — in both covered seating and lawn areas — the venue is a fixture on the national touring circuit. Initially called the Coral Sky Amphitheatre, the concert showplace is part of the South Florida Fairgrounds.

Why it's important: When the Cruzan opened in the mid-1990s, Palm Beach County finally had something that Miami and Fort Lauderdale didn't: namely, a big-league outdoor theater.

To this day, Florida residents to our south and north drive for hours to hear such prominent acts as the Dave Matthews Band, Radiohead and Janet Jackson perform. And let's not forget that the Spice Girls made their American debut at this amphitheater in 1998.

Mary and Bob and Montgomery at the opening of Palm Beach Opera's 44th season, in 2005. Bob, who died in 2008, served as chairman of the opera board for 25 years. He and his wife donated millions to local cultural organizations.

Palm Beach Daily News

Palm Beach Opera   WEST PALM BEACH

Year founded: 1961

Key details: The nearly half-century-old company presents at least three operas each season at the Kravis Center, bringing in star talents from the Metropolitan Opera and leading European opera houses. Palm Beach Opera also hosts a nationally prominent vocal competition.

Why it's important: Few regional opera companies in Florida — or the rest of the country — produce opera on as grand a scale as this hometown troupe. Among the singers it has presented over the years: Luciano Pavarotti, Placido Domingo and Beverly Sills.

Norton Museum of Art

WEST PALM BEACH

Year opened: 1941

Key details: The museum's permanent collection consists of more than 5,000 works, split among European, American, Chinese and contemporary art. In addition to its original Art Deco/Neo classical building, the museum now encompasses the more modern-style Gail and Melvin Nessel Wing, which opened in 2003.

Why it's important: The Norton, founded by the late industrialist and art collector Ralph Hubbard Norton, is the largest art museum in Florida. But it's also one of the most prominent in the Southeast. It has landed several prominent touring exhibitions, including one in 2009 devoted to works by painter Georgia O'Keeffe and photographer Ansel Adams.

Tim Stepien/The Palm Beach Post   *C.J. Walker*

Left: Laura Allen in the Frederick and Patricia Supper Garden inside the Norton Museum of Art. Her wedding and reception were held there in 2009. Right: The staircase of the Norton's Gail and Melvin Nessel Wing, which opened in 2003.

Richard Graulich/The Palm Beach Post

Alexander W. Dreyfoos Jr. in the Kravis Center concert hall that bears his name. Each year, the number of events hosted at the Kravis exceeds 800, and the West Palm Beach performing-arts center attracts more than 500,000 patrons. A major donor to cultural groups, Dreyfoos also has a school named after him: the Alexander W. Dreyfoos Jr. School of the Arts in West Palm Beach.

Maltz Jupiter Theatre

Year opened: 1979

Key details: It originally started life as Burt's place — that is, the Burt Reynolds Dinner Theater. Today it's no longer affiliated with Reynolds, and it no longer serves dinner. However, the Maltz Jupiter Theatre does serve a steady stream of musicals and plays; plus, it runs a bustling theater training program for kids.

Why it's important: (for two reasons): The legends who once appeared there (think such Reynolds cronies as Dom DeLuise and Charles Nelson Reilly), and the potential future legends who are now appearing there.

Raymond F. Kravis Center for the Performing Arts

WEST PALM BEACH

Year opened: 1992

Key details: The $100 million center consists of three theaters: the 2,193-seat Alexander W. Dreyfoos Jr. Concert Hall, the flexible 300-seat Rinker Playhouse, and the outdoor Michael and Andrew Gosman Amphitheatre. The Cohen Pavilion, a combination banquet, arts-education and administrative facility, is the most recent addition to the center.

Why it's important: In less than two decades, the Kravis, named in honor of the late oilman and part-time Palm Beach resident Raymond F. Kravis, has established itself as *the* cultural gathering place in Palm Beach County. Among the big-name performers who have graced its stages: Frank Sinatra, Mikhail Baryshnikov, Liza Minnelli, Itzhak Perlman, Jimmy Buffett and Bill Cosby.

Caldwell Theatre Company

BOCA RATON

Year opened: 1975

Key details: Now located at a new 333-seat theater, the company, which started life at a local college, has a subscription base that has been as high as 7,500 theater-goers.

Michael Hall, founding artistic director.

Why it's important: Named after businessman James R. Caldwell (the man behind the Rubbermaid brand), the Caldwell was arguably the first company to bring contemporary drama (mixed with the occasional classic) to Palm Beach County. It also became a true home for South Florida's growing base of theatrical professionals.

The new Boca Raton Museum of Art opened at Mizner Park in January 2001.

Boca Raton Museum of Art

Boca Raton Museum of Art

Key details: The museum's roots reach back to the late 1940s, when a group of socially active women — including Hildegarde Schine and Roberta MacSpadden — formed a club to build a library and arts center. Eventually, they found a spot in Addison Mizner's Old Floresta neighborhood, the former site of his 1926 radio station WFLA — "The Voice of Tropical Florida." The four Art Deco-style radio antennae bases still stand on the museum grounds and today serve as stately bases for sculptures in an outdoor sculpture garden. The museum expanded again in 2001, with the opening of a 44,000-square-foot museum in Mizner Park.

Key works: The permanent collection now numbers more than 4,000 works, including the Dr. & Mrs. John J. Mayers Collection of Modern Art and more than 50 works by modern masters including Degas, Matisse and Picasso.

Boca Raton Museum of Art

Mrs. Arnold MacSpadden (left), with Mrs. Horatio Ebert and Mrs. J. Meyer Schine at a 1956 Art Guild fundraiser.

Henrietta, Countess de Hoernle

Thank You, Countess

Countess *Henrietta de Hoernle*

Looking back at a century of growth for Palm Beach County, one woman has distinguished herself as an avid humanitarian dedicated to improving the lives of so many. We thank you for your vision and generosity, Countess de Hoernle.

Boca Raton Community Hospital Foundation • Northwood University
Boca Raton Historical Society • Boca Raton Museum of Art • Centre for the Arts at Mizner Park
Junior League of Boca Raton • YMCA of South Palm Beach County

Rice Family

GONE FISHIN'! Eight-year-old twins Greg (left) and John Rice along the Southern Boulevard causeway in West Palm Beach in 1960. They were fishing with "Captain Jack," who did a TV fishing report. The 2-foot-10-inch Rice brothers, listed in the *Guinness Book of World Records* as the shortest twins on the planet, became self-made millionaires and local celebrities. They are best-known for their Hulett Pest Control commercials. John died in 2005 at 53.

LITTLE BIG MEN

John and Greg Rice personify the county's can-do spirit.
As one friend said:
'You could always count on those guys to support whatever it was that was good for the county.'

John Rice's memories of Palm Beach High, 1969:

Since I'm only 3 feet tall, my memories of Palm Beach High School are — well, it was a long walk up the hill from the band room to the library. When we started, they thought it was going to take us longer to make the changes between classes.

But I guess we didn't do a lot of walking ... everybody and their brother comes up to us and says, "Hey, I used to carry you on my shoulders from class to class." Those guys were my taxi back then.

In the late 1960s, we went through some rapid changes in integration. I remember the riots and having the police and their full riot paraphernalia ...

The thing I miss the most is the brownies at the Campus Shop. They were the best in the world. I'd give $1,000 now for that brownie recipe.

— *From a 1988 Palm Beach Post interview*

Greg Rice (left) and John Rice at Palm Beach High School, 1969 >

The Palm Beach Post

By PAUL LOMARTIRE
The Palm Beach Post

Dr. Jennings Derrick took care of so many children, rich and poor, in Palm Beach County in the 1950s that his longtime office manager called him "Palm Beach's doctor."

"He was a doctor to the stars," Jeri Baysinger remembers. "The Kennedys. The Shrivers. He cared for Caroline Kennedy. And he cared for kids out in Belle Glade. He took care of everybody."

Including a pair of identical-twin dwarfs, born five minutes apart on Dec. 3, 1951, at St. Mary's Hospital. Their mother, a young woman from Delray Beach, named them John and Greg Rice, then took a good look at them, and disappeared.

Dr. Derrick did the opposite: He made a promise, that day, that he would always care for those tiny boys. If God had forced them to bear such a physical burden, he would help heal the emotional one.

For the first eight months of the twins' lives, hospital nurses and nuns took turns as mothers while Dr. Derrick searched for a foster home. When John and Greg were 8 months old, a social worker found Frank and Mildred Windsor.

Mildred's big heart was well-known around sleepy Lake Worth in 1952. If parents were in a jam and ended up in jail, the police knew where to drop off their kids.

A devout Pentecostal, Mildred was willing to take in foster kids to live with her daughter, Betty, 14; and son, J.D., 12. Frank worked at a place that made jalousie windows.

Yes, she would take the Rice babies, who were destined to be split up as wards of the state.

"Mildred called my mother and said, 'You've got to come over and see my boys,'" recalled Betty's friend Helen Saxon. "When we went over, she had them lying in the same crib, one at each end. They were precious."

Mildred died of ovarian cancer

David Spencer/The Palm Beach Post

Greg (left) and John Rice sport SunFest beads on Clematis Street in 2002. The twins were identical only in looks. Right-handed John, 5 minutes older, was the risk-taker. Left-handed Greg is more cautious. John figured out, when the boys were young, that "If we're ever going to be anything in this life, we've got to learn to run our mouths."

when John and Greg were 8. Her daughter, Betty, finished raising them. And just as Helen said, everyone was crazy about them.

The smallest kids at Palm Beach High always commanded a big crowd. They played cymbals in the school band.

"It was so funny — because John and Greg were so small and the cymbals were so big," said former County Commissioner Ken Foster, who grew up rooting for a rival team, the Belle Glade Rams. "But their personalities were electric, even in a stadium."

From those early days at school, they loved Palm Beach County, Foster said: "You could always count on those guys to support whatever it was that was good for the county."

John and Greg became millionaire salesmen and two of the most popular

guys in the county.

Their size hooked you. Their skills sold you: From the *Tonight Show* to *Real People* to the local *TV Parade of Homes* that the brothers kicked off in 1980 to today's Hulett Pest Control ads.

The Rice brothers made about 40 pest-control ads over a 20-year period, and syndicated them. As a result, almost all of America has seen John and Greg carrying on their comical battle with termites.

When John died during surgery for a broken leg in 2005, the entire community mourned.

Especially Greg, who spoke at John's funeral about how John loved to make people laugh. "If you see people smiling, there's John," Greg said. "Because that's what John is."

Burt Reynolds on Jupiter:

'IT'S A MAGICAL, WONDERFUL PLACE'

'We had some terrific actors who came down here, who trusted me, and who fell madly in love with Jupiter and the beach and the turtles and all those things that we live here for. It was amazing.'

Photo by Chris Matula
The Palm Beach Post

MEMORIES

WHY WE LOVE WHERE WE LIVE

BURT REYNOLDS: *'This is where I found peace'*

Loren Hosack/The Palm Beach Post
Burt Reynolds at his Jupiter Farms ranch in September 1999. The ranch had a "gas station set." Reynolds — Palm Beach County's most famous resident — is a hometown boy who still loves to come home.

Burt Reynolds as an FSU football star...

...and a proud member of Palm Beach High School Class of 1954.

From his 1994 autobiography, *My Life:*

"The first time I actually saw the ocean was on Highway A1A in Jupiter. It was so green and beautiful. Little did I know what a big part of my life the little town of Jupiter would become someday. In those days, it was a truckstop...

"As advertised, Riviera Beach was right on the water, too...When we arrived, the small town had a few thousand residents and two trailer courts: The Sea Breeze and Star Camp. With few belongings, we bought an old trailer and moved into — you guessed it — Star Camp.

"Most people believed paradise was actually 7 miles south and over the bridge — the exclusive island of Palm Beach...None of that interested me as much as the swampy wilderness to the west. You could've offered me the largest mansion in Palm Beach, and I would've turned it down in favor of the mysterious woods that ran all along the northern shore of Riviera and the Everglades to the west."

1954

Palm Beach High's "Best All Around" — Mary Alice Sullivan and Burton "Buddy" Reynolds. Mary Alice later married and divorced — to great publicity — tire heir Russell Firestone Jr.

1953 Mo Mustaine (No. 64, left) and his good pal Buddy (center) with the Palm Beach High football team.

Our Buddy: Burt Reynolds

By CHRISTINA WOOD

Burt Reynolds isn't the only celebrity who got his start in a small town, but he is one of the very few who always came home.

The Hollywood legend was born in Waycross, Ga., but he's been hanging his hat in Palm Beach County ever since his father, Burt Sr., went to work for the Riviera Beach Police Department in the late 1940s.

"I didn't know until I was almost 30 that I was from 'Riv-ee-era' Beach," Reynolds now jokes.

2004 Burt and Mo at FSU, where Burt played football on scholarship until an injury ended his career.

< **Bud and I met in 1949 at Central Junior High.** We met at football practice; Bud was our fullback, and I was halfback. We had a lot of fun. We both made the All-Star team but lost to Conniston in the Palm Bowl game. Football was Bud's sport. He was very good and very fast. He went on to become All-Southern in high school.

We always were roommates on away games. We tried our best to get some girls up to our room, but it never worked as we had some tough coaches. Bud lived in Riviera Beach; his dad was chief of police. Bud taught me how to drive in his dad's car.

Since he's become a famous movie star, he is still a neat guy, and my wife and I have been to Bud's house in Hobe Sound hundreds of times.

Bud and I also own a *Smokey and the Bandit* car together. It's a restored black 1977 Pontiac Firebird Trans-Am with a V-8 engine and a T-top — just like in the movie.

The car stays up at Bud's place.

— MO MUSTAINE

1991

Watson B. Duncan III, third from left, is honored by former students: actor Burt Reynolds, author Terry Garrity (who wrote the 1969 best-seller *The Sensuous Woman*) and actor Monte Markham, another Palm Beach High graduate. PBJC literature teacher Duncan encouraged Reynolds and Markham to pursue acting.

"Everybody called it 'Riv-era,' and they called us 'conchs.'"

In the 1970s, Reynolds was drawn to the charm of Jupiter. "Somebody in Hollywood asked me, 'Where is Jupiter?' I said, 'Well, you go to Mars and you turn right until you hit Jetty's (waterfront restaurant). It's a magical, wonderful place ...

"I've always come back, even when I was doing two-and-a-half pictures a year. This is where I found peace.

"Whatever success I had, I wanted to share it. I wanted to give something back."

Over the years, he did just that — from the dinner theater he ran here in the 1970s and '80s to film productions he brought to the region and the master-acting classes he currently teaches at the Burt Reynolds Institute for Film and Theatre Training in Jupiter.

"I had the theater for seven years. I remember the first opening night; we had an incredible cast that included Sally Field and Tyne Daly. There were a lot of people who had never seen live actors before who came and loved it.

"I was really proud of some of the things we did. They weren't the usual dinner-theater fare. We had some terrific actors who came down here, who trusted me, and who fell madly in love with Jupiter and the beach and the turtles and all those things that we live here for. It was amazing."

Reynolds' first taste of success came much earlier, though: as a first-team All-State, All-Southern tailback at Palm Beach High.

"I had quite an amazing class in high school. My best friend was Dick Howser, the one the baseball stadium at Florida State is named after. I mean, what are the chances that two best friends would go on — one to a career in motion pictures and television, and the other to become a Major League Baseball player who was Rookie of the Year, manager of the New York Yankees, and then took the Kansas City Royals to the World Series?

"I also ran around with this guy, Mo Mustaine. I always thought that was the best name. I got a football scholarship and Howser got a baseball scholarship. But Mo didn't get a scholarship even though he was a terrific athlete.

Burt's museum

Memorabilia at Jupiter's Burt Reynolds & Friends Museum includes the canoe he used in the 1972 movie *Deliverance* and photos and souvenirs from *Smokey and the Bandit* and *Smokey and the Bandit 2* (left). The original *Smokey* was 1977's second-highest-grossing movie, after *Star Wars*, and made the 1977 Pontiac Firebird Trans-Am a top seller. Also at the museum: Reynolds' Golden Globe for best supporting actor (for *Boogie Nights*), football jerseys from Reynolds' days at Palm Beach High School and the revolver, money clip and badge used by Reynolds' father, who was police chief of Riviera Beach (below).

Gary Coronado/The Palm Beach Post

Burt Reynolds' father, Burt Sr., served as police chief of Riviera Beach in the 1950s. "It's never a picnic being the police chief's son," Burt wrote in his 1994 autobiography, *My Life*. "Yet, in my eyes, no man was greater than my dad. Nobody stood taller or stronger."

We all felt quite bad for Mo — but it turns out we didn't need to. Mo ended up as an electrician; he started his own company and ended up with more money than any of us. We laugh about it now."

Reynolds' career path took a sharp and surprising turn following a football injury at Florida State University and an English-literature class with Watson B. Duncan III at Palm Beach Junior College. Since then, he has had his name on everything from movie marquees to shiny statuettes.

When Palm Beach County put his name on a 35-acre waterfront park in Jupiter, however, he knew he had achieved a much broader measure of success.

"I was so floored and touched when they put my name on the park. I was trying not to be flip about it, but it is wonderful to have your name on something that you didn't pay for. I love this town. When I go somewhere like the hardware store, people who are just people come over and say hello.

"When I lived in California, Gregory Peck was my neighbor. I had tremendous respect for him, but he was always 'Mr. Peck.' With me, it's always been 'Hey, Burt!' or 'Good to see you, Burt' or 'I knew your dad, Burt.' I've always been approachable. I like that."

Christina Wood is a freelance writer in Delray Beach. Parts of this interview originally were published in art&culture of Palm Beach County, a 2009 magazine produced by the Palm Beach County Cultural Council and Passport Publications.

Living with the stars: Our world was a stage

By JIM "JIM BOB" CRABTREE

As the children of Paul and Mary Crabtree, my brothers and sisters and I grew up in the 1950s and early '60s around the Palm Beach Playhouse and the Royal Poinciana Playhouse.

For me, Palm Beach was Little League and the Worth Avenue Merchants under the irascible yet loving eye of O.J. Senecal of the Palm Beach Police Department. It was an idyllic life — four houses from the ocean — at Oahu, a three-story "cottage" on Sunset Avenue. It was burgers at Green's Drug Store, and sandlot baseball on the grassy corner by The Biltmore and the bridge.

It was cracking coconuts on the sidewalk, drinking the milk and digging out the meat. It was mockingbirds mocking my dad's signal whistle, calling a false alarm to us kids to come home. It was the Dominican nuns and the scores of Rosarian girls with whom I shared the stage, and fell in unrequited love, in *The Perils of Pinocchio* and *Dreamland, USA*.

Paul Crabtree

It was Cardinal Newman High School football with Coach Sam Budnyk — with two-a-day practices during a tropical August — and golf at The Breakers with Dad and Dr. Raymond Roy. It was Latin Mass and Latin class — mostly As but a big bad algebra D.

We never knew how perfect it was, how rich and remarkable a family life we lived — secure, busy, beloved. Helen Hayes and Liberace were just people we met at the Playhouse. Gypsy Rose Lee was just pal Eric's mom. Eva Gabor was Mom's good buddy. Billie Burke was a flighty, forgetful lady who bloomed miraculously on opening night of my first play as an actor, age 8.

There was nothing quite as idyllic as Palm Beach summers — the town quiet and empty, a bicycle and baseball paradise. Nothing quite as glamorous as opening night at either theater, fussed over by Messmore and Sepha Kendall, thrilled when Frank Hale pulled off a 10 from his money clip.

I even got to perform with Helen Hayes — in *Mrs. McThing*.

"You've done this before," I said to Miss Hayes at age 10 when we first sat down to read *Mrs. McThing*, and I realized she was *good*.

"Yes," she said, "I've done it before. And I love Palm Beach."

So do I — even now.

Crabtree is now the producing director of the Cumberland County Playhouse in Crossville, Tenn., founded (along with the Palm Beach Playhouse and the Royal Poinciana Playhouse) by his father, Paul.

Crabtree Family

1955 Helen Hayes with Jenny Hecht (daughter of playwright Ben Hecht) and Jim Bob Crabtree, in costume for *Mrs. McThing* by Mary Chase, author of *Harvey*.

The Palm Beach Post

Early 1970s

Opening night at the Royal Poinciana Playhouse in Palm Beach is such a big deal that it's covered by the local press. Ted Kennedy escorts Mary Sanford (left) and his mother, Rose, to an evening of theater.

The zenith of happiness?
Our own TV

By BARBARA STARKEY HUBBARD

Linda Willson grew up across the street from me in Northwood Hills in West Palm Beach. We went to school together — all the way from Mrs. Moyle's kindergarten class to Palm Beach Junior College.

If we don't see each other for a long time, we pick up right where we left off.

We have the Southern bond — our mothers are Southern, and we were raised that way. We both love the genteel ways and men with manners. We love Sunday-afternoon drives and chatting with friends over a glass of iced tea. There are no friends like old friends.

Like Linda Willson and me.

After Linda's mom passed away a couple of years ago, I started remembering the things Linda and I did when we were kids.

My father Raymond Starkey was in the meat-packing business, and every Friday night, we patronized his clients. Most of them were in Palm Beach, so we had to gussy up, look good, put on our best behavior and eat like nice people.

I loved Petite Marmite. It means "Little Pot" in French, and the owners were my parents' friends, the Pucillos.

For dessert, Petite Marmite waiters would bring out ice cream with Crème de Menthe on top. It was so pretty that my father said it was all right to eat — no alcohol in it. If my father said there was no alcohol, there was no alcohol. He didn't lie; he was my father.

A few days later, while I was over at Linda's house, I remarked to Mr. Willson about the dessert. He said that Crème de Menthe was a cordial, and it had alcohol. I can still see myself turning red and saying,

"No, it doesn't. My father said so." Mr. Willson laughed, and I got so mad.

He used to drive us to school until a friend got a car. He sold insurance and wasn't home much. Mrs. Willson was home all the time, and I'm sure she was tired of me coming over every day.

That's right — every day after school. Linda had television, but we didn't.

My father was waiting for TV to be "perfected" (whatever that meant), so Linda and I sat in front of that box and watched *American Bandstand* every day. We had so much fun.

She had cookies, and I had oranges. I wonder why I'm fat and Linda is skinny. Maybe it's because I would trade one orange for three cookies.

'Such a wonderful place to grow up'

Our house was on the corner of 36th Street and Eastview Avenue, on the coastal ridge, one of the highest points in Palm Beach County.

This incredible altitude provided us special joys: For one, our house had a basement, which was perfect for slumber parties. And two, we had a wall in front where people could sit, and a sidewalk that curved down the hill.

Wow! A curvy sidewalk! We made scooters out of anything that would roll.

Linda's brother, Manning, and his friend, Glen Burgenhouser, were older, and they knew how to use a hammer. Their scooters were made of wooden crates with skates

Photos from Barbara Starkey Hubbard

Linda Willson (left) and Barbara Starkey Hubbard, who grew up together, are still friends.

'There we were in the pool when I spied the Herrington TV truck fly up 36th Street. There was only one place that truck was going — my house!

'I shot out of the pool and made it home just in time to hear the doorbell ring. I watched as the big swivel Motorola was put in its special place in the living room.'

on the bottom. You know the ones? Get out your skate keys and hope your shoes don't fall off.

My father made me one out of wood and baby-buggy wheels. I could sit up, hold on to the ropes and go down the hill. There were lots of skinned knees and elbows, bumps on our heads and broken sprinklers, but there was no deterring us. Such a wonderful place to grow up.

Sundays were quiet days for church, fried chicken and afternoon rides. Linda and I would sit in the back seat, and off we'd go. We went different places. One favorite spot was Kelsey City, where there were snakes in the roads.

There was no actual Kelsey City then — the town became Lake Park — but there were concrete arches at the entrance to the old city, and we would find snakes sunning themselves in the middle of the streets because there weren't many houses.

We always ended up at Howard Johnson's at Belvedere Road and Dixie Highway in West Palm Beach. We'd start to order, and Linda would ask, "What's the budget?" The budget was an ice cream soda. I miss Howard Johnson's hot dogs, clam rolls and ice cream. Where did they go?

It's a lesson. Nothing lasts forever. I wish it did.

Summer 1958: Finally, our TV arrives

Television was a huge part of our lives. It was new and exciting. My father read the *Saturday Evening Post* and *Colliers Weekly*, tinkered down in the basement or listened to the radio for entertainment. Television was much better than those things.

I remember the day our television came. It was the summer of 1958. Linda and I were swimming in Tommy Dioguardi's pool. Can you believe it? Someone had a pool in their yard.

This was incredible to us. We learned to swim at the Mayflower Hotel in Palm Beach. It seemed like every kid in West Palm Beach paid 10 cents for swimming lessons on Saturday morning.

Lido Pools was on the beach in Palm Beach. There was a tunnel from the pool to the beach with water to

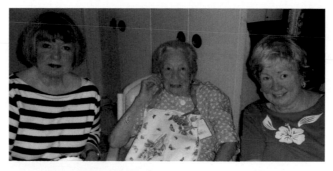

Lois Mercer is flanked by her daughters Betty Ann Starkey (left) and Barbara Starkey Hubbard in their childhood home.

wade through so that sand was not tracked in.

Summers were spent in the water. You must remember: We lived in Florida and no one — I mean *no one* — had air conditioning.

Mrs. Dioguardi was very nice to us. We'd knock on the door and ask if we could swim in her pool, and she always said it was all right. Mr. Dioguardi was a contractor, and he built our house. Maybe that's why she let us swim when we wanted to.

There we were in the pool when I spied the Herrington TV truck fly up 36th Street. There was only one place that truck was going — my house!

I shot out of the pool and made it home just in time to hear the doorbell ring. I watched as the big swivel Motorola was put in its special place in the living room.

I want to mention two funny things about the Dioguardis and the Herringtons.

Billy Herrington and I were born on the same day at Good Samaritan Hospital: Sept. 6, 1945. Judy Cook had a crush on him and told me years later. Tommy Dioguardi taught driver's ed at John I. Leonard, and two of my three daughters took him.

When one of them said, "Mr. Dio-

Photo by J.D. Vivian/The Palm Beach Post
Barbara Starkey Hubbard grew up in 3702 Eastview Ave. in West Palm Beach. The home sits on the coastal ridge, one of the highest areas in the county.

guardi said …" I knew it was Tommy. I went to the school to meet the teachers, and it was so nice to chat like old times.

I like old times.

I kept my class picture from sixth grade at Northmore Elementary School for almost 50 years, and I'd still have it except for a fire at my house in 2004.

Tommy Dioguardi is in that picture. He's standing next to Mrs. Bowles, the principal. Tommy became a championship swimmer — thanks, I'm sure, to that pool in his back yard.

So many of the friends I still have today are in that class photo. In my eyes, they haven't changed.

There's Robert Terwilliger, my first date in the seventh grade. We went to the Halloween dance. His father drove, and I wore a gray dress with a big orange sash.

I see Jimmy Sleeth, who I danced the maypole with in fifth grade. There's Sandy Moss and Frankie Yelverton. We used to pay a quarter to watch them kiss.

John Leeder and I were in love and planning to go to the moon together. We tricked-or-treated that year. I loved to go to his house because his parents were fascinating. They were hippies before there were hippies.

There's Barbara Knapp, who became a teacher.

Linda Willson is sitting next to Douglas Manske in the back.

I can blink and go right back to that classroom. We had so much fun as kids.

Fun sticks with you. So do friends.

Linda Willson lives in Sarasota now. But next time I see her, it will be like we had just come home from school, and I had skipped across the street to watch *American Bandstand*.

It will be like old times … the moments that live forever in our hearts.

My Cinderella night as homecoming queen

By BILLIE JO McFEE SWILLEY

What was it like to be homecoming queen for Seacrest High School in 1953? Hmmm … where is that old senior-year high school scrapbook? Ah, ha, the attic.

As I run to the garage, pull down the stairs and scramble up the ladder, my mind drifts back to what life was like in the sweet little town of Delray Beach that I loved so much.

In the attic, I see the clearly marked box with a big eagle on it (our mascot symbol was the Seacrest Seahawks). I slowly blow off the dust and open the box containing so many wonderful memories of our high school and my early courtship with my husband, Del.

Let's see — freshman year, a big green "S" with many bars for years in the band, the "S" letter for swimming. Gosh, a band medal slips onto the floor, and I remember how hard our band members worked to earn the "superior" rating in the State Band Contest. And here is a real gem: a postcard with six girlfriends in bathing suits on the front. (Wish I was that size again!)

Homecoming was an important time for all high schools in those days. In 1953, we were once again playing Lake Worth High, our arch-rival. For the first time in Seacrest High School History, could we beat the Lake Worth Trojans?

The homecoming queen was selected by the entire student body, and the senior class had selected four girls to run for queen. My competitors included a gorgeous girl from Boca Raton who had already won many beauty contests (and would go on to become the fifth runner-up in the Miss America Contest a few years later), the president of the Student Council, and one of the editors of the yearbook.

I had very little hope that I could win, but I did have a secret weapon: the band members!

I had been in the band for 12 years. We grew up together, and we were like family. Also, my best friend, Nancy, was the very popular head cheerleader. I was feature twirler and did the choreography for the 10-member majorette squad, so I was busy.

About a week before homecoming, my next-door neighbor, who went to private school, came

Billie Jo McFee Swilley

Billie Jo McFee and Del Swilley

1953   2006

1953   Being homecoming queen of Seacrest High (top) was just one of Billie Jo McFee's high-school highlights. In 1953, her prom date was the prom king, Del Swilley, who grew up in Boynton Beach. In 2006, they celebrated their 50th wedding anniversary (right). They have three children, several grandchildren and a host of hometown memories.

'My husband and I have lived in south Palm Beach County since 1936 and have watched as our little county moved from a sweet little sleepy Southern community to what we have today. I grew up in Delray Beach, and my husband grew up in Boynton Beach.

We were high school sweethearts. He was the football captain; I was the drum majorette. My dad was the only baker in south Palm Beach County in the 1930s and early '40s and also a councilman in Delray in 1942.

My mother sold his baked goods until they sold their business — Bon-Ton Bakery — and she worked as a real estate broker until she was 93.'

— BILLIE JO MCFEE SWILLEY

Billie Jo McFee as a majorette (above). She recalls that she was elected homecoming queen by one vote. "Delray Beach of the '30s, '40s and '50s was truly a Norman Rockwell city," Billie Jo says.

Beach beauties: Billie Jo McFee (right) with friends from Seacrest High, on spring break in Delray Beach. From left, they are: Jeri Bradfield, Meta Schrodel, unidentified girl, Dorothy Steiner (who was fifth-runner-up in the Miss America contest in 1957, Billie Jo says), Shirley Barker and Billie Jo, who now lives in Boynton Beach.

over and casually asked what I was going to wear to the dance. I showed her what I had. She shook her head, thought a minute and said, "I'll be back in a few minutes."

Now, understand that this lovely girl had a closet-ful of clothes. Her dad owned a large trucking firm, and money was no problem. In a few minutes, Betty returned with the most beautiful white strapless gown I had ever seen. It fit perfectly. Mama called Betty's mom to be sure it was OK for me to borrow such an expensive dress. It was.

I had my shoes. But Betty said the earrings I had did not match, so we hit Mama's jewel box. Nothing!

About that time, a real estate client of mother's stopped by the house for a visit. I was still in *the dress*, and she loved it. She said rhinestones would show up on the football field better than pearls. Later that night, she returned with a beautiful set of rhinestone earrings and a necklace. The only thing I had to buy was a hoop skirt. *Hoorah!!*

The band performed a pre-game show before every home game, and the first quarter went by real fast. Then I got nervous. It was half-time, the band was performing, I was twirling; then the band was off the field, and I was running to the band house to change into my beautiful dress while the Lake Worth band was doing its half-time show.

I ran down the path with my shoes in hand, got to the goal posts with the rest of the homecoming court, and was pulling on my shoes as Miss Cannon walked over to give out the stoles. There were three green stoles, and one white velvet stole for the queen.

The cheerleaders were close by watching, so that they could run back to the crowd and tell them who the queen was.

I never dreamed I would win, so I was speechless when Miss Cannon looked at me, said "Congratulations, Honey" and handed *me* the coveted white stole.

The next thing I knew, my best friend, Nancy, almost knocked me down with a hug and a kiss. Then off she went, running down the sidelines, yelling, "Billie Jo! Billie Jo! *Billie Jo!!*"

I don't remember walking onto the field and taking the seat of honor on the 50-yard line. My mother and daddy came down to give me a hug and kiss, and our great little football team won the game: 20 to 14. We had beaten Lake Worth High!

The president of the Student Council gave me a little football charm, and my date gave me the charm bracelet to go with it.

I was Cinderella at my ball. I will never forget that night. What a joy!

What's a '60s teen to do? Head downtown

By PENNY GREENBERG MURPHY

When I grew up in the 1950s and '60s, we were a small community — no Interstate 95, no mall. Life ended at Military Trail.

I started at Conniston Junior High in 1960. On Saturday mornings, we would hop on the bus and meet boys on Clematis Street for the afternoon. Usually that meant buying lunch at the Woolworth's counter and an afternoon movie at either the Palms or the Florida Theatre.

"Downtown" (as it was known at that time) was booming. There were a few shoe stores, three five-and-dime stores, a Walgreens, several dress stores, Anthony's for men's and women's fashions, Myers Luggage, Harris Men's Store and, of course, my family's business, the Pioneer Co. (now Pioneer Linens).

My time at Forest Hill High School was just like the movie *American Graffiti*. The coolest thing to do was to cruise by The Hut, our local drive-in. Parking there was a trick, though. Two cars parked, one behind the other, in one spot.

You did not want to hear the waitress call "Car out!" That meant you had to back out — with the drive-in's tray still attached to your car — in order to let the car in front out. If the metal tray fell off your car, it crashed to the ground, making a loud noise that was embarrassing.

We met all our friends at The Hut, and that included students from Palm Beach High, our rival school. It was one big party.

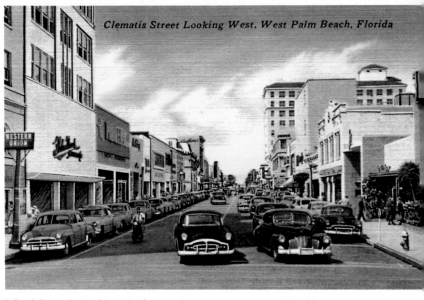

1940s Early Clematis Street, shown on a postcard, looking west. The Florida Theatre (far right) is now the Cuillo Centre for the Arts. Pioneer Linens (left) is still there.

1952
Lois Greenberg with daughter Penny and son George Jr. at their home at 921 Almeria Road in West Palm Beach. The Greenbergs' family business, Pioneer Linens, was founded by Penny's grandfather, Max, in 1912.

Greenberg family

1940
Elsie Greenberg with her son George (Penny Greenberg Murphy's father) during a visit home around 1940. He was stationed in Virginia, serving in the U.S. Army Quartermaster Corps. George Greenberg and his Pioneer Linens proved to have staying power — he was informally knows as "The Mayor of Clematis Street."

Establishing the county's first synagogue

George Greenberg ran his family's Pioneer Linens, on Clematis Street, for more than

Max Greenberg

seven decades, until just two months before his death at 92 in 2007. "The Mayor of Clematis Street" was a living link to Palm Beach County's

early merchants, as well as to its early Jewish community. In fact, Greenberg's father, Max, helped to establish the county's first synagogue, Temple Beth Israel, in 1923. George was its first Bar Mitzvah, five years later. From those modest beginnings, the county's Jewish community has grown to become the fourth largest in the country, behind only the New York, Chicago and Los Angeles areas. About one in five county residents is Jewish.

Karen Marcus: Dancing at the Lot Hop and the Music Casters

We were one of the first 10 families to move to North Palm Beach. It was so undeveloped in 1957 that my dad could land his plane next door to our house to drop off his laundry.

In middle school, I would walk from my house in North Palm Beach to my best friend, Sue Kuebler's, house in Lake Park. We'd walk to Riviera Beach and cross the bridge and go to the beach on Singer Island.

Karen Marcus

We could walk up U.S. 1. There was really no traffic because it was only two lanes. We'd go to the beach to watch our friends surf. We'd hang out at the Dairy Belle. It's still there on Broadway.

Edward M. Eissey was my principal at Howell Watkins Junior High and then he was my principal at Palm Beach Gardens High. When I went to Palm Beach Junior College, he showed up as president! I graduated from high school with his son, Mike, and we all still laugh about that.

I started high school at Riviera Beach High School. Then they split us up, and I was among the first group of students at Gardens High. I graduated in 1970.

We started the Teens Unique club in 1968. It was all north-county teens, and the most popular thing was the Lot Hop — dances held in the parking lot at the Palm Beach Gardens Public Works Department on Burns Road. We also used to dance at the Music Casters. It was in a cool little shopping plaza, Bazaar International, across from what is now the Port of Palm Beach. It had a

Tulino Family

1950s

Robin, Faith and Karen Tulino in North Palm Beach. Their mother, Fran, recalls: "In March 1957, we moved into our house on Bay Road. They had a parade of homes here, and we bought it from H&D Construction. Eight years later, we bought the home where we live now a few blocks away."

Look! Dad just parked the plane on the lawn!

Joe Tulino was one of Pratt & Whitney's first Florida employees. The Hartford, Conn.-based Pratt & Whitney — a world leader in the design, manufacture and service of aircraft engines — liked the wide open spaces of northern Palm Beach County in 1956, when they hired Tulino. "The original office for Pratt was downtown on Datura Street on Nov. 1, 1956. There were seven of us. There was me, a general manager, a financial officer, a personnel manager and a couple of others. We hired," Tulino recalled. "I used to take the company Jeep out there on the Beeline Highway, which was a dirt road. In early '58, we ended up out where Pratt & Whitney is now. I worked as a test engineer on the RL-10 rocket engine. They still use the RL-10 for the space shuttle." Joe and Fran Tulino (left) and their three daughters moved to North Palm Beach when Northlake Boulevard was just a two-lane, shell-rock road. It was so deserted, Joe could land the plane next to their house to drop off his laundry (above).

huge Eiffel-like tower and a train going around it.

I was like the mother of our high-school group. I had a car, and I was the best driver. My dad had a black 1960 Oldsmobile convertible that I'd drive. I could put 11 girls in it. We'd stop and get a dollar's worth of gas and drive around with the top down all over North Palm Beach, Palm Beach

Gardens, Riviera Beach.

My dad used to take my family on Sunday rides. One day, he took us to Palm Beach. We had the top down and saw John and Jacqueline Kennedy. We said hi. He was also in a convertible. He said hi.

— KAREN TULINO MARCUS

Marcus was elected to the Palm Beach County Commission in 1984 and is due to serve until 2012.

The Palm Beach Post

1997 Chief Engineer Frank Gillette shows off the small group of tools required for maintenance on the F119 fighter engine developed by Pratt & Whitney. "I came to Pratt & Whitney in 1962," Gillette said in 2009. "I've been everything from chief of structures and chief engineer to director of engineering. Even now, I'm still a consultant. Many of the projects we worked on were top-secret — I couldn't even tell my wife about them."

The rocket scientists

John F. "Jack" McDermott

Jack McDermott in 1976. He started with Pratt & Whitney in 1941 and came to Florida in 1958.

I'd say the project I'm proudest of is the work we did on the J58 engines that powered the SR-71 Blackbirds. This was a reconnaissance plane that *cruised* at the unprecedented sustained speed of 2,200 miles per hour — or more than mach 3, which means it cruised at more than three times the speed of sound.

The trick was to design the engine so that it didn't make the plane burst into flames. It had never been done before and hasn't been done since. The Blackbirds used to fly at tremendously high altitudes over Russian air space to keep an eye on what the Soviets were doing. I used to say, "Blackbirds cruise at the speed a bullet is fired out of a rifle."

The Palm Beach Post

1980 A crowd looks over an F-15 jet after a demonstration at the Pratt & Whitney plant, which was so remote in the early years that staffers often saw alligators.

Walt Bylciw

Walt Bylciw

What best illustrates our passion was how we created the F119 engine for fighter jets.

The Department of Defense wanted to upgrade the F100 engine. Pratt & Whitney and General Electric competed to develop a new one.

For more than four years, we ate, drank and slept this project. We were awarded the contract on April 23, 1991 — my wedding anniversary.

We're proud of our deep roots in Palm Beach County.

Pratt & Whitney has been proud to call Palm Beach County home ever since it landed here in 1958. Congratulations on the last 100 years to the community that helped us develop and test aerospace engines for the U.S. military, the world's airliners and America's space exploration programs. And, we're already working on the new technologies that will shape the next 100 years.

 It's in our power.™

 **Pratt & Whitney**
A United Technologies Company

Pretty baby

Before SunFest, there was the Seminole Sun Dance — a festival and parade that lured thousands to downtown West Palm Beach from 1916 to 1950. One of the highlights was the Baby Beauty Contest. The winner in 1921 was Dorothy Donnelly, born Nov. 7, 1919, in Palm Beach at her grandfather's house on the Clarke Estate. John B. Donnelly managed the Clarke Estate.

My mother attended grade school and high school in Palm Beach County. After graduating from Florida State College for Women (now Florida State University), my mother moved to Chicago, where she met my father, J.T. Baldwin. My parents spent their winters in Palm Beach at my mother's childhood home on Park Avenue. My mother passed away in 2007.

— PAT BALDWIN

Baldwin family

1921   Dorothy Donnelly, first place in the baby contest at the 1921 Sun Dance Festival in downtown West Palm Beach.

Educators and entertainers: The Ecklers of West Palm Beach

William "W.B." Beecher and Harriet Fowler Eckler landed in West Palm Beach in 1916, after traveling by boat down the Intracoastal Waterway from New Smyrna Beach.

W.B. quickly established his reputation as an architect and builder, with projects such as the West Palm Beach Woman's Club, at Clematis Street and Flagler Drive; and the Lake Worth Casino.

Harriet, a highly regarded educator, established the first private school in West Palm Beach: Eckler Private School, above the Grace Miles Studio of the Dance on Iris Street.

Children of many pioneer families attended Eckler Private School, which Harriet eventually moved to a large building off Olive Avenue to accommodate her growing enrollment.

The Anthonys, the Andersons, David McCampbell (who married Jean years later and had been the first boy to kiss her at age 13; he also was a World War II Medal of Honor winner), Louis Clarke Duberry (whose family operated the ferry service on Lake Worth), Ralph Kettler, the Curries, Judge James Knott, Dr. Annette Rhem, and scores of other students learned reading, writing, math, Latin, French, deportment, elocution and critical thinking from Mrs. Eckler and her staff.

Grace Miles told Harriet that Jean was "born to dance," and she quickly became an accomplished performer with dreams of becoming a "Broadway star." After graduation from Palm Beach High School in 1929, where she was selected Cutest Girl by the senior class, she and her mother boarded a train for New York City. Jean was selected for an innovative dance troupe that eventually became the Rockettes.

After 10 years, she came home and opened her own studio, Eckler School of the Dance, behind the old Ranch's Drug Store on Conniston Road. "Those recitals were just as exciting and professionally staged as a New York musical," remembers Edith Anderson Harris, whose father was a West Palm Beach town manager and whose family still owns the J.C. Harris Co. and the Harris Building on Clematis Street.

In the finale of her career, the 1960s and '70s, Jean became director of Opportunity Inc. Boys & Girls Club, founded by Winifred Anthony. Its mission: to aid children, of working mothers, who needed a home away from home after school and during summer vacations. Jean was a perfect fit for the job. After all, she herself was a single working mother of six children.

— CYNTHIA L. STOWE

Cynthia L. Stowe is the daughter of Jean Eckler McCampbell. Stowe is the English Department co-chair at Jupiter High School. She has two sisters, who live in North Carolina; and three brothers in this area: Bill Quigley, a Realtor with Illustrated Properties and the former percussionist for Neal Smith's Orchestra; John Quigley, former director of public relations for WPTV-Channel 5; and Jim Quigley, former mayor of Greenacres.

Seminole Sun Dance Parade, 1919: Mrs. Harriet Fowler Eckler, who had the first private school in West Palm Beach (left), with some of her pupils. They dazzled the crowd dressed as vegetables that year.

Jean Eckler (center) as a Rockette: Brown eyes and a big smile.

Eckler family

Opportunity Inc. Boys and Girls Club, 1959: Jean Eckler McCampbell (center) smiles the same smile she flashed as a Rockette as the children give her a certificate of gratitude on her birthday, June 29. She was married to Capt. David McCampbell, war hero, whose name graces the Palm Beach International Airport terminal. (Opportunity Inc. is a charity to help families co-founded in 1939 by Winifred Clarke Anthony, the daughter of Louis S. Clarke, the inventor of the first gear-driven automobile.) Jean's oldest son, John, is the tall boy in back toward the right, wearing a crew cut and striped shirt with a collar. Her son, Billy, is the boy wearing a striped shirt and two-tone shoes (left, front) and pointing his toe — mimicking the pose his dancer mother sometimes used when she was photographed.

1966

Jimmy Shirley

Jimmy Shirley delivers his paper route.

Rain or shine, 'The Palm Beach Post' is on time

This picture was taken in front of my grandparents' house in 1966. I delivered *The Palm Beach Times*, the afternoon paper, in Pahokee from 1965 to 1966.

The weekend papers were dubbed *The Palm Beach Post-Times*, and on Saturday, I delivered them in the afternoon. But on Sunday, I had to get up about 3 or 4 a.m. in order to have all the papers delivered by sun-up.

The paper route began after school let out, which was 3 p.m., and I would usually finish by 5 p.m. My grandparents' house was the next-to-last stop.

— JIMMY L. SHIRLEY JR.

Jimmy L. Shirley Jr. was born in 1954 in Pahokee. His father, Jimmy L. Shirley, had moved to Pahokee at age 1 in 1926. His mother, Nina Francis Russom Shirley, born in 1932, was one of the first sets of twins born in Pahokee.

Integration pioneer: My family's roots go from the Styx to the schools

My great-grandmother, Priscilla Peppers, came to West Palm Beach in the late 1800s because her husband, Thomas Peppers, worked for Flagler's railroad. My father, George Ward, worked in Palm Beach riding a bicycle carriage. My mother, Lenora, was a domestic at the Whitehall Hotel and the Biltmore Hotel.

I went to segregated elementary schools — Pleasant City, Lincoln Elementary in Riviera Beach, Roosevelt in West Palm Beach — before sixth grade at St. Ann Catholic School. That was in 1960. Anthony Dyett, Lorraine Stevens and I were the first black students at St. Ann.

Our families went to the Catholic church for blacks, Blessed Martin de Porres, under the Palm Beach Lakes Boulevard overpass on 12th Street.

My sister, Constance Ward, was three years ahead of me at Cardinal

1968

Zenetta Ward Miller: Cardinal Newman yearbook, 1968

Newman. She graduated in 1965 and, like me, became a teacher.

I graduated from Cardinal Newman in 1968. Samuel Thomas was one of the first black teachers at Cardinal Newman when I was there. He taught science. He is an attorney now.

— ZENETTA WARD MILLER

Ward Miller, who taught for 34 years in Palm Beach County, lives in West Palm Beach. She got her first teaching job from Ed Eissey when he was principal of Palm Beach Gardens High School. Zenetta and her husband, retired teacher Willie Miller Sr., have two children and six granddaughters who live and work in Palm Beach County.

Historical Society of Palm Beach County

Thomas and Priscilla Peppers in the Styx in Palm Beach, 1890s. Their daughter, Inez, right, was Zenetta Ward Miller's great-aunt.

'We had to rely on the graces of white people'

By JUDGE EDWARD RODGERS
As told to Paul Lomartire

Separate was not equal when I moved to West Palm Beach in 1950.

I came to West Palm Beach after graduating from Howard University in 1949 as a political science major. This was the home of my wife, Gwendolyn Baker. After selling insurance for the Afro-American Life Insurance Co. — it was 25 cents weekly, sold only to black people — I took a job teaching veterans at night school at segregated Industrial High School. It's now U.B. Kinsey Elementary. All the black kids, from West Palm Beach all the way north to Jupiter, went to Industrial.

In 1951, brand-new Roosevelt High School at 15th Street and Tamarind Avenue replaced Industrial. I became a vocational teacher/guidance counselor at Roosevelt. I helped students find jobs as apprentice plumbers, electricians, office workers.

Back then in the summer, you could walk down the street in West Palm Beach's black section, and you wouldn't miss any of the Brooklyn Dodgers games on the radio — because everyone was rooting for Jackie Robinson. He was the first black to break Major League Baseball's color barrier.

In West Palm Beach, at Third and Rosemary, everyone was pulling so hard for Jackie that the pool hall was named The Dodgers Dugout.

Jackie Robinson was the Barack Obama of the late 1940s for us.

The big difference — whether it was Jackie Robinson or Ed Rodgers — is that, to be the first, we had to rely on the graces of white people. Barack Obama didn't have to do

that. He took his case to the people and convinced the masses that he was the best guy.

1960: For blacks, no Bar exam required

In 1960, I quit teaching to go to law school at Florida A&M University. No white universities in Florida would admit me because of my color.

When I went off to law school, the few black lawyers we had in West Palm Beach never had to pass the Bar. All they needed was a couple of white attorneys to say they were of good moral character.

If they had graduated from an accredited law school, which was usually up North, they were automatically admitted to the Bar with the whites' recommendations, because the state had no law schools for blacks.

That's why FAMU got a law school.

When I graduated in 1963 from law school, we had to pass the Bar just like everyone else. But none of the teachers who taught us had ever passed the Bar.

Congressman Alcee Hastings was one of my five fellow law school classmates.

My personal history then became one of area "firsts": first black prosecutor in Palm Beach County, first black county judge, first black circuit judge, first black chief judge of the circuit court, first retired Palm Beach County judge to have a post office named for him.

I hope President Obama's election means we've reached the day when we stop noticing when a black person is the first black in whatever appointment or profession. I hope we'll stop hearing the punctuation: "The first black to ..."

Ed Rodgers, 81, who lives on Singer Island in Riviera Beach, was raised in Pittsburgh during the Great Depression. He worked in the steel mills, like his parents, before joining the Navy during World War II. He retired from the bench in 1995 but has not yet retired from public service.

"Whenever someone asks about something that probably will never happen, they'll say: 'That'll happen when hell freezes over' or '... when pigs can fly' or '... when it snows in Palm Beach.' I've always said: 'It'll happen when a black man is president.' Well, I've seen it snow in Palm Beach, and I went to Washington, D.C., and saw Barack Obama sworn in as the 44th president of the United States. I haven't seen pigs fly or hell freeze over. Yet."

— JUDGE EDWARD RODGERS,

who blazed a trail of Palm Beach County "firsts" — first black prosecutor, first black county judge, first black circuit judge, first black chief judge of the circuit court, first retired Palm Beach County judge to have a post office named for him.

Gwen Baker Rodgers: She grew up on Rosemary Avenue in West Palm Beach and was honored in 2006 by Howard University, which named a room in her honor. Mrs. Rodgers started the Charmettes service club in her Riviera Beach living room in 1951. Her aim: to provide opportunities and support for young black women. The Charmettes have contributed more than $300,000 to Howard University's Cancer Research Center. Mrs. Rodgers died of cancer in 1994.

In West Palm Beach in 1950, blacks were not allowed to:

■ Be treated at Good Samaritan Hospital — not even black hospital employees. "If they cut their hand in the kitchen, they were taken over to St. Mary's Hospital," recalls Rodgers.

■ Try on clothing in department stores. Blacks could buy, but if an item was the wrong size, they could not return it.

■ Travel freely after dark in any white areas, "or there was a 95 percent chance the police would stop you," Rodgers says.

■ Swim in the city pool or play on the municipal golf course.

First lady of fishing: Kay Rybovich

By WILLIE HOWARD | The Palm Beach Post

This painting of Kay's husband, John Rybovich – 'The Master and His Sailfish' – hangs above her bed.
"Every night, it's the last thing I see. I say, 'Goodnight, darling. Tight lines!'"

Kay Rybovich lives in a penthouse with a magnificent water view.

"I always look out on the ocean," she says. "How could I resist? I look out to see if any boats are out there."

Wherever she looks, whatever she does, her life comes back to three things: water, boats — and the man who took her fishing almost every Sunday for 50-some years. He was John Rybovich Jr., the renowned Palm Beach County boat-builder.

They met at a dance at the Palm Beach Yacht Club a few years after Kay had graduated from Palm

Beach High School in 1934.

Already, Kay's love for the water had been instilled in her.

Both her grandfather and her father had been sea captains. Her uncle, Gus Jordahn, was famous in Palm Beach in the '20s for his Gus' Baths, a complex of three swimming pools and shops at the eastern end of Worth Avenue.

"He was quite the character," Kay says of her Uncle Gus, a Denmark native who owned the Rainbo Pier in Palm Beach and was founder of the "Cowboys of the Sea," a group of ocean lifeguards who rescued hundreds of swimmers.

When "Captain Gus" wasn't

Taylor Jones/The Palm Beach Post
"Oh, it was wonderful to catch those big fish!": Kay Rybovich at her penthouse apartment at McKeen Towers in West Palm Beach.

saving people, he was entertaining them by diving off the pier and swimming to the shore.

"Sometimes people did it with him," Kay recalls.

The former Katherine Jordahn, now 92, moved here in the spring of 1924 when she was 6. Her father, a Navy sea captain, had died from dysentery after drinking water in France during World War I. "He was 38, a young life," she says.

The cold New Jersey weather made young Katherine sick. So her mother, Beatrice Swenson Jordahn, came south with her four children to be near her brother-in-law, Gus.

Gus' Baths became Kay's playground. "It cost a quarter for adults and a dime for kids, but I didn't have to pay the dime!" she says, smiling.

Later, fishing — and one particular fisherman — became her love.

On their first date, John Rybovich invited her to go fishing. She caught a sailfish.

"I couldn't wait to show everybody that I caught this beautiful fish," Kay recalls. "He released it."

She was upset, until her future husband explained the need to release sailfish alive so that they could reproduce and continue to be enjoyed by others.

His ocean-conservation ethic continued throughout their marriage and his career: builder of cutting-edge fishing boats, tournament angler, fishing columnist and president of the West Palm Beach Fishing Club.

John worked at his family's successful boat-building company, Rybovich & Sons Boat Works, with brothers Emil and Tommy.

"I was very proud of him," Kay says. "He was a fine person. When he asked me to marry him, I thought, 'Gee, I'd love to marry you.'"

John Rybovich died in 1993. The couple have two children, John Jordahn Rybovich and Sally Altizer, both of North Carolina.

"I sure miss him," she says. "I miss the fishing, too."

They'll be together again, she says — out at sea, where John's ashes are and where hers will be one day.

"I'll call you," she says, "and tell you what the fish are doing."

Kay and John Rybovich with Kay's big catch in the early 1940s: "It would have been a record, but it missed because of its curved bill," Kay says.

Kay Rybovich

'I will fish also'

During the 1950s, while John Rybovich was making a lot of waves in ocean conservation, tournament fishing and boat-building, Kay Rybovich was making some fishing history of her own.

During the 1955 International Light Tackle Sailfish Tournament in Palm Beach, Rybovich and other women were allowed to fish on the fourth day of the tournament, called "Ladies Day."

She decided to form a women's fishing group: "We thought it would be more fun to fish for three days than one."

The next day, she met with Denny Crowninshield and Ginny Sherwood at the Sailfish Club in Palm Beach. They started the International Women's Fishing Association (IWFA), an organization that still holds tournaments, promotes conservation and awards scholarships to marine-science students. "It also stands for 'I will fish also,'" she quips.

In October 2008, Kay Rybovich was inducted into the International Fishing Hall of Fame in Dania Beach for her forward-thinking work organizing the IWFA.

'Hemingway was charming'

Kay and John Rybovich visited Hemingway at his home in Cuba. Hemingway agreed to sponsor the Old Man and the Sea trophy for the West Palm Beach Fishing Club's annual Silver Sailfish Derby. "Hemingway was charming," Kay recalls. "He was always happy to see us. We liked him because of himself, not because he was famous."

IN CUBA: John Rybovich and Ernest Hemingway in the 1950s. Rybovich was inducted into the Fishing Hall of Fame posthumously in 1998. Other members include Zane Grey, Ted Williams, Curt Gowdy, Roland Martin, Bill Dance and Hemingway.

Keepers of the flame

The Palm Beach Post

VERA FARRINGTON

'African-Americans played a big role ...'

The S.D. Spady Museum (above) is Vera Farrington's canvas.

As president of Expanding and Preserving Our Cultural Heritage, Farrington has a mission: to showcase Delray Beach's black leaders.

She and other EPOCH members have filled the house on Fifth Street (once owned by Carver High School Principal Solomon D. Spady) with photographs and artifacts from early black settlements in Delray Beach: The Sands, where white sand blanketed the ground like snow; and Frog Alley, where frogs flooded the neighborhood after a hard rain.

Farrington was born in West Palm Beach but moved to Delray Beach when she was 5. She was a teacher for decades, before retiring and dedicating her time to preserving history.

"African-Americans played a big role in making Delray Beach what it is today," Farrington said in 2006, "and everyone should know that."

The Palm Beach Post

EVEREE JIMERSON CLARKE

'The children ... are my ministry'

Pleasant City isn't marked on maps anymore. But Everee Jimerson Clarke is determined to keep it alive.

Fifteenth Street to 23rd Street, Dixie Highway to the railroad — "That was Pleasant City," Clarke said in 2004. The West Palm Beach neighborhood was settled in 1905 by black laborers hired to build Palm Beach. By 1926, when Clarke was born, Pleasant City was a prosperous black enclave.

"My father, William Jimerson, was a minister. I was taught by him to honor people, to respect people, to render service back to the community. That's what I've tried to do my whole life," said Clarke, who now runs the Pleasant City Family Reunion Committee & Heritage Gallery. "The children who come here are my ministry."

Gary Coronado/The Palm Beach Post

Ineria Hudnell inside her West Palm Beach home, with a portrait of her, painted by one of her art students, behind her. The art teacher and her postal-worker husband were one of the first to move into homes in the new Palm Beach Lakes development in the 1960s. They raised their son there. Today, Hudnell has five grandchildren, nine great-grandchildren and one great-great-grandchild — and an amazing legacy. She has been collecting photos and clippings about the area's black history for more than six decades.

INERIA HUDNELL

'God has me here for a reason'

Palm Beach County's black history lives on hundreds of dog-eared poster-boards leaning on virtually every inch of wall in the narrow hallways and living room of Ineria Hudnell, an 88-year-old walking time machine.

Even during three decades as a schoolteacher, and in the three decades since she retired and became a widow, she has served as a historian.

She says it's because she believes God had a plan for her. But it's also because no one else has done it.

"I was interested in reading and finding out about history," Hudnell said in 2003. "I had no idea I would end up with this much."

FROM THE INERIA HUDNELL COLLECTION

Undated photo of students "waiting to ride the new bus at Roosevelt High School."

Cornelious Richardson Sr., the first black deputy in Palm Beach County, worked in the 1920s and '30s, transporting criminals from the local jail to the state prison in Raiford, Ineria Hudnell says.

Roosevelt High School's 1965 basketball team with Coach Sam Marshall (inset). Marshall coached Roosevelt High to seven consecutive regional basketball championships and two state titles in the 1950s and 1960s. In 1979, he became a member of the Palm Beach County Sports Hall of Fame's third inductee class.

The Palm Beach Post

1982 The divorce case of newspaper heir Herbert "Peter" Pulitzer (left) and Roxanne Pulitzer became infamous — with lurid testimony about drugs, debauchery and the use of a trumpet as a sex toy. With Joe Farish as her attorney, Roxanne insisted she was the dutiful wife trying to save a marriage to a much older husband. She later immortalized the 1980s Palm Beach lifestyle in her 1988 best-seller, *The Prize Pulitzer*, telling stories of "fishbowls of cocaine."

'I practiced law to do right by my clients'

I've had lots of interesting clients over the years. Probably the most famous divorce case I handled was the Pulitzers in the early 1980s — Roxanne and Peter. I was friends with both of them, and they both wanted me to represent them. But Roxanne called first.

Joe Farish

All Roxanne asked for was custody of the kids and reasonable child support, but Peter wasn't having it, so it became all-out war — but only on Peter's side! Roxanne refused to let me attack Peter. She took a beating in the press, and her public partying certainly didn't help her image — or our case — but she never wanted to be vicious toward Peter.

I never practiced law for the money. I made my money in other ventures: real-estate developments; radio stations; a Lincoln-Mercury dealership; citrus and cattle farms.

I practiced law to do right by my clients. My philosophy is simple: Be a professional. I compare it to golf: If you're on a par 5, put the ball in the hole in five strokes or less. Too many lawyers want to take eight or 10 strokes — and charge them all to the client.

I always believed that if I could settle my clients' problem with a single letter or phone call, then I had earned my keep.

— JOE FARISH,
famed West Palm Beach attorney. He came to West Palm Beach at age 4 in 1925 and graduated from Palm Beach High in 1938. After serving in World War II, he earned his law degree and went into practice with his father. "In 1948, I was elected municipal judge," he recalls. "In those days, being a municipal judge was a part-time job, so I was still able to practice law. That was the first local election in which blacks were able to vote, and I was endorsed by black leaders."

'I can't imagine living anywhere else'

By PHIL LEWIS
As told to Steve Dorfman

After high school at St. Ann's, I attended Georgetown University in Washington, D.C., for a year — but that was it. I didn't want to go back, and they didn't want me back. I began working for my father, Frank Lewis. That was like a university in itself!

My father was, among other things, a very ambitious developer. Over the years, he had bought thousands of acres of land down here, most of it in Riviera Beach, then set up the infrastructure: plumbing, water, sewage, drainage, power grids, etc.

Before he put me into that end of the business, though, he had me working on his ranch in what would later become Atlantis. The work on that ranch left me always smelling like manure.

Phil Lewis

The first time my father sent me to a public bidding on a parcel of beachfront land in Riviera Beach, I was literally "straight off the farm" — cowboy boots and all! The other bidders were none too pleased to see me (or probably smell me!). But to my father's credit, he let me go through the process and learn my lessons — and we won the bid that day.

One of the things I'm proudest of is helping to create the South Florida Water Management District. It's not something people necessarily think about or notice on a daily basis: You just turn a faucet or press a button, and water pours out, right? Well, it's a lot more involved than that, and it's so vital to our way of life.

I love South Florida and can't imagine living anywhere else. I know that most South Floridians feel the same. In 2004, after we got hit back-to-back by Hurricanes Frances and Jeanne, I saw a TV news reporter interview a local homeowner. The first storm had damaged one part of his house; the second storm had damaged a different part of his house.

The reporter said to him, "Sir, you must be devastated. How are you able to deal with it?" But the man just cheerfully replied, "Ma'am ... that's just the price of living in paradise."

Phil Lewis served in the Florida Senate from 1970 to 1980 and was Senate president in 1979-80.

Pay it forward: 'Friends don't charge friends interest'

Here's a story that might explain why I'm so attached to Palm Beach County and the people who live here: After Faye and I were married, we needed $2,200 for the down payment on our house, and we didn't have anything saved up.

Ed Eissey

So I asked my father if he could lend us the $2,200. Many years later, I would learn that my father didn't have anywhere near that kind of money, but he didn't hesitate at all — he just said, "Sure."

My father then went to talk to his good friend Carl Robinson. Carl was a black man who owned several grocery stores. In those days, it was uncommon for blacks and whites to socialize, much less to be good friends. But my father and Carl were great friends.

So my father explained to Carl why he needed $2,200, and Carl gave it to him on the spot. My father asked how much interest he should pay. Carl replied, "Please — friends don't charge friends interest."

More than two decades later, after I became president of Palm Beach Junior College, I had the pleasure of telling this story to Carl's daughter-in-law, Trinette Robinson, who taught there.

— EDWARD M. EISSEY

Eissey moved to Palm Beach County in 1933 when he was 5. He served as president of Palm Beach Community College from 1978 to 1997, and the north campus of the school is named for him.

Ineria Hudnell Collection

Early 1930s

FOURTH OF JULY PARADE: Carl Robinson was a prominent grocer — and sponsor of this parade car — in West Palm Beach's black community. From the late 1800s to the 1960s, West Palm Beach's blacks lived in three neighborhoods: Northwest, Freshwater and Pleasant City, all west of Dixie Highway. Businessman John Collie headed up a prominent black family. His son, Warren, became a dentist. Warren's daughter, Laurita Collie Sharpp, remembers the Northwest neighborhood: "Carl Robinson's market was on Third Street. Going north toward Fourth Street was Ned's Shoe Shop and Chester's Bar." In 2002, Sharpp donated her private collection of photographs and diaries to the Historical Society of Palm Beach County.

The Pompeys of Delray Beach

Years ago, C. Spencer Pompey walked in late to a faculty meeting at then-Carver High School in Delray Beach, looked across the room and saw his future wife.

"I wish he was here to tell the story," Hattie Ruth Pompey said. "He used to say he looked over at me and said, 'Ah, that's the one.'"

At the time, she was Hattie Ruth Keys — daughter of the Rev. J.W. Keys, preacher at Mount Olive Baptist Church — who had moved his family to Delray Beach in 1926, when Ruth was 3.

She graduated from Carver High School in 1941, then returned to teach and run the library at her alma mater.

True to his word, Spencer Pompey married Ruth — and also became one of the most influential civil-rights leaders in Palm Beach County. Ruth keeps his photograph and his memory alive in her home, which faces Pompey Park in Delray Beach.

The Palm Beach Post

Ruth Pompey in her Delray Beach home with a portrait of her late husband, C. Spencer Pompey.

C. Spencer Pompey:

■ Served as an educator for more than 40 years at Carver High and other schools. At Carver, he taught social studies; became its basketball, track and football coach; then its principal.

■ Filed, with two other black teachers, a class-action lawsuit in 1942 against the Palm Beach County School Board, because black teachers earned less than their white counterparts. Mr. Pompey persuaded the NAACP to send a lawyer to help. He was Thurgood Marshall, who later became the first black justice on the U.S. Supreme Court. Marshall won the case.

■ Fought to open Delray Beach's whites-only beach to blacks in the 1950s.

■ Pushed for the first organized recreation programs for the city's black children.

Jack and Barbara Nicklaus: Champs for the children

By DAVE GEORGE | The Palm Beach Post

How it came to be that legendary golfer Jack Nicklaus, back during the years when Lyndon Johnson was president, chose Palm Beach County as his home is a fish story at heart.

The Golden Bear first rented a place in Pompano Beach around the time he turned professional in 1961. He needed a winter-time base of operations for a golf career born in snowy Ohio. Plus, Jack and his father Charlie wanted ready access to the ocean for the fishing excursions that filled their fun time.

"We didn't like the inlet out of Lighthouse Point, though," Nicklaus said. "It was too tough. So the next year, my dad and I bought a house down on the south side of Fort Lauderdale, which was all right for fishing. But there weren't that many fish down there, and I was 45 minutes from the nearest golf course without traffic. So I said, 'This doesn't work.'"

A pro-am he played at the new Lost Tree Village Club in North Palm Beach turned the tide. Nicklaus was 23 and already the winner of a U.S. Open and a Masters title. Some of the members asked him to move to Lost Tree, joining PGA Tour veteran Cary Middlecoff. As an incentive to try it out, an honorary club membership was offered to the young star.

"I said, 'Why don't you give the membership to my dad?'" Nicklaus recalled. "'I'd rather pay my dues. Then I can complain like everybody else.'"

Complaints? Not from our end. Jack and Barbara Nicklaus have made a beautiful name for themselves in this community.

Young patients in our area who are dealing with pediatric cancer and other traumatic illnesses benefit greatly from the work of the Nicklaus Children's Health Care Foundation.

The Benjamin School, a well-respected institution for college-bound students, was just a little kindergarten-through-sixth-grade operation until Jack and Barbara put their fund-raising energy behind it and cemented a long-term educational plan for their growing family.

The school now offers classes from kindergarten through 12th grade. Jack and Barbara maintain close ties and often show up to watch their grandchildren participate in school and athletic

The Palm Beach Post

1971 KEY TO THE CITY OF PALM BEACH GARDENS: In March 1971, Palm Beach Gardens declared "Jack Nicklaus Week" and gave the golfer a key to the city. From left: Councilman Tom Prentiss, City Manager Robert Carlson, Councilman John Orr, Jack Nicklaus, Mayor James DeLonga, Vice Mayor Walt Wiley and Councilman Craig James. This is one of hundreds of photos from the collection of Wiley, who served Palm Beach Gardens from 1970 to 1978 as councilman, vice mayor and mayor. Wiley worked at Pratt & Whitney from 1960 to 1993.

The Palm Beach Post

1999

Barbara and Jack Nicklaus in the garden of their home in Lost Tree Village in North Palm Beach. Nicklaus loves to garden and experiment with plants at home. As he said in 1999: "If you're going to get into golf courses, especially designing them, you have to care about the surroundings." Barbara added: "When Jack decides to do something — anything — he does it 100 percent." The couple married in 1960, after their junior year at Ohio State University.

The Palm Beach Post

2004

To help children whose parents can't afford health care, Jack and Barbara Nicklaus started a foundation to build the Nicklaus Children's Hospital at St. Mary's Hospital. "It was a dream of ours," Barbara said at the dedication of the four-story, 81-bed hospital.

activities.

These are the better known of the Nicklaus philanthropic efforts locally; many more are not publicized at all. Add in all of the Golden Bear's world-wide golf course design and related business ventures with long-time headquarters in the county, and it's impossible to measure what would have been lost if Nicklaus had invested the bulk of his life and energy in some other sunny spot on the map.

'Lost Tree was convenient for me to practice.'

"It really had nothing to do with Palm Beach County or anything else," he said, "but the fishing was better up here. The Gulf Stream came in close, and we enjoyed that. My dad liked to fish, and I liked to fish.

"Lost Tree was convenient for me to practice. We started spending pretty much from September to June down here, because we didn't think it was fair to take the kids in and out of school."

Then there was the house overlooking the water, built in 1970 as an upgrade from a smaller Lost Tree home.

Now, after four decades of family memories, beginning with a chaotic move-in — with three small children — at Christmas-time, there is no budging Jack and Barbara from that house on the water, with the boat docks and the pool and the tennis court and the love.

"We redid the house about four years ago," said Jack, "and of course, every architect wanted to knock down the house. I said, 'No, no, no. Come on, guys, this is the house we raised our five kids in.'

"All I wanted to do was to change it from the way we lived with five kids to the way we live today. So we gutted the inside of it and redid the house on the inside. It's terrific."

It is home, more than anything else, and that keeps the Nicklaus children close as well.

"Jackie built a house across the street from us," Jack said. "Gary's building at the Bear's Club (in Jupiter). Steve's building at the Bear's Club. Nan is at Seminole Landing, which is very close. Michael's still got a place at Lost Tree.

"We like it here. I have no desire to go anyplace else. I keep going around the world, and I keep saying, 'You know, I've seen a lot of places, but I've never seen a better one.'"

The more deeply the Nicklauses are involved, the better it gets. Their name is on the athletic facilities at Palm Beach Community College's Palm Beach Gardens campus, for instance.

Jack has long been involved, too, with the PGA of America's efforts to introduce kids to golf, including the creation of the Barbara & Jack Nicklaus Junior Golf Endowment Fund.

That commitment to children is the legacy that Nicklaus will leave to Palm Beach County — far beyond the prestige of having the winner of a record 18 major professional championships as a neighbor.

"It's always been about kids with my wife," Jack said, "and that's been good with me. It was not something we could have said that we don't want to do anymore. We've got a lot of kids. We've got 21 grandkids. I mean, good gracious, what's more natural than being involved with kids?"

So said the Golden Bear, speaking from the North Palm Beach base that has been a very natural habitat for 44 of his 69 years.

Dorothy McDonald Wilson
Dorothy McDonald on the slide at Phipps Park in the 1950s.

'It was a great time to be a kid in Palm Beach County!'

I was born at 5:15 a.m. in Good Samaritan Hospital on Dec. 19, 1951. It was a very special time to be born at Good Sam. My mother, Ethel, remembers the nurses carrying candles and singing *Away in a Manger* as they walked down the corridors of the maternity wing. I left the hospital on Christmas Eve and went across the street to my first outing: the *Hetzel Brothers Christmas Pageant*. It became a yearly tradition.

My first daughter, Christy, would be born in the same hospital in 1969. It was quite a busy place that week as Jack Nicklaus' son was born at the same time. They were across the hall from me and had tons of visitors! My second daughter, Tara, would be born at Bethesda Hospital in Boynton Beach in 1971.

I remember going to Lido Pools in Palm Beach and to the "Tea Room" at Burdines with Mom and Aunt Frances. I lived in Lake Worth, and it was a great time to be a kid in Palm Beach County! We lived at the Lake Worth Casino pool all summer!

My girlfriend, Nancy Ebersold, and I used to ride horses from west Lantana Road all the way to the beach. We would stop and let the horses go for a swim in Lake Osborne. Lantana Road was a quiet, two-lane road back then.

— DOROTHY MCDONALD WILSON

The Bakers: Legacy of law enforcement

My mother brought me to West Palm Beach in 1928 when I was 8 months old. We lived with my grandmother, whose house was on top of the hill on Evernia Street — one of the highest spots around!

George Bell Baker

When the offices of *The Palm Beach Post* were on Datura Street, my cousins and I would watch in that direction from the top of Evernia Street hill for the red-and-black hurricane warning flags.

My Grandfather Baker (George Bell Baker) was the first sheriff of Palm Beach County after it was formed out of Dade County.

My uncles also played important roles in Florida history:

Robert C. Baker (Bob): succeeded his father George as sheriff of Palm Beach County. Robert was well-known for his pursuit of the Ashley Gang in the 1920s.

L.R. "Jack" Baker: a former Palm Beach County state attorney, legislator and sheriff in the 1940s.

John Edwin Baker Sr.: a former state senator from Lake County, Fla.

— PATRICIA F. COBB, *West Palm Beach*

1931

Patricia Ferner Cobb (left) and her cousin, Leola Baker, whom Patricia called "Owo." "We were in a Tom Thumb wedding at the Methodist Church on Hibiscus that day," Patricia recalls. "Leola was born at Good Samaritan Hospital during the 1928 Hurricane!" Patricia's memories include visits from Seminole women, who would come to West Palm Beach from the Everglades to sell huckleberries. "I remember being somewhat frightened of them, as their dress was so different and their hairdos so strange," Patricia remembers. "But my grandmother was very friendly to them, and they always seemed to seek her out."

Cobb Family

Her motto: 'Live, learn and pass it on'

My father, Buster Robert Lowe Sr., was born in West Palm Beach. My mom, Janie, was born in Georgia. Later she moved to West Palm Beach to live with her sister. She met Dad at the Sunset Cocktail Lounge just after World War II.

Lowe

Our relatives would either come from West Palm Beach to visit us in Belle Glade on weekends, or we would travel to West Palm Beach to visit them.

My father discovered largemouth-bass fishing in Lake Okeechobee when he was around 9. I think that's why he decided to raise his family around the lake.

— DR. CATHERINE LOWE

Dr. Lowe, an ophthalmologist who lives in West Palm Beach, is president of the Artists Showcase of the Palm Beaches and a former chairwoman of the Palm Beach County Cultural Council.

The baby picture of me in my mom's arms was taken across the street from where we lived in the summer of 1953 — Royal Palm Way in Belle Glade — in front of a beautiful hibiscus tree. A friend of my mom asked her to dress me up so that she could take our picture. You can see me beckoning for my sister, Gwendolyn, to come to me. You also can see the ribbon and the back of her head at the bottom of the picture.

Lowe Family

get your groove back

 **Always ORIGINAL**

SHOPS

RESTAURANTS

ART GALLERIES

COFFEE HOUSES

NIGHT CLUBS

NEIGHBORHOODS

STREET FESTIVALS

LIVE THEATER

GREENMARKETS

WPB LIBRARY

FOUNTAINS

PLAZAS

WATERFRONT

PROMENADES

ICE CREAM PARLORS

BOAT DOCKS

BIKE PATHS

DOWNTOWN DEVELOPMENT AUTHORITY

Shaping a Dynamic Downtown

THE CLEMATIS DISTRICT

Jeff and Emma Sullivan
West Palm Beach

DOWNTOWN WEST PALM BEACH

Wayne DuBois, Allan DuBois and Cary Braswell (from left) are members of a pioneering pepper-growing family. They are shown here at the DuBois & Son packing house in Boynton Beach.

Lannis Waters
The Palm Beach Post

HOW WE WORK

THE INDUSTRIES THAT FUEL OUR GROWTH

<1: Test pilot Rick Becker walks away from an S76 B helicopter at the Sikorsky Development Flight Center in West Palm Beach in March 2009. Sikorsky Aircraft Co. began making and testing helicopters — including the U.S. Army's workhorse, the Black Hawk — in West Palm Beach in 1979.

2: Curtis Lewis, owner of Okeechobee Steak House, shows off the house specialty. Lewis' dad, Ralph, opened Okeechobee Steak House in 1947, and it's been in the same place and under the same family management since. In the early years, it was called the "Okeechobee Drive In," and there was no Palm Beach Lakes Boulevard. "Past Military Trail, Okeechobee was a two-lane dirt road," Lewis recalls.

3: In 1954, William and Lillian Stevens founded Stevens Bros. Funeral Home in West Palm Beach at 17th Street and Tamarind Avenue, with their sons Eugene A. and Roderick H. Stevens serving as the first funeral directors. This photo is from 1960. The funeral home remained in the Stevens family until 2000.

Roderick W. Stevens, son of Roderick H. Stevens, served as funeral director until 2007, when he moved on to Shuler's Memorial Chapel in Mangonia Park.

4: "Our mission has been to continue to grow with the community," says Robert Hill, president and chief executive officer of Bethesda Memorial Hospital in Boynton Beach, which turns 50 in 2009. Hill, pictured in the MRI suite in a 1998 photo, started at Bethesda in 1971 and is the only decades-long-serving hospital chief executive in Palm Beach County.

5: Jose Angel Chicas of Murphy Construction helps rebuild the Lake Worth Pier in October 2008. It took 15 months and $3.4 million to rebuild the pier after Hurricanes Frances and Jeanne broke it apart in 2004. Murphy Construction Co. was founded in 1924 in West Palm Beach by Martin E. "Pat" Murphy.

6: Honeybells: Tourists call them "those sweet bell oranges from Florida" — but honeybells are actually mineola tangelos, a cross

between a grapefruit and tangerine. The late Ed Cushman, who founded Cushman Fruit Co. in West Palm Beach in 1945, gave honeybells their name.

7: Ernest Burkhardt's store in 1919, at Dixie Highway and Southern Boulevard. Ernest was the brother of Louis Burkhardt, who settled on the shores of Lake Worth in 1893.

8: Founders of the Gunster law firm, the oldest commercial law firm in Palm Beach County: (top row) David S. "Bud" Yoakley, Joseph F. Gunster, Marshall M. Criser; (bottom row) J. Kenneth Williamson, A. Obie Stewart, George William Hersey III.

9: T.J. Cunningham Sr. (seated) is one of the attorneys who helped dismantle segregation in Palm Beach County. The Cunningham family is still prominent in the local legal community: (from left) T.J. "Jimmy" Cunningham, Kimberly Cunningham Mosley, Latricia Cunningham Donley, Mallorye Cunningham-Curtis and Malcolm Cunningham.

10: Dr. Coleman, the pharmacist,

and R.L. Saunders, the owner, at Palm Garden Drug Store on Third Street and Rosemary Avenue in West Palm Beach in the 1930s.

11: Robert Bertisch, executive director of the Legal Aid Society of Palm Beach County since 1981, poses for a photo in front of the Palm Beach County Courthouse in 2000, when he won the Alpert Jewish Family & Children's Service Advocate of the Year Award. When Bertisch joined Legal Aid, the organization had a staff of 10 and a budget of $200,000. Today the staff of 85 includes 36 full-time attorneys and a budget of $6.8 million.

12: County Judge Cory J. Ciklin (now a judge for the 4th District Court of Appeals) presides over the domestic-violence court in 1998. In 2008, the Palm Beach County Clerk & Comptroller's Office summoned 155,700 jurors, processed 8,788 marriage licenses and filed 558,779 new cases.

13: The Palm Beach County Convention Center (foreground) opened in 2004.

Sources: Roderick Stevens, The Palm Beach Post, the Bush family, the Burkhardt-Jackson family, Gunster law firm, the Ineria Hudnell collection

PALM BEACH COUNTY'S TOP 3 ECONOMIC DRIVERS:

- FARMING
- CONSTRUCTION
- TOURISM

'There's some satisfaction in growing food for people.'

**— FRITZ STEIN, lifelong Glades farmer.
In this 2005 photo, he is standing in a sugar warehouse in Belle Glade.**

Fritz Stein's grandfather, Hans, came to the Glades as a farmer and rancher in 1915. Today, Fritz Stein Jr. operates Stein Sugar Farms Inc., an 800-acre sugar-cane farm in Palm Beach County, as well as a 3,300-acre cattle ranch in Highlands County. The Steins' agricultural legacy has expanded to a fourth generation: Son Fritz III, known as "Sonny," manages Stein Sugar Farms Inc.; son Stewart manages Wedgworth Farms and grows sweet corn and beans; son Tim sells farm chemicals for Wedgworth's Inc.

PALM BEACH COUNTY:
NO. 1 FOR FARMING IN FLORIDA

Palm Beach County leads all counties east of the Mississippi in total agriculture sales. It is first in the nation in the production of sugar cane and sweet corn.

It leads the state in the production of rice, bell peppers, lettuce, radishes, Chinese vegetables, specialty leaf vegetables (arugula, for example) and celery.

Number of farms
1,263

Land in farms and nurseries
468,810 ACRES TOTAL

Sugar cane: 397,916 acres
Vegetables: 33,483 acres
Pasture: 18,334 acres
Nurseries: 7,278 acres
Sod: 7,121 acres
Citrus: 4,428 acres
Bees: 116 acres
Fish: 51 acres
Ostriches: 39 acres
Miscellaneous: 36 acres
Numbers have been rounded

The county's farming industry includes
- Three major sugar-manufacturing mills
- One sugar refinery
- 14 fresh-vegetable packing houses
- 600 horticultural nurseries
- Plus … a major hydroponic growing operation, a rice-processing and -packaging mill, an agricultural-by-product electrical cogeneration plant, and a major sugar and molasses port shipping facility.

Photos from The Palm Beach Post

Palm Beach County crop sales

VALUE AT
FARM LEVEL, 2007-08

Sugar: $552.8 million
(total sugar value, including refining)

Vegetables:
$211.6 million

Nurseries: $151.7 million

Sod: $20.66 million

Citrus/tropical fruits:
$4.7 million

Miscellaneous crops:
$2.15 million

Beef: $369,000

Numbers have been rounded

TOTAL:
$944 million

Source: Palm Beach County Cooperative Extension Service

Sources: Palm Beach County Property Appraiser's Office, 2007 Census of Agriculture, Palm Beach County Business Development Board

George Wedgworth in a 2002 hand-tinted photograph: His father, Herman, developed ways to use fertilizer to boost farming in the Glades.

Secrets of the soil: How one family changed farming

By SUSAN SALISBURY | The Palm Beach Post

For almost 50 years, George Wedgworth has presided over the Sugar Cane Growers Cooperative of Florida in Belle Glade. He came to the Glades at age 2, and except for the years spent obtaining an agricultural-engineering degree in Michigan, he has never left.

From his rural spot, the cooperative's founder, a 1946 graduate of Belle Glade High School and now in his early 80s, has been on the front lines of the sugar industry's biggest battles: political, environmental, economic and labor.

The cooperative was founded in 1960 when Wedgworth and 53 other growers of sugar and vegetables banded together to harvest, process and market their crops.

"Growing vegetables is more like Las Vegas. You can make a bundle, or you can lose it. Sugar cane is a more stable, hardier crop," Wedgworth explained recently.

The Sugar Cane Growers Cooperative might never have come into existence if George's father, Herman Wedgworth, had not moved to Belle Glade in 1930 to become a plant pathologist at the University of Florida's Everglades Experiment Station. (Today the facility is called the Everglades Research and Education Center.)

Within two years, he had quit his $1,800-a-year job and started his own vegetable farm. His research would prove to be key to Palm Beach County becoming the nation's winter-vegetable capital.

"In the early days, the only land that would produce vegetables was the high-in-minerals soils that came from the waters of Lake Okeechobee — the overflow around the edge. You could not grow produce out any further.

Dad came here to help figure out why (farmers) could not grow beans on what was called 'sawgrass muck,'" Wedgworth said.

Herman Wedgworth and a number of other researchers found that the soil was deficient in a variety of minerals, such as copper and manganese. Thus, the answer to greater vegetable production lay in enriching the soils. Using proper fertilization, the sugar-cane and vegetable industries were able to expand onto the sawgrass muck.

In 1938, tragedy struck the Wedgworth family on a day that George will never forget. His father was crushed by the frame of an ice machine.

"I was with my father when he got killed. He was at the (vegetable) packing house, and a crane was lifting a 10-ton ice machine. My cousin and I

Herman and Ruth Wedgworth

were playing in the packing house. I heard the accident," George said, choking up.

His mother Ruth, who already was keeping the books, took over running the farm while raising three children alone. From both his parents, George Wedgworth learned to face challenges and to work hard.

Wedgworth and his wife Peggy, who met in the ninth grade, live in Belle Glade in the one-story concrete-block house that Ruth Wedgworth built in 1941. They raised their two sons and two daughters there.

Today their youngest son, Dennis, runs the family businesses, including Wedgworth's Inc., the state's largest fertilizer company; and Wedgworth Farms, a 5,000-acre sugar-cane farm.

George explained, "Agriculture, we think, is an honorable profession that provides people with food. We think we are responsible and have changed our ways to try to show the public that we have had a good record. We have lowered the phosphorus level (in Lake Okeechobee). The water is cleaner leaving the farming region than what we get out of the lake."

Wedgworth Family

Ruth Wedgworth in the fields during corn harvesting in the 1950s.

'It was wild and beautiful then, like some foreign, tropical land, far from the city we see today.'

— DIANE BENEDETTO, *about early Boca Raton*

Boca Raton Historical Society

Imogene 'in the pines,' 1923

Boca Raton was well-known for its pineapple crop — or "pines" — when Imogene and Buddy Gates posed on Frank Chesebro's pineapple land south of today's Camino Real. Their father, H.D. Gates, came to Florida in 1907, and the family settled here in 1914, when he built a bungalow for his family on the Palmetto Park Plantation. Imogene lived here through the eighth grade, then went to boarding school in Orlando and pursued a dancing career in Miami. She returned to Boca Raton in 1965 as Diane Benedetto, wife of Joseph Benedetto, and they opened Chez Joey restaurant. She turned 93 in April and still cries every time she thinks of Petey, her pet raccoon, who she rescued when he was a baby.

This shot is from Diane Benedetto's dancing career in Miami — a long way from her days as a pioneer girl.

Boca Raton Historical Society

THE KAMIYA CHILDREN WERE AMONG IMOGENE'S CHILDHOOD FRIENDS: From left, *circa* 1915, they are Mishi, Rokuo and Masa (also known as Suga). They lived in the Yamato Colony. "Their family lived as they had in Japan," recalls Diane Benedetto. "They slept on pads, and they ate with chopsticks. All the Japanese families farmed, and they were excellent at it."

Diane Benedetto on her childhood:

"My father owned 28 acres of land ... the plantation stood on the north side of Palmetto Park Road by the bridge. The road was named by my father after his plantation. It was wild and beautiful then, like some foreign, tropical land, far from the city we see today. Across the canal was a lovely lagoon. It is my favorite memory, that peaceful lagoon. I sat on the banks, filled with wonder, watching the fiddler crabs. I would try to catch one for Petey, my pet raccoon. The only way to get to our town was by train, and you never knew where you might be let off, baggage and all. The train just slowed down and you jumped off, with your luggage thrown off after you."

A Rich History of Progress.

A Future Bright with Promise.

The Fanjuls: A sugar dynasty for 50 years

By SUSAN SALISBURY | The Palm Beach Post

When brothers Alfonso "Alfy" Fanjul Jr. and J. Pepe Fanjul fled Cuba in 1959 as Fidel Castro's revolutionaries seized power — and their family's assets — they knew they wouldn't return.

Alfy, then 21, remembers telling his father, "Your job is Cuba. My job is America."

Left behind were the family's 10 sugar mills and 150,000 acres. Their only remaining money: some investments outside Cuba. The two brothers knew that it was up to them to rebuild the family's sugar business, literally from the ground up, in western Palm Beach County.

"The responsibility we had was enormous. You had to feed yourself also. We had to be careful not to lose the money. We were playing with the cookie jars," Alfy Fanjul said from the company's corporate headquarters on Clematis Street in West Palm Beach.

Alfy, now in his early 70s, is chairman and chief executive officer of the recently renamed Fanjul Corp., formerly known as Flo-Sun. Fanjul Corp. is the parent company for its Florida Crystals Corp. and Central Romana Corp., Dominican Republic. Pepe, 64, is vice chairman, chief operating officer and president.

Now, 50 years later, their Florida holdings include 155,000 acres in Palm Beach County, plus two sugar mills and a refinery. Worldwide, they own another two sugar mills and seven more refineries, as well as 250,000 acres in the Dominican Republic.

Altogether, the company produces 4.5 million tons of refined sugar. How did the Fanjuls do it?

"The first thing we purchased was 4,000 acres of land from Alex Ramey. This was at $215 an acre. We had a family group that bought it," said Alfy. "It was a struggle for many reasons... "We bought four sugar mills from Louisiana. We dismantled them there, put

Alfonso "Alfy" Fanjul, chairman and CEO (left); and J. Pepe Fanjul, vice chairman, COO and president of Florida Crystals Corp., at their office in West Palm Beach. The portrait behind them is of their father, Alfonso Fanjul Sr.

Taylor Jones
The Palm Beach Post

them on a barge and brought them to Florida. To build a sugar mill directly on the muck was very difficult. We made an island of rock and sand that was large enough for the foundation for the mill."

He remembers walking around the hundreds of pieces of mill equipment laid out on the ground at Osceola: "I told Frank Casablanca, the engineer, that it looked like an old rusted Erector set. I said, 'Frank, do you really think you can put this back together again?' He said, 'Don't worry about it. I can do it.'"

That first Florida crop was a success,

producing 10,000 tons of raw sugar that had to be sent out of state to be refined.

Today there are three sugar mills in Palm Beach County: The Fanjuls have two; the Sugar Cane Growers Cooperative of Florida has one. U.S. Sugar Corp. has one, in Clewiston, in neighboring Hendry County.

The company kept growing through the 1970s, but still the Fanjuls were cautious.

"We were careful. I remember one of the new sugar people who had gone to the same banks we had gone to, who said, 'You could borrow more money than you are borrowing.' My response was, 'I am more concerned with the money I can pay back than with the money I can borrow,'" Alfy said.

In 1984, they made a major corporate acquisition: Okeelanta, south of South Bay.

Their younger brothers Andres and Alex also work in the business. So do Pepe's son Pepe Jr., Alfy's son-in-law Luis Fernandez, and their cousin Johnny Fanjul.

Their sister Lian Fanjul de Azqueta presides over New Hope Charities, which provides a variety of services in western Palm Beach County.

"We had to make it work," Alfy Fanjul said. "In life, the most important thing is to plan for the future."

Pepe Fanjul said, "Agriculture is an integral part of Florida and the future of Florida and, frankly, of the United States, too. Some people would like to make South Central Florida a national park. I don't think that is going to happen. We need to make sure our kids do not have to go to another state to get a job."

Bruce R. Bennett/The Palm Beach Post

Style and charity

Emilia Fanjul (center) with daughter Emilia Fanjul Pfeifler (right) and daughter-in-law Lourdes Fanjul. The photo was taken at the Palm Beach home of Emilia and J. Pepe Fanjul. Lourdes is married to J. Pepe Fanjul Jr. The three women enjoy supporting worthy causes, such as Emilia's Everglades Preparatory Academy in Pahokee. "My family has always been involved in education," says Emilia Fanjul, whose grandfather headed the chemistry department at the University of Havana. "My grandfather and my mother instilled in me the feeling that education always helped you overcome whatever obstacles you have in your life."

Fanjul Family

Alfonso "Alfy" Fanjul Jr. in the early 1960s, surveying the depth of the muck in a sugar-cane field.

Clouds are reflected in the water of an A. Duda & Sons farm in Belle Glade.

A. DUDA & SONS
His celery is his signature

Drew Duda

Celery is the crop that built Drew Duda's family's business, A. Duda & Sons, now the county's largest grower of vegetables and sugar cane — with 27,000 acres in and around Belle Glade. Founder Andrew Duda immigrated from Slavia in 1909 and, after years of struggling, incorporated the business in 1926.

Celery is still Duda's signature crop, although two-thirds of the company's Palm Beach County acreage is in sugar cane. When it comes to radishes, the state has just three remaining growers: Duda; third-generation grower Rick Roth of Roth Farms; and the Hundley family of Hundley Farms, in the Glades since 1935.

Lannis Waters/The Palm Beach Post

GREEN CAY FARMS
A little green west of Boynton Beach

Ted Winsberg (above) used to grow 800,000 boxes of vegetables each year. He shut down his farm in 2000 — selling 175 acres to Palm Beach County for what is now the Green Cay Wetlands and Nature Center, and another 43 acres to a developer for housing. His daughter Sylvia Winsberg Jameson and her husband still run a 20-acre tree farm on the land. And Ted and his wife, Trudy, also provide 10 acres rent-free to Nancy and Charlie Roe, who grow vegetables for locals. "It's what Trudy and I want to do," Winsberg said. "People will be able to see what farming was here."

ERICKSON FARM
In the family since 1911

Dale Erickson

When Swedish immigrants Elfrida and Alfred Erickson and their family arrived on the eastern shore of Lake Okeechobee in 1911, it was by boat. No railroad or highways existed, and Lake Okeechobee was a natural lake that afforded pristine views.

Using a 10-foot two-man saw that remains in the family today, Alfred and his eldest son Karl cleared the land and planted crops. The farm passed to Floyd, the youngest of the Ericksons' children, who planted tropical fruit trees, mainly avocados. Today, Floyd's son Dale runs the farm, with help from his daughters and grandson. They still specialize in mangos, avocados, carambolas, and other fruits and vegetables.

Meghan McCarthy/The Palm Beach Post

Dick Bowman (left) has lived on Smith Sundy Road his entire life, and he and wife Theresa are raising their two daughters (Meaghan, left, and Cailean) there. A 1935 wood-frame house where Dick and his sister Susie Bowman were raised remains on the property.

Billy Bowman recalls that, in the 1950s, Palm Beach County was home to close to 50 dairy farms plus dairy processors such as Alfar Creamery and Boutwell Dairy. He remains active in the dairy industry, serving on the board of McArthur Dairy, which milks 8,000 cows.

'I had agriculture in my blood'

William "Billy" Bowman was the last dairy farmer in Palm Beach County when, in 1995, he closed up what had been a 1,600-cow operation on Smith Sundy Road, west of Delray Beach.

Following a $38 million land sale to Palm Beach County for its Agricultural Reserve in 1999, Bowman became a cattle rancher in Okeechobee County in 2001. He and wife Dari maintain a primary residence in Tequesta.

"It gave us the chance to go from 900 acres to 4,700 acres," said Bowman of the 7-square-mile Taylor Creek Ranch in Okeechobee.

The transition from dairy farming to cattle ranching gave Bowman more time to enjoy life and throw more of his legendary barbecues, many of which are fund-raisers for politicians and charities.

"Dairy cows have to be milked seven days a week — and through hurricanes. You don't have to worry about beef cows during hurricanes," said Bowman, whose father Gene retired from the dairy business in 1964.

Today, Bowman's son Richard "Dick" Bowman continues the family's agricultural tradition by growing 900 acres of peppers, squash and cucumbers. Dick also owns a 100-acre nursery with more than 40,000 landscape trees. It's appropriately named Beefy Tree Farms.

Dick Bowman has lived on Smith Sundy Road his entire life, and he and wife Theresa are raising their two daughters there. A 1935 wood-frame house where Dick and his sister Susie Bowman were raised remains on the property.

"I had agriculture in my blood. I wanted to stay in the agricultural business and saw the development going on," Dick Bowman said. He figured that his farm would help satisfy the need for trees.

His nursery is one of about 600 in the county — making ornamental horticulture a major industry here.

"It's not a business that someone can just get into, due to the capital," Dick Bowman said. "The agricultural industry is passed from generation to generation."

John D. MacArthur

Quirky and colorful, he put northern Palm Beach County on the map

If Palm Beach and West Palm Beach mean Henry Flagler, northern Palm Beach County means John D. MacArthur. He stands second only to Flagler in importance among the region's developers.

Both were self-made millionaires who grew up poor, and both were sons of preachers. But while Flagler was refined, MacArthur was rumpled and ornery, and he favored blue collars over bluebloods.

He awoke at 4:45 every morning, smoked three to four packs of cigarettes a day, drank 20 cups of coffee and enjoyed the occasional scotch.

MacArthur sold mail-order insurance in Chicago before coming down in 1955 to collect on a loan.

He took control of 80 percent of Lake Park and all of what he would name North Palm Beach. He kept buying, adding thousands of acres. He founded Palm Beach Gardens in 1959 and decided to stay and watch it grow.

When MacArthur died in 1978, he was the second wealthiest man in America.

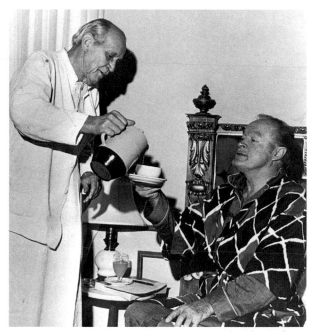

The Palm Beach Post

As a publicity stunt, MacArthur pours coffee for Bob Hope at Mr. Mac's Colonnades Hotel on Singer Island. The developer is wearing his typical casual duds. Once, when asked why he dressed like a bum, MacArthur explained, "Sometimes it's better to feel like a bum than a millionaire."

With TV shows like *Flipper*, Mr. Mac wanted to lure tourists. "Come see scenes right out of *Flipper*, come see the Everglades made famous in *Gentle Ben*, come see wildlife like in *Daktari* — and then go try to win a set of Samsonite luggage on *Treasure Isle*," Sherman Adler recalls. "Meanwhile, you can stay at the world-famous Colonnades Hotel, play golf on the PGA courses, then go over to a Disney-like park we envisioned for PGA Boulevard."

Memories of Mr. Mac and me By SHERMAN ADLER

John D. MacArthur had a dream — to use TV to sell the wonders of Palm Beach County — and he hired me, a young NBC sales executive, to do it.

Mr. Mac had been inspired by three days that he spent with Walt Disney, scouting land for the latter's new dream: Disney World.

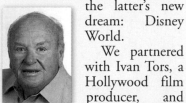

Sherman Adler

We partnered with Ivan Tors, a Hollywood film producer, and soon Palm Beach County was getting a national TV audience — thanks to the hits *Flipper*, *Gentle Ben* and *Daktari*.

But it was a revolutionary game show — *Treasure Isle*, the first game show ever played outdoors — that promised to bring tourists and young home buyers to Singer Island and to MacArthur's Colonnades Hotel and his PGA golf courses.

The year was 1967. Imagine the publicity machine that we were creating for South Florida tourism: We had three prime-time shows, plus a daytime game show five days a week.

The *Treasure Isle* concept was that couples would compete, paddling boats around a lagoon we built in back of the Colonnades. Once they got to "Treasure Isle," they'd dig for buried treasure. John Bartholomew Tucker, a well-known TV personality, was the host.

The show lasted one season.

But my memories of the brilliant, challenging, completely original Mr. Mac remain a treasure.

Ahoy, contestants! Dressed in yachting attire, *Treasure Isle* host John Bartholomew Tucker sped around the Singer Island set in a mini-speedboat and announced his arrival with the blow of a loud horn. Meanwhile, the theme song touted the beauty of "sunny Florida."

Welcome home to Wellington

Wellington's population has jumped more than tenfold since 1980, when 4,622 people called the western suburb home. Today the estimated population is 55,076.

In this 2005 photo inside Wellington's Olympia development, Socki Berg bites into a slice of pizza while Zachary Howard swings.

Carolyn Drake/The Palm Beach Post

RISE OF THE WEST

The Palm Beach Post

1971: H. Irwin Levy (center) breaks ground on a Century Village expansion with pitchman Red Buttons (left) and state Sen. Tom Johnson by his side. Levy's concept of Century Village was "to provide a way of life, more than just housing."

H. IRWIN LEVY

He created Century Village and changed the face of Florida

In 1968, he looked at 680 acres of ranch and swamp land in suburban West Palm Beach and saw a retirement haven. Memories of summers in the Catskill Mountains became endless summers in Florida. With Red Buttons as his pitchman, Levy sold nearly 8,000 one- and two-bedroom condominiums in about four years. Another Century Village opened in suburban Boca Raton, and two more in Broward County. Copycats followed. Florida began to gray in a big way. In October 1997, Levy formally sold the villages' holding company and name.

How did Wellington and Royal Palm Beach go from country bumpkins to municipal powerhouses?

THE VISION OF SAVVY INVESTORS AND DEVELOPERS:

■ In 1956, Samuel Nathan Friedland — founder of Food Fair grocery stores — bought 65,000 acres of farmland that would eventually become Royal Palm Beach, The Acreage, the J.W. Corbett Wildlife Refuge and home to Pratt & Whitney.

■ When Guerry Stribling started putting the community of Wellington together in 1977, marketing consultants told him: "Build for the young." Everyone else had their sights set on retirees.

Stribling, who died in May at 75, was project manager for Wellington's earliest developers: Investment Corp. of Florida and Gould Florida Inc.

Gould Chairman William Ylvisaker took the vision even further: Let's create suburbia with an elegant and sporty twist.

He redrew Wellington's master plan to create the 2,200-acre Palm Beach Polo and Country Club.

"We were pushing to bring show horses in because that's where the real money is," Stribling said.

Jess Santamaria

■ Jess Santamaria saw a "sleepy little town" when he came to Royal Palm Beach in 1974. Later, he pooled money from friends to buy 14 acres at Southern and Royal Palm Beach boulevards. He wanted a grocery store there, but Publix and Winn-Dixie said no because the land was in "the boonies."

Santamaria turned to Darrell Miller of Miller's Supermarket, who finally agreed to open a store in 1982 after Santamaria got to know him over coffee nearly every week for more than six months. Eventually, Fidelity Federal bank, McDonald's and a gas station came to the corner, too.

Santamaria also was busy in real estate, partnering with Wally Sanger to build about 3,000 homes in Wellington, Royal Palm Beach and The Acreage. Now, as a Palm Beach County commissioner, Santamaria has a new mission: "Congestion is there. I'm trying to slow it down."

— Mitra Malek

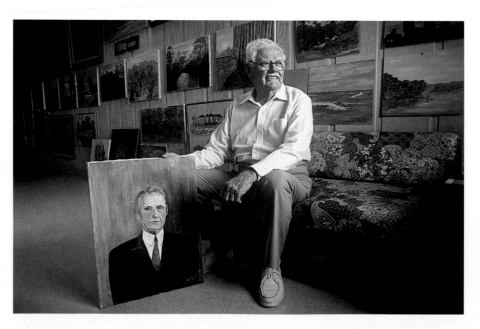

Allen Eyestone/The Palm Beach Post

Maria Illiano rides Hell Boy while competing at the Winter Equestrian Festival in Wellington in February 2009.

*'We gradually became a metropolis.
Now we have everything out here we need.'*

— SAM LAMSTEIN,

mayor of Royal Palm Beach from 1982 to 1990. The village's population jumped from 4,000 to 15,000 during his tenure. Due to Lamstein's persistence, the western communities got their own hospital — Palms West — in 1986, and their own county commissioner in 1990.

< ARTHUR W. 'BINK' GLISSON

He saw potential in the swamp

In 1951, C. Oliver Wellington told Glisson, his family friend, to buy 10,000 acres of swamp land south and west of today's State Road 80 and U.S. 441. Skeptics doubted that the property, much of it under water, would amount to anything. Nevertheless, Glisson, a native Floridian and an environmentalist, thought it would — and it did, with the help of the Acme Improvement District, which Glisson launched as its first employee and then ran for decades. "He was really the keeper of the land for the Wellington family," said his wife, Joan Glisson. Glisson came to be known as the unsung founder of Wellington. He also painted scenes of old Florida and collected artifacts, which he donated to the Bink Glisson Historical Museum at the South Florida Fairgrounds' Yesteryear Village. Here, Glisson shows off a painting he did of C. Oliver Wellington. Glisson died in 2000.

1992, Loren Hosack/The Palm Beach Post

Thom Smith/The Palm Beach Post

GENE MISCHE AND WILLIAM YLVISAKER

Wellington's ultimate horse people

Ylvisaker (right), who has served as president of the U.S. Polo Association at various times, brought polo to Wellington — which now hosts some of the most prestigious tournaments in the world. "He knew that if he started the polo club, not only would he be able to create a community that had a wonderful quality of life, but that, in the long run, real estate would benefit — and the whole western communities did," said Laurie Ylvisaker, his daughter. Ylvisaker persuaded show-jumping producer Gene Mische (left) to bring the world-renowned Winter Equestrian Festival to Wellington. At the time, Mische looked around and thought: "There's just a bunch of sand dunes. I said to Bill, 'What are you smoking?'" The first equestrian festival, in 1979, lasted one week and hosted 300 horses. Today the Winter Equestrian Festival runs for as long as 12 weeks with several thousand horses.

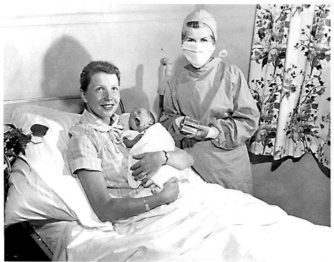

Bethesda Memorial Hospital

Bethesda Memorial Hospital

In 1959, Jeffery Errol Snow was the first baby born at Bethesda Memorial Hospital, which had just opened in Boynton Beach. In 2008, 3,149 babies were born at Bethesda. This flagship of the Bethesda Healthcare System has its own "baby" planned: In fall 2009, construction is slated to begin on an 80-bed hospital west of Boynton Beach.

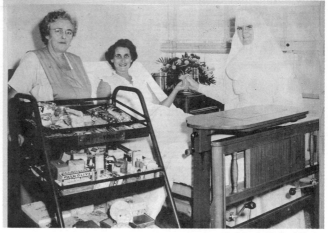

St. Mary's Medical Center

St. Mary's Medical Center

Mrs. George Kairalla of West Palm Beach has just had her seventh child, Samuel, at St. Mary's Hospital — an occasion that was so notable that it made the newspaper. With her in this 1952 photo are Mrs. William B. Shields (left) and Sister Ann Patrice — but not baby Samuel, who must have been resting elsewhere. Mrs. Kairalla's six prior children also had been born at what is now St. Mary's Medical Center, in West Palm Beach. In 2008, 3,923 babies were born at St. Mary's.

Baby, baby, baby!

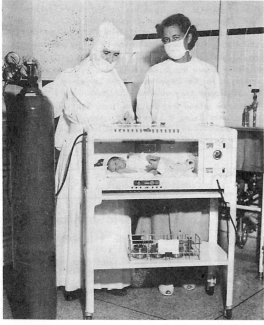

St. Mary's Medical Center

St. Mary's Medical Center

A tiny Donald J. Roberts, weighing 4½ pounds at birth, lies in an incubator. With him in this undated photo are Sister Ann Patrice (left) and Mrs. John P. Butler. More babies are born at St. Mary's than at any other Palm Beach County hospital, with Bethesda second, Wellington Regional (with 2,668 births in 2008) third, and West Boca Medical Center (with 2,146 births in 2008) fourth.

Historical Society of Palm Beach County

Pine Ridge Hospital

For about 40 years, starting in 1916, blacks were treated at one hospital: Pine Ridge. The hospital, at 1401 Division Ave. in West Palm Beach, was originally made of wood but rebuilt in 1923. One of the prominent doctors who cared for patients at Pine Ridge Hospital, which closed in 1956, was Dr. Philip Lichtblau, a white orthopedic surgeon who also treated some of the area's most notable residents, including John F. Kennedy, Jack Nicklaus and Hank Aaron.

We're here for your entire family.

From Our Family to Yours

As the first hospital in South Palm Beach County, our dedicated team of physicians, nurses and healthcare professionals has cared for this community since 1959. Today, we're a 401-bed comprehensive medical facility with 525 physicians in 40 specialties…all here to provide world-class medical care to you and your family!

Bethesda Memorial Hospital
50 years of caring

Our comprehensive healthcare services include:

24-hour Emergency Department • 24-hour Pediatric Emergency Department • Bethesda Heart Institute
Certified Primary Stroke Center • Comprehensive Cancer Center, *an Affiliate of the H. Lee Moffitt Cancer Center & Research Institute*
Cornell Institute for Rehabilitation Medicine • Centers for Advanced Imaging • Center for Women and Children
Driskill Endovascular Center • Women's Health Center • Wound Care and Hyperbaric Medicine Program

Call for a FREE Physician Referral Today!
561-737-7733, ext. 4499

2815 South Seacrest Boulevard • Boynton Beach, FL 33435 • (561) 737-7733 • www.BethesdaWeb.com

HEALTH HEROES

Mom – 1919

< MILLIE GILDERSLEEVE

Pioneer midwife

A freed slave from Georgia, Gildersleeve came to the "Lake Worth Region" in 1876 with the Dimick family. She became a midwife to Richard Potter, the area's first doctor. When it was time for a pioneer baby to be born, Dr. Potter would sail up to Millie's wharf (she had a waterfront home in what is now Riviera Beach), toot his whistle, and Millie would scurry out with her instruments. She died in 1950. Many of her descendants — and the descendants of the babies she delivered — still live in West Palm Beach.

DR. CLARENCE 'CARL' BRUMBACK

County's first director of public health, a position he held from 1950 to 1986

He helped to lead the fight against diseases, from polio to AIDS, and to provide care to the county's migrant population.

Despite racial segregation at the time, he helped to improve access to care for blacks in the county. Dr. Brumback also assisted in helping to establish a child guidance center that

Dr. Brumback

later became the 45th Street Mental Health Center and is now called the Oakwood Center.

DR. JEAN MALECKI

Director of the Palm Beach County Health Department from 1988 to 2009

She will be remembered for overseeing the county response to the 2001 fatal anthrax attack in Boca Raton. But she also made the county's first pediatric AIDS diagnosis, and she battled instances of unsafe drinking water in West Palm Beach and the Glades.

Dr. Malecki

In addition, Dr. Malecki was instrumental in forming the county trauma system, putting fluoride into the public water supply, and providing care to thousands of uninsured residents each year. She also confronted health threats from malaria to tuberculosis to typhoid fever, and established the Florida Public Health Institute in Lantana.

FLORENCE WATTON LINDROSE

'Doctoring' Pahokee's pioneers

Florence, born in Allenhurst, Fla., in 1883, moved to Pahokee as a young bride near the turn of the century. She became the local midwife, treating snake bites and "doctoring" pioneers who became ill with fever. She also farmed her own land and gave birth to six children. Later she managed a family-owned supply store and cooked for the men who lived at the fish camps (including her first husband, Axel Jensen, and second husband, Ernest Lindrose). She lived to be 102.

CARIDAD ASENSIO

Co-founder of the Caridad Health Clinic

Asensio

She began working with migrant families in 1971 as a community health worker for the Palm Beach County School District. In 1989, she helped to found the clinic, west of Boynton Beach, which provides free medical and dental care to thousands of migrant workers and their families and other working poor. The clinic, now called the Caridad Center, has a small paid staff but also relies on volunteers.

DR. THOMAS LEROY JEFFERSON

A county 'first'

He became West Palm Beach's first black doctor in 1912 and was nicknamed the "Bicycle Doctor" because he was frequently seen cycling around town with his black medical bag.

Dr. Jefferson

We Are Our Brothers' / Sisters' Keeper

"The Strong & The Fortunate Have An Obligation To Protect & Assist The Weak & Less Fortunate Among Us Until They Are Able To Help Themselves."

When We Take Care of Each Other - We All Win;
If We Don't - Eventually, We All Lose.

Together, We Can Make Palm Beach County
The Great County It Was Meant To Be For All.

Jess R. Santamaria

BUILT TO LAST

Been around for 70-plus years?
These Palm Beach County businesses have, too.

1893
Lainhart & Potter Inc., a building-materials company, is founded in West Palm Beach by George W. Lainhart and George W. Potter.

1894
Greenleaf & Crosby Co., a jewelry store, is founded in Palm Beach, in the Royal Poinciana Hotel, by Damon Greenleaf and J.H. Crosby. Betteridge buys the company in 2006.

1895
Anthony's Ladies Apparel is founded in West Palm Beach by Gus Anthony and his brothers.

1896
The Breakers, a luxury resort and hotel, is founded in Palm Beach by Henry Morrison Flagler.

1897
Daily Lake Worth News — renamed **Palm Beach Daily News** in 1899 — is founded in Palm Beach by brothers Joel and Bobo Dean.

Greenleaf & Crosby opened its first fine jewelry store in Jacksonville in 1868 and came south when Henry Flagler opened his luxurious Hotel Royal Poinciana. In the early days, the jewelers sold rare birds and artifacts along with jewelry. Today, the store is famous for precious jewelry like this $370,000 diamond ring designed by Nicholas Varney.

1902
Ahrens Cos., a construction firm, is founded in West Palm Beach by George W. Ahrens and son Frank F. Ahrens.

1903
J.C. Harris Co., a men's-apparel store, is founded in West Palm Beach by James Calvin Harris.

1909
Jones, Foster, Johnston & Stubbs P.A. has evolved from a law firm founded by H.L. Bussey in West Palm Beach.

1916
The Palm Beach Post begins daily publication in West Palm Beach. It has evolved from a weekly newspaper, Palm Beach County, founded in 1909 in West Palm Beach by Donald H. Conkling.

Richard Graulich/The Palm Beach Post
THE BREAKERS HOTEL IN PALM BEACH: To the west of this twin-towered gem is The Breakers golf course, the oldest existing golf course in Florida and now a championship-level par-70. Paul Leone, president of The Breakers Palm Beach and Flagler System Inc., has spearheaded renovations at the historic Italian Renaissance-style resort since 1994.

1912

Lake Worth Herald has evolved from a newspaper founded in Lake Worth by Harold J. Bryant and William F. Greenwood.

Museum of the City of Lake Worth

This 1914 photo (above), looking east down Lake Avenue, shows (left) the office building of Bryant & Greenwood, a development company; and (far right) the office of the *Lake Worth Herald*.

1912 VIEW OF THE BREAKERS PIER: The Breakers and the Hotel Royal Poinciana boasted entertainment from fishing to Fifth Avenue shops. (One shop featuring "the latest French novelties" was run by "Madame Najla Mogabgab.")

The Palm Beach Post

MANY LIVES: The Dade County State Bank building was Johnnie's Playland in the 1960s.

First bank: The Dade County State Bank building, founded in 1893, was originally on Palm Beach. It was floated over to West Palm Beach in 1897 and had various locations and lives — including as Johnnie's Playland. Today the building is on Flagler Drive and houses the Palm Beach High School Museum. For decades, the largest bank based in Palm Beach County was Fidelity Federal. Fidelity was acquired by National City in 2006, and National City is now part of PNC. "We are bringing in all of the services of National City, and we will keep our local decision-making," Vince Elhilow, Fidelity's chairman, president and CEO, said in 2007. Fidelity was founded in 1952.

1952: West Palm Beach Federal Savings & Loan, forerunner of Fidelity Federal, opens on Datura Street.

Good
Samaritan
Hospital
opened with 35
beds in 1920.

Generations of Palm Beachers have enjoyed Testa's strawberry pie, blueberry pancakes and more. Michele Testa (left) started with a soda shop and cafe, then moved to Royal Poinciana Way (vintage menus shown here).

Bush Family

BUSH FAMILY: Bush's Market, on North Dixie Highway in West Palm Beach, 1931: This business is now Bush Brothers Provisions. Pictured here (from left) Dr. Dodd and his wife, Mr. and Mrs. Tom Turner, John and Sebell Bush, and Harry L. Bush. In back is Jack Giddings.

1912
Pioneer Linens, a linens and bedding store, is founded in West Palm Beach by Max Greenberg.

1917
Farm Credit of South Florida, an agricultural credit association, is founded by farmers in South Florida.

1919
Plastridge Insurance is founded in Delray Beach by Pierce Brennan and A.E. Plastridge.

1919
Ferrin Signs Inc., a signage company, is founded in West Palm Beach by Ike E. Ferrin.

1920
Good Samaritan Medical Center is founded in West Palm Beach.

1921
Halsey & Griffith, an office-supplies and photocopier retailer, is founded in West Palm Beach by William L. Halsey and John L. Griffith.

1921
Michele Testa Sr. arrives in Palm Beach and opens a small soda fountain. In 1946, **Testa's Restaurant** moves to its present location at 221 Royal Poinciana Way.

1923
Kassatly's Inc., a retail store, is founded in Palm Beach by Sam Kassatly.

1923
U & Me Moving and Storage is founded in West Palm Beach by Herbert A. Spencer.

1924
Murphy Construction Co. is founded in West Palm Beach by Martin E. "Pat" Murphy.

1924
Myers Luggage is founded in West Palm Beach by Toby and Selma Myers.

1924
Sewell's Hardware is founded in West Palm Beach by Worley L. Sewell Sr.

1925
Bush Brothers Provisions Co., a meat and provisions wholesaler, is founded in West Palm Beach by John M. Bush and son Harry L. Bush.

• History In The Making •

Celebrating 100 years of Palm Beach County

1909 · 1919 · 1929 · 1939 · 1949 · 1959 · 1969 · 1979 · 1989 · 1999 · 2009

Dancers from the Thomas Dance Studio inside the Lake Worth Casino, 1950s: (from left, on the floor) Joan Lee Nichols, Carol Coston, Doris Gregory (seated in middle), Marion Wilson, Virginia Sullivan Thomas. In the middle, being held up, is Wilma Jean Fizell, and Gay Hulme Mueller is being tossed above. George Fizell is standing at left, and Douglas Brown is at the front right. The men in the center are unidentified.

Mercer Wenzel, a department store, has been a fixture on Atlantic Avenue in Delray Beach since 1958. Zuckerman's department store had been in this spot since 1927.

Rudolph Tomasello and his pest-control truck in 1928 in West Palm Beach.

1925
Cheney Brothers Inc., a food-service distributor, is founded in West Palm Beach by Joe Cheney.

1925
Coleman Funeral Home is founded in West Palm Beach by George P. Coleman.

1925
Florida Power & Light Co. has evolved from an electric-utility company founded in South Florida.

1925
Gracey-Backer Inc., an insurance company, is founded in Delray Beach by Matthew Gracey III.

1925
Gunster, Yoakley & Stewart P.A. has evolved from a law firm founded in West Palm Beach by John Kenneth Williamson.

1926
Boca Raton Resort & Club, a luxury resort and hotel, is founded in Boca Raton by Addison Mizner.

1926
Colony Hotel & Cabaña Club is founded in Delray Beach by Alfred T. Repp.

1926
Thomas Dance Studio is founded in Lake Worth by Grace Thomas.

1927
Boynton Landscape Co. is founded in West Palm Beach by James Sturrock.

1927
Lesser, Lesser, Landy & Smith, a law firm, is founded in West Palm Beach by Joseph Lesser.

Joseph Lesser

1928
Tomasello Pest Control is founded in Palm Beach by Rudolph Tomasello.

1932

Divine, Blalock, Martin & Sellari, an accounting firm, is founded in West Palm Beach by Wilbur F. Divine III.

1932

MacLaren Sign Co. is founded in Delray Beach by Robert I. MacLaren.

1932

Wedgworth Farms, a sugar-cane and rice-growing company, is founded in Belle Glade by Herman and Ruth Wedgworth.

1932

Wedgworth Inc., a fertilizer company, is founded in Belle Glade by Herman and Ruth Wedgworth.

1934

Hand's Office Supply has evolved from an office-supplies store founded in Delray Beach by Lauren Hand.

1938

St. Mary's Medical Center is founded by the Franciscan Sisters of Allegany (New York). It is the oldest faith-based hospital in Palm Beach County.

Acosta Family

Growth of the Hispanic Chamber of Commerce

At the April 5, 1976, ground-breaking for José Martí Park, Armando Acosta (second from left) reads a proclamation honoring the "Apostle of Cuban Liberty." Nine Cuban organizations, including the Pro-Cuba Association and the Latin Chamber of Commerce, cooperated with the City of West Palm Beach on the project. The Latin Chamber of Commerce — now the Hispanic Chamber of Commerce of Palm Beach County — has about 400 members. Among those attending the ceremony is West Palm Beach Mayor James Adams (fifth from left). José Martí Park, on North Flagler Drive between Second and Third streets, is sometimes used to hold rallies and as a staging point for marches.

A look at Delray Beach's Atlantic Avenue in the 1950s.

Atlantic Ave. Business Area, looking east, Delray Beach, Florida

Delray Beach Historical Society

< Delray Beach High School's first graduating class, 1915: (from left) Ben Sundy, Betty Ferguson, Lauren Hand and Bill Sperry. Hand grew up to serve as city clerk and treasurer and as managing editor of the *Delray Beach News*. In 1934, he started the Delray Book Shop, which the locals called "Hand's." Today that store is Hand's Office Supply, a landmark on Atlantic Avenue. It is now run by the Cook family. Lonnie Cook Sr. came to Delray Beach in 1911, and the first person he met was Lauren Hand. Hand ended up selling his business to Lonnie Cook Jr. Today, Lonnie's son, David, runs the business.

The Anthonys:
In fashion for 114 years

By ELIOT KLEINBERG | The Palm Beach Post

There was a time when one member of the Anthony family would greet a sunrise — while surrounded by women's wear — and another would chase the sunset on horseback.

The Anthonys' ranch and grove are gone. But the retail-store chain, now called Anthony's Ladies Apparel, has survived the 1896 downtown fire, the boom and bust, war, changing tastes and the flight to the suburbs.

Anthony's even had its name printed on the folders in which students received their report cards, recalls West Palm Beach lawyer Bill Sned, the grandson of Emile D. Anthony, who ran Anthony's from 1914 through World War II.

An Anthony has been an original settler, an early merchant, a grower, a rancher, a banker, a West Palm Beach mayor, a director at Good Samaritan and St. Mary's Medical centers or their auxiliaries, and the Norton Museum of Art.

In short, "Anthony" has been a household name in Palm Beach County since back when, pretty much, every household knew each other's name.

"We used to go to the airport and see everybody we knew," Sned said. "Now you don't know anybody. It is sad because it went from a small town to a big metropolis. Times change."

The Anthonys opened their clothing store in 1895. It's West Palm Beach's second-oldest business, behind the Lainhart & Potter lumber firm. Anthony's is credited with popularizing the "Poinciana uniform" — navy blazer, white pants and straw-boater hat — worn by fashionable gents at the turn of the 20th century and later.

Three generations have run Anthony's, which celebrated its centennial in 1995. Anthony's Ladies Apparel has 11 locations in Florida; three are in Palm Beach County.

In the early 1940s, the family began buying land in Royal Palm Beach. Eventually, they would own a 760-acre ranch. They also ran Anthony Groves, selling oranges alongside their kitschy gift-shop-and-alligator exhibit.

Sned, 63, and the other Anthony children frequently went out to the family ranch to ride horses. When he was about 12, he recalled, "a

Photos from Anthony Family

Gertrude Holden, wife of E.D. Anthony Sr., in her wedding dress, 1906. Her grandchildren called her "Ahwoo," and her husband called her "Mama Dear." As Betsy Anthony, her daughter-in-law, recalls: "She was a Southern, genteel lady. Her three sons went by to see her almost every day, and every Sunday night, Ahwoo had the children and grandchildren over for sandwiches and cake."

little Piper Cub (airplane) came and landed — made a hard landing. It was Oliver Wellington. He owned the Flying Cow Ranch next to ours. He was out of gas. We sold him $3 worth of gas.

Yes, *that* Wellington. As in the county's 37th municipality.

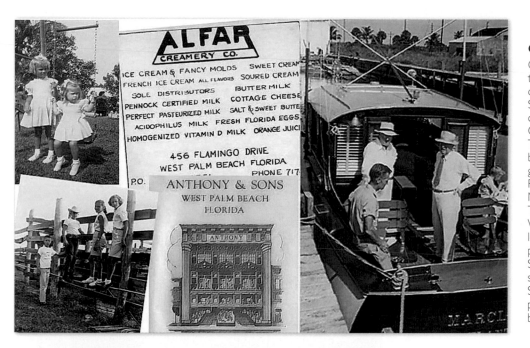

Collage of Anthony memories

Cornelia "Neeli" Anthony Reamer put together these photos of family significance. Clockwise from top left: Marcia Sned and cousin Lynne Anthony model dresses made by their Grandmother Gertrude Anthony in the 1940s. The Alfar Creamery ad is important because E.D. Anthony Sr. took the grandkids to Alfar dairy in Flamingo Park every weekend. The yacht is the Marcia II, owned by Neeli's uncle, Oscar Thompson of Atlanta, who was visiting West Palm Beach. The Anthony & Sons logo is from an early envelope and pictures the flagship store on Clematis Street in the 1930s. The ranch photo shows Marvin Anthony, Marcia Sned, Sunny Spires Dixon and another friend posing on the fence at the ranch that became Anthony Groves, *circa* 1950s.

< Emile D. Anthony Sr. and his wife, Gertrude, with their children (from left) Carl, Emile Jr., M. Pope ("Ham") and Cornelia in 1924. Emile Sr. eventually turned over the Anthony's stores to his children. Today, Anthony's is run by Ham's son, Pope.

Marvin "Ham" Anthony and his sister, Cornelia, in the 1920s. When Ham's wife, Betsy, first arrived in West Palm Beach in 1951, she recalls: "Everyone knew Ham Anthony. He would get letters addressed simply to 'Ham Anthony, West Palm Beach.'" He served as mayor of West Palm Beach in the 1970s.

LOOKING ACROSS LAKE WORTH, FROM WEST PALM BEACH, FLA.

110204

Flagler Drive has long been a scenic promenade, thanks to efforts by early residents such as Gus Anthony, Emile Anthony's older brother. This 1926 view shows the twin-towered Biltmore hotel in Palm Beach (left) and the Whitehall hotel at right (a hotel addition had been built onto Henry Flagler's mansion), with the Hotel Royal Poinciana in between. Anthony's flagship store was on Clematis Street, which was bustling in the mid-20s (facing page, top right).

'Mr. E.D. Anthony says'

From 1947 to 1949, Emile DuBose Anthony Sr. wrote small articles titled 'Mr. E.D. Anthony Says' in *The Palm Beach Post* about local history. The clippings were transcribed by Cornelia Anthony Reamer.

Here are excerpts:

■ "Way back in 1902, A.P. ("Gus") Anthony, founder of Anthony's, was president of the City Council of West Palm Beach. Mr. Flagler had built Whitehall, and he had moved the railroad bridge from where the George Washington Hotel now sits to the site of the present Flagler Bridge. Gus was most enthusiastic about a Lake Shore Drive along the west shore of Lake Worth. He had to have a starting point and labored hard on the idea. Finally, he succeeded in buying for the city from the railroad riparian rights from the north corner of the present George Washington Hotel to the Flagler Bridge at a cost of $2,250. This was the beginning of Flagler Drive in West Palm Beach. Public opinion has sustained every effort to extend it since that small beginning."

■ "I remember when most of the residents of West Palm thought the Everglades began at the west end of Clematis Street, where the Seaboard Freight Depot now stands. In those days they thought of all this part of West Palm Beach as an island, exactly as we now regard Palm Beach … the impassable saw-grass marshes beyond were caused by the overflow of Clear Lake and other lakes east of the watershed. … Lake Avenue was named for an actual lake, which was where Howard Park is now. All the north end of Lake Avenue was part of the lake. All this was changed by the West Palm Beach Canal, which lowered the water table and made all this territory into land suitable for present developments."

■ "About 1912, (Harold) Bryant and (William) Greenwood were the master promoters and developers of Palm Beach County's history. They bought up great tracts of Everglades land at Okeelanta (entirely under water at that time). They sold tracts and gave away lots at Lake Worth; then to make good their development, they got behind the building and expansion of the City of Lake Worth. They were the most resourceful developers to ever operate here. Above all else they were real advertisers who knew how to publicize a city and make it grow. Our sister City of Lake Worth owes a deep debt of gratitude to Bryant and Greenwood, promoters and developers."

The Chamber of Commerce of the Palm Beaches and its Board of Directors Congratulate Palm Beach County on its 100th Birthday

401 North Flagler Drive • West Palm Beach, FL 33401 • (561) 833-3711 • chamber@palmbeaches.org • www.palmbeaches.org

Richard Graulich/The Palm Beach Post

The main Florida Atlantic University campus, in Boca Raton: The university offers more than 140 degree programs and 18 NCAA sports on seven campuses.

PALM BEACH COUNTY'S
COLLEGES and UNIVERSITIES

Florida Atlantic University

Into the 1960s, North Florida politicians ran the state and, even though Florida was becoming "bottom-heavy," resisted expansion to the south. The last straw was in 1956, when the state established a college in Tampa and had the nerve to call it the "University of South Florida." Boca Raton leaders lobbied hard, and the first four-year state college south of Tampa opened in September 1964, with President Lyndon Johnson cutting the ribbon. In addition to its Boca Raton main campus, FAU now has three campuses in Broward, two in St. Lucie County and one in Jupiter. It now boasts 27,000 students and is challenging the dominance of its counterparts to the north. And it has become a major research site; Scripps Florida is based at its Jupiter campus.

This photo of Christine Lynn is inside the Christine Lynn College of Nursing at FAU, a new facility that received an award in 2006 for its green design principles.

Marymount College/College of Boca Raton/Lynn University

The Boca Raton school was founded in 1962 as Marymount College, a two-year Catholic institution for wealthy girls. It was run by nuns who protested the Vietnam War, organized migrant workers to vote and led a Passover seder on campus — all laudable, but not the kinds of activities that drew support from old-line Boca. By 1971, Marymount was $6 million in debt. The school became the College of Boca Raton in 1974 and, in 1991, was renamed Lynn University in honor of its top donor, insurance magnate Eugene Lynn, who gave several $10 million gifts. Lynn died in 1999. Enrollment has risen from 230 in 1971 to about 2,400 today.

Palm Beach Junior College/Community College

This wasn't just the county's first college; it was the first in Florida. It opened in October 1933 with 41 students, in a building next to what was Palm Beach High School. In 1948, it moved to Morrison Field, now Palm Beach International Airport. PBJC was at Lake Park Town Hall from 1951 until it moved to its suburban Lake Worth location in 1955. The school's student body grew during the next two decades from 600 students to more than 8,000. In the two decades after that, it ballooned to 51,000; added campuses in Boca Raton, Palm Beach Gardens and Belle Glade; and changed "Junior" to "Community."

Northwood Institute/University

Northwood Institute opened in Alma, Mich., in 1959. The West Palm Beach site opened in 1984; it now has about 750 students. There also are campuses in Texas and Switzerland. Northwood, which specializes in business management and entrepreneurship, became a university in 1994.

Damon Higgins/The Palm Beach Post

Palm Beach Community College students Brittany Kroop and Bryan Kinnee-Crowley chat with Gov. Charlie Crist in July 2009 at PBCC's Palm Beach Gardens campus. Crist was meeting with biotech companies, and the students said they were using enzymes to break down cells in applesauce to make apple juice. Biotech jobs are key to Palm Beach County's second century.

Thomas Delbeck
Palm Beach Atlantic University's DeSantis Family Chapel.

Palm Beach Atlantic College/University

In 1959, the Florida Baptist Convention wanted to create a second affiliated college — the other was Stetson University — and looked to South Florida. Palm Beach Atlantic College opened on Sept. 4, 1968, with 114 students. In 2002, PBAC became Palm Beach Atlantic University. It now boasts 35 buildings on 27 acres of prime downtown West Palm Beach land, plus satellite campuses in Wellington and Orlando. PBAU has a student body of about 3,300.

Greg Lovett/The Palm Beach Post

The first graduation ceremony at PBAU's Lloyd L. Gregory School of Pharmacy, 2005: (From left, front) Mylinh Duong, Hew Fong and Joseph Frappier cheer fellow classmates.

Sikorsky is pushing the limits of helicopter speed with its X2 prototype. The tail rotor faces backward, like the propeller on a boat, to provide push for the aircraft.
Sikorsky photo

IT HAPPENED HERE FIRST

By STACEY SINGER | The Palm Beach Post

The IBM personal computer was invented here.

But that 1981 world-changer is neither the beginning nor the end of Palm Beach County's history of innovation.

Some of America's most amazing technical advancements — from superconductors to submarines to engines that powered the supersonic Blackbird jet — happened here.

It's a story that is seldom told, because much of the innovation went into secret military projects.

Palm Beach County's history of innovation began in 1942. That's the year when Boca Raton became the training ground for microwave radar, the MIT technology credited with turning the tide of the war.

In 1958, Pratt & Whitney spread out on rural land 15 miles west of West Palm Beach. The company developed a hydrogen-fueled rocket engine called the RL 10, which went on to power a

generation of satellite launchers, moon missions and shuttle boosters.

By the late 1960s, Palm Beach Gardens had put its stamp on transistors, integrated circuits, and the fledgling computer and semiconductor industries, thanks to the growth of RCA and ITT.

They were followed by the arrival, to the south, of IBM. On the company's Boca Raton campus, innovations in robotics and business computing unfolded, culminating in the unexpected success of the personal computer.

The industries — and the numbers of Palm Beach County residents they employed — have waxed and waned, but the innovation has never stopped.

Today, for example, Sikorsky is developing a new generation of computer-guided Black Hawk helicopters, and is pushing the envelope on helicopter speed with a new, propeller-tailed technology called X2.

Nearby, a Pratt & Whitney spin-off company called Coastal Optical Systems is making lenses that are able to focus on targets large and small, from high-powered missile-defense lasers to photon-emitting DNA tags.

In 2009, the Scripps Research Institute at Scripps Florida opened a 30-acre campus in Jupiter — where molecular biologists hope to find the next generation of cancer-fighting drugs, age-defying medicines and clean fuels.

These researchers will soon be joined by biochemists and engineers from the Max Planck Society, who plan, among other things, to develop new methods for tracking the movement of molecules in living systems, as well as unraveling the mysteries of the brain.

Thus, the innovation continues.

And Palm Beach County's second century promises to become the Century of Bioscience.

1942

Radar goes live. An airstrip built for wealthy resort-goers in Boca Raton is taken over by the U.S. Army. It becomes a training center for MIT-developed **microwave radar**. Pilots use the technology to curb U-boat attacks on Atlantic shipping and to make bombing strikes more precise. Florida Atlantic University now sits on part of the former base.

1958

Pratt & Whitney establishes a rocket- and jet-engine research-and-development plant in rural north-central Palm Beach County.

1961

RCA builds an electronics-manufacturing plant in Palm Beach Gardens.

1963

Pratt & Whitney's **RL10 engine** — the world's first liquid-hydrogen-fueled rocket engine — makes its first flight powering an Atlas-Centaur rocket. Since then the RL10 has provided propulsion for a variety of rockets, including Atlas, Delta, Saturn and Titan.

1966

ITT Semiconductors opens a plant in West Palm Beach.

RCA is granted a contract with the U.S. Navy to maintain and operate the **Atlantic Undersea Test and Evaluation Center** at Andros Island in the Bahamas.

1970

IBM opens its 620,000-square-foot complex in Boca Raton. In a manufacturing plant there, the **IBM System/ 360 Model 20** is built. Other computers are developed and built there, including the 1130, the System/3 and the Series 1.

1973

Pratt & Whitney wins a contract to develop an **air-to-air laser gun**.

ITT is making semiconductors in West Palm Beach.

TOP SECRET NO MORE

From radar to rockets, how the county changed technology

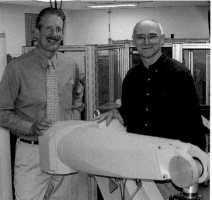

Scripps
Orthopedic surgeon Dr. Andrew Hodge (left) and Harry W. Orf, Ph.D., vice president of scientific operations at Scripps, with a robot that performs experiments.

1974

Metallurgists at Pratt & Whitney develop a method, called **"powder metallurgy," for making super-alloys.** The alloys are used to make stronger military jets.

RCA's Solid State Division in Palm Beach Gardens begins making semiconductors for consumer electronics.

1978

IBM opens the Advanced Manufacturing Systems unit, where **robotics systems are developed to build other machines**. IBM robotic arms are used to help make Ford Tempo and Topaz components, as well as General Dynamic and Boeing aircraft parts.

1979

Sikorsky Aircraft Co. begins **making, improving and testing helicopters** 15 miles west of West Palm Beach, including the U.S. Army's workhorse, the Black Hawk.

1981

IBM's Entry Systems Division in Boca Raton releases the **first personal computer**. It's not anticipated to be a big seller — at $2,665 (monitor sold separately). However, its runaway success causes IBM employment in Boca to peak at 9,600 by 1985.

1983

Motorola opens a pager plant in Boynton Beach. Two years later, it introduces **Baby Beeper**, the smallest pager to date. But by 2004, Motorola closes pager production here.

Late 1980s

Pratt & Whitney develops **mirror-cooling systems** that make possible the super-powerful lasers needed for President Ronald Reagan's "Star Wars" Strategic Defense Initiative.

1990s

Sikorsky develops the S-92 in Palm Beach County. It's a **19-person chopper** popular with oil companies and corporate fliers.

2003

Coastal Optical Systems, a Pratt & Whitney spin-off firm, delivers the first of two lenses designed to focus a **jet-borne laser gun**, a 21st-century weapon now in development by a consortium of Boeing, Lockheed Martin and others.

2004

Recruited to Florida by Gov. Jeb Bush, the nation's largest independent biomedical research organization, **The Scripps Research Institute**, establishes a branch in Palm Beach County.

2008

The Scripps Research Institute receives an $80 million grant from the National Institutes of Health to expand its molecular screening program, which uses Florida-based robotics and other technologies — **tools for exploring biology at the molecular level**. The Max Planck Society prepares to launch a research program in temporary laboratories next door.

Greased lightning

By STEVE DORFMAN | The Palm Beach Post

Pratt & Whitney has been instrumental to Palm Beach County's growth — and to our nation's security.

Pratt engineer John F. "Jack" McDermott said the company came here for a few reasons: "One, our engine-testing made lots of noise, so we needed more room to spread out and stop annoying our neighbors. Two, it was hard to find engineers in those days. But when we ran ads looking for engineers to work in Florida, we received a great response. And three, those were the Cold War days, and our government wanted our facilities to be, let's say … a little more off the beaten path."

In 1958, if you transferred down to Florida from Pratt & Whitney's headquarters in Connecticut, "the guys back in Hartford would look at you like a wayward family member," McDermott, who retired in 1985, said. "But we had such an *esprit de corps* when we started down here — it was like, "We'll show them!""

Show them they did!

The Palm Beach Post

U.S. Rep. Paul G. Rogers (left) views a J58 jet engine (used to power the SR-71 Blackbird) during a Pratt & Whitney open house in November 1973. "The trick was to design the engine so that it didn't make the plane burst into flames. It had never been done before and hasn't been done since," says Jack McDermott. "The Blackbirds used to fly at tremendously high altitudes over Russian air space to keep an eye on what the Soviets were doing." The SR-71 Blackbird was in service from the mid-1960s through the 1990s.

MORE THAN THREE TIMES THE SPEED OF SOUND: The J58 engine developed by Pratt & Whitney in Palm Beach County in the 1960s powered the SR-71 Blackbird reconnaissance aircraft (above). "I used to say that Blackbirds cruise at the speed a bullet is fired out of a rifle," says Jack McDermott. "Blackbirds flew at the unprecedented sustained speed of 2,200 miles per hour — more than mach 3, which means it cruises at more than three times the speed of sound."

Here are a few of the amazing innovations in jet and rocket engines that Pratt & Whitney developed here:

■ RL10 engine, which launched its first payload into Earth orbit in 1963.

■ RL10's dual models currently power the latest versions of the Atlas and Delta launch vehicles.

■ Pratt & Whitney Rockedyne still produces the improved-durability, liquid-oxygen and liquid-hydrogen turbopumps for the space shuttle's main engines. As the shuttle accelerates after launch, the turbopumps deliver liquid fuel to the shuttle's three main engines at a rate that would drain a standard residential swimming pool in less than 25 seconds.

■ Developed and tested the J58 jet engine, which powered the SR-71 Blackbird reconnaissance aircraft. The Blackbird cruised at more than three times the speed of sound and still holds multiple aviation records, set in the 1960s, for speed and altitude.

■ Developed and tested the F100 family of jet-fighter engines, which power all of the U.S. Air Force's F-15 Eagles and most of the F-16 Fighting Falcons.

■ Developed and tested the F119 jet engine that powers the U.S. Air Force's F-22 Raptor — the world's most advanced production engine for stealth technologies and vectored thrust.

A strong community is our greatest asset.

We believe communities are built on the goodwill and energy of the people who belong to them. That's why we're proud to honor Palm Beach County's rich history and support the communities that have developed as a result. PNC congratulates Palm Beach County on its 100 year anniversary.

For more information, visit pnc.com.

LEADING THE WAY

CON PDF 0409-0119

LEGACY OF LUXURY

THE ESTATES AND NEIGHBORHOODS THAT DEFINE THE PALM BEACH LOOK

Addison Mizner

"Mizner is the first architect of significance to work primarily in Florida," says historian Donald Curl. With his romantic flair and Mediterranean Revival style, Mizner is the man behind many of Palm Beach's greatest estates.

Mizner's story, page 249

The grand staircase of Eastover (facing page), Harold S. Vanderbilt's mansion in Manalapan, leads to a second floor living room. When this photograph was taken, in the early 1990s, owners Mel and Bren Simon had changed the estate's name to Villa di Venezia. The estate was designed by Maurice Fatio.

The Palm Beach Post

Maurice Fatio

Matinee-idol looks combined with polished European manners and consummate skill made Swiss-born architect Maurice Fatio not only the man to invite to 1920s house parties but to design the house as well.

In the 1930s, he designed homes in Manalapan for Harold S. Vanderbilt and his sister, Consuelo Vanderbilt Balsan. Although best-known for a refined Italian Mediterranean style, Fatio also worked in other styles. "The Reef," a Palm Beach oceanfront house designed in 1937, won a gold medal at the Paris International Exhibition for being "the most modern house in America."

Marion Sims Wyeth

Two years after arriving in Palm Beach in 1919, Marion Sims Wyeth was hired by Marjorie Merriweather Post to design her first Palm Beach house. By 1923, he was working on what would become Mar-a-Lago, although he later confided that its boisterous architecture "isn't my taste."

During Wyeth's long career, he designed more than 100 homes in Palm Beach in a wide variety of styles, including 45,000-square-foot Cielito Lindo for Jesse Woolworth Donahue, as well as the Florida Governor's Mansion in Tallahassee and Doris Duke's Shangri-La in Hawaii.

John Volk

When Austrian-born architect John Volk arrived in Palm Beach near the end of the first Florida Land Boom, he designed the Spanish-style houses that were still the rage. But as the boom turned to bust, Volk began designing less-opulent Georgian- and British Colonial-style homes, which brought the white-tile roof to Palm Beach. He designed more than 2,000 homes and commercial buildings, most of them in Florida and the Bahamas. In addition to homes on nearly every residential street in Palm Beach and many in historic neighborhoods (see page 253), Volk helped create Lost Tree Village in North Palm Beach.

Castles
IN THE SAND

By BARBARA MARSHALL | The Palm Beach Post

In Palm Beach, history hides behind tall hedges.

Beyond those fierce stands of ficus are the mansions that created the resort style of architecture known around the world as "the Palm Beach look."

The houses seem old and venerable today, but when their builders arrived in Palm Beach at the start of the Jazz Age, everything was brand-new. That included social codes, dress codes — and much of the money. The stuffy resort life that had centered around the big hotels was over. Members of new high society wanted to party in their own back yards.

And these new mansion builders wanted homes as jazzy as the age.

Architects Addison Mizner, Maurice Fatio and Marion Sims Wyeth responded, designing immense castles, in the midst of the wild beach jungle, in a dizzying combination of Mediterranean styles. There, the owners of these party palaces lived in walled splendor for the three short months of the Palm Beach winter season.

Except for Mar-a-Lago, the largest estates fell to bulldozers in the 1950s and '60s. But many other mansions survived, even if their once-vast grounds became subdivisions.

Here's a peek behind the hedges of 10 of Palm Beach's most spectacular 1920s mansions still in existence.

The towers of Mizner's magnificent Casa Nana, between Worth Avenue and Southern Boulevard. This grand old estate is for sale for $72.5 million.

Historical Society of Palm Beach County

Former Kennedy Estate
1095 N. Ocean Blvd.

Monterey Rd.

N. Lake Way

N. Ocean Blvd.

Palm Beach Country Club

N. Lake Way

N. Lake Way

N. County Rd.

Lake Worth Lagoon

N

Atlantic Ocean

Palm Beach

MAP AREA

MARTIN

Lake O.

PALM BEACH COUNTY

HENDRY

BROWARD

Bradley Pl.

Royal Poinciana Way

Former Estée Lauder House
126 S. Ocean Blvd.

Cocoanut Row

Barton Ave. **2**
3

Royal Palm Way

S. County Rd.

El Sarmiento
140 S. Ocean Blvd.

S. Ocean Blvd.

Everglades Golf Course

El Salano
720 S. Ocean Blvd.

Banyan Rd. **4**
5

Cielito Lindo
122 Kings Rd.

Casa Nana
780 S. Ocean Blvd.

Kings Rd.

6

7

Southern Blvd.

Mar-a-Lago
1100 S. Ocean Blvd.

Casa Apava
1300 S. Ocean Blvd.

S. Ocean Blvd.

8

AIA

Il Palmetto
1500 S. Ocean Blvd.

9

The former Kennedy Estate is now named Castillo del Mar, but it still houses most of the Kennedys' original furniture.

Richard Graulich The Palm Beach Post

1. Kennedy Estate

The family hasn't owned it for more than 10 years, but this house on North Ocean Boulevard will always be known as the Kennedy Estate. Originally called La Guerida, the 11-bedroom home was built by Addison Mizner in 1923 for department-store tycoon Rodman Wannamaker. Joe Kennedy purchased it for $120,000 in 1933.

During the brief, bright years of Camelot, it was the winter White House, where newly elected John F. Kennedy chose his Cabinet and worked on his inaugural address. Its oceanfront lawn was the scene of the famous Kennedy football games.

After her husband's death, Rose Kennedy continued to spend time in Palm Beach, visited frequently by various family members. After she died, the un-air-conditioned, increasingly ramshackle estate housed rotating gangs of Kennedy kids on spring break. In 1991, it was the scene of the police investigation into a rape allegation made against William Kennedy Smith, who was acquitted of the charge.

In 1995, the Kennedys sold the furnished house for $4.9 million to John and Marianne Castle, who began an extensive restoration using Mizner's original plans. They changed the name to Castillo del Mar but kept most of the Kennedys' furniture.

David Spencer/The Palm Beach Post
The front entry of the John and Marianne Castle home.

Jackie, JFK, John Jr. and Caroline Kennedy at the gate of the estate on Easter Sunday in 1963.
Davidoff Studios

Katherine Fay family photo

Here's how the Kennedy kitchen looked over the Easter week-end in 1963. Kathy Fay (standing) and her sister, Sally (at left), were guests of President Kennedy and his wife, Jackie. Caroline (back) and John-John joined in the coloring of Easter eggs. "This was a magical moment in my teenage life," said Fay, who now lives in Delray Beach. Her father, Paul, was one of JFK's best friends and an usher at his wedding.

David Spencer/The Palm Beach Post

David Spencer/The Palm Beach Post

The kitchen in the John and Marianne Castle residence (above).

In addition to Castle family photos in the living room (left) is a photo of JFK and his son, taken at the mansion when it was owned by the Kennedys.

Palm Beach Daily News

"I did not get there by wishing for it, or by dreaming it, or hoping for it. I got there by working for it," said business-woman Estée Lauder.

The Estée Lauder House today.   *Richard Graulich/The Palm Beach Post*

2. Estée Lauder House

It was built by Marion Sims Wyeth in 1938 for Mrs. Francis A. Shaughnessy. The late cosmetics queen and her husband, Joe, purchased this Neoclassical oceanfront home in 1964. In later years, the couple came to Palm Beach in December, staying until April. Its current owners are their son, Leonard Lauder, and his wife, Evelyn, who completed a renovation that won the Ballinger Award for preservation in 1999.

In 1923, Anthony J. Drexel Biddle Jr. built his home just north of Palm Beach's midtown public beach. In 2008, current owners David and Julia Koch added the house next door (at left) for staff quarters and a children's playhouse.

3. El Sarmiento

For $5 in 1969, the public could stroll through this 32-room home, past its six fountains and antique Spanish tiles, during that year's Palm Beach Garden Club home tour. Its owner at the time was Alexander Kirkland, whose second wife was stripper Gypsy Rose Lee.

The Jazz Age mansion was built by Addison Mizner in 1923 for Anthony J. Drexel Biddle Jr., who was married to tobacco heiress Mary Duke. Biddle became ambassador to several European governments during World War II and, later, ambassador to Spain.

By the early 1990s, 16,000-square-foot El Sarmiento had been "architecturally vandalized," according to a New York designer renovating the house for new owners. That face-lift, in which 14 small bedrooms became six large suites, earned El Sarmiento its first Ballinger

David Koch

Award from the Palm Beach Preservation Foundation in 1991.

In 1998, oil tycoon David Koch paid $10.5 million for the estate. Last year, he and his wife, Julia, completed a $12 million restoration, which won the Preservation Foundation's 2008 Ballinger Award.

PALM BEACH ESTATES: MEMORIES

'My father worked with Addison Mizner'

My father, Albert Tatoul, came to Palm Beach in the 1920s to work as a salesman for Addison Mizner. He later opened his own shop on Worth Avenue, where he specialized in furniture for the Florida outdoor lifestyle.

He was also Addison Mizner's friend, and my father helped him to develop products for Mizner Industries. When the Mizner bubble burst, my family moved back to New York City, where I was born. So I never met that "bigger-than-life" gentleman, Addison Mizner.

We returned to Florida in 1939, and growing up in the Palm Beaches in the 1940s and '50s was as good as it gets.

— DR. WARREN P. TATOUL

Dr. Tatoul is a former mayor of North Palm Beach. He and his wife, Judy, now live in PGA National in Palm Beach Gardens.

Robert and Warren Tatoul as members of the local Messenger Corps during World War II: "We lived at 303 Royal Palm Way. During WW II, a small Army base was built on the north end of the island to protect the inlet. The beaches were patrolled by Coast Guardsmen in search of Nazi spies being sent ashore from submarines. We were part of the Messenger Corps of local boys. Part of our training was to sneak through the woods, undetected. Our rewards included trips to both the Palm Beach military camp and to Camp Murphy in Hobe Sound. We also helped to serve military personnel on Sundays at the V for Victory Soldier Canteen on the corner of Worth Avenue and County Road."

El Salano's famous former owners include Addison Mizner, Harold S. Vanderbilt, Brownie McLean, and John Lennon and Yoko Ono. Renters include Florida Gov. Claude Kirk and *Hustler* publisher Larry Flynt.

Richard Graulich
The Palm Beach Post

4. El Salano (John Lennon House)

Best-known as the house John Lennon and Yoko Ono owned briefly in the early '80s, El Salano was supposed to be Addison Mizner's own home. After building it in a "jungle setting" in 1919, he sold it to a persuasive Harold S. Vanderbilt, who had Mizner add a large new living room and swimming pool.

Vanderbilt spent winters there in the 1920s, but when the town refused to close South Ocean Boulevard in front of his house (as the town had done for the wealthy residents on North Ocean Boulevard), he built a larger mansion farther south in Manalapan.

In the 1960s and '70s, El Salano's 22 rooms were a top society party destination when John "Jock" and Brownie McLean owned the house. (The McClean

Brownie McLean in 1960.

family once owned *The Washington Post* and the Hope Diamond.) It was also the scene of raunchy photo shoots for *Hustler* magazine when Brownie unknowingly rented the estate to the magazine's publisher, Larry Flynt. Florida Gov. Claude Kirk stayed in the house the Christmas before his 1967 inauguration. McLean sold the estate to Lennon and Ono, who vacationed there for about two weeks one winter but never moved in. Ono renovated the house after Lennon's death, then sold it for $3.15 million.

'I thought I was talking to the gardener,'
said a neighbor, who met John Lennon during the two weeks he and Yoko Ono stayed at El Salano.

Davidoff Studios
In 1973, John Lennon visited Palm Beach with his son Julian.

5. Casa Nana

Addison Mizner built this house with its two-story, Venetian-style loggias and an open circular stairwell in 1926 for George Rasmussen, the founder of the National Tea Co., who named it after his wife. The living room contains a circa-1550 fireplace King Henri II of France had made for his mistress, Diana de Poitiers. The fireplace's engraved double Ds refer to her; the H above stands for the king.

In addition to the original circular stair tower leading to an oceanfront master suite, the 30,000-square-foot estate has nine bedrooms, 14 baths, and a movie theater with tiered seating for 12.

Its former owners include Mary Woolworth Donahue, a host of early Chicago TV shows, who married the heir to the dime-store fortune and once rented the house to Adnan Khashoggi before selling it for $3 million in 1980.

Bud Paxson, founder of Paxson Communications; and his wife, Marla, owned Casa Nana in the late 1990s and early 2000s. They hosted a 2000 fund-raiser for George W. Bush's presidential campaign there before selling it furnished for $30.25 million in 2003.

Casa Nana is once again for sale, this time for $72.5 million.

Garden parterres set the formal tone at Casa Nana, with its unique two-story Venetian-style loggias.

Richard Graulich/The Palm Beach Post

THEN: At Casa Nana (above), the living-room fireplace was too tall for the room, so Addison Mizner reconfigured the antique fireplace.

NOW: (right) The 15th-century fireplace is still the focal point of the room, along with the home's antique European "linen-fold" paneling.

Robert Brantley Photography, Delray Beach

MATTHEW 5:3-12

The Beatitudes

³ "Blessed are the poor in spirit, for theirs is the kingdom of heaven.

⁴ Blessed are those who mourn, for they will be comforted.

⁵ Blessed are the meek, for they will inherit the earth.

⁶Blessed are those who hunger and thirst for righteousness,

for they will be filled.

⁷ Blessed are the merciful, for they will be shown mercy.

⁸ Blessed are the pure in heart, for they will see God.

⁹ Blessed are the peacemakers, for they will be called sons of God.

¹⁰ Blessed are those who are persecuted because of righteousness,

for theirs is the kingdom of heaven.

¹¹ Blessed are you when people insult you, persecute you and falsely

say all kinds of evil against you because of me.

¹² Rejoice and be glad, because great is your reward in heaven,

for in the same way they persecuted the prophets

who were before you."

Palm Beach Prayer Team Ministries, Inc.

P.O. Box 2586, Palm Beach, FL 33480

561-882-1660

PRAYER OF SALVATION

At this time, if you desire to be set free in your soul, simply bow your head, confess your need for salvation, ask God to forgive your sins and then open your heart to receive His Son, the Messiah, and He will send His spirit as a seal, and you will be able to begin a new life with Him in "the Promised Land", here on Earth while being sanctified by His word with the hope for a future in Heaven.

JOHN 3:3

• Reference: New International Version

6. Cielito Lindo

One of the largest of Palm Beach's Jazz Age palazzos, the 45,000-square-foot "Little Bit of Heaven" was originally sequestered in the midst of 16 lush ocean-to-lake acres. Built by Marion Sims Wyeth in 1927 for dime-store heiress Jessie Woolworth Donahue, the 135-room mansion was "one of the finest Hispanic-American houses in that land of magical dwellings — Palm Beach," enthused *Arts & Decoration* magazine the following year, citing its distinctive Moorish brickwork and wooden window grills.

But in 1948, after the suicide of her husband, James, Jessie sold the house to developers, who subdivided the property and built Kings Road straight through the middle of her former living room. Wyeth himself devised a plan to save the original mansion by breaking it up into five separate homes. Yet Cielito Lindo was so large that one of these "smaller" homes (on the south side of Kings Road) still contains 20 rooms — and retains the name, Cielito Lindo.

Tops of columns (right) in the entrance foyer were uncovered when a mezzanine floor was removed during a renovation and restoration.

Robert Brantley Photography, Delray Beach

Kings Road

Once secluded on 16 acres just north of Southern Boulevard, Cielito Lindo was broken up into five houses in the late 1940s, when Kings Road was built through the middle of the home's former living room.

Growing up inside a Fatio mansion: 'Exquisite'

In 1928, William McAneeny, president of the Hudson Motor Car Co., hired my father to be caretaker for his estate on Palm Beach — Casa Della Porta, a famous estate designed by Maurice Fatio. I was 9, so my job was to open the house for airing every day. I had to open and shut all the windows in the main house to keep the air from getting musty. I also used to earn 50 cents to wax and polish the tile floors on the pavilion. Many things in that home were exquisite. The doors in the dining room were two very ornate doors. They were hand-carved in Italy. Each panel had a scene with buildings and people on it. The doors fascinated me.

I used to love living there at the estate. On a hot day I would take a book to the tower room and sit on the windowsill reading and watching the boats on the ocean.

We used to pick a wicker basket full of roses every day to bring to our teachers. Boy, those teachers loved the Frazier girls.

I also used to play the organ. It was a Skinner pipe organ, the most expensive kind available. In my 20s, Mother would let me use the Wedgwood China and expensive glassware and host my friends. I did all the dishes, and I am proud to say I never broke a thing.

I had a big thrill recently when I toured the estate with Alexandra Taylor, Maurice Fatio's daughter. She had never even seen the estate before, and it was so exciting to tell her how I had lived there for some 20 years.

— REBECCA FRAZIER PETERSON

Rebecca Frazier at the pavilion gate of Casa Della Porta, *circa* 1940s (above). Rebecca's family moved to West Palm Beach from Tennessee in 1925. They stayed in the Whitehall Hotel during the 1928 hurricane. Rebecca's father, Carlos, became caretaker for Casa Della Porta, a Maurice Fatio estate on Via del Mar in Palm Beach. The front entrance of the estate (right) is particularly noteworthy.

In the 1920s it was common for residents to go to the beach in their clothes. Carlos Frazier (left) also took his copy of *The Palm Beach Post*. Also in photo, from left: friend India Ackerman, Mildred Frazier, Cecile Whitworth Frazier, Frances Frazier and Rebecca Frazier.

Elaborate carved ceilings, here in the loggia, were restored thoroughout Casa Della Porta in Palm Beach.

Stephen Leek/Palm Beach Daily News

The Mar-a-Lago Club's pool, on the west side of the famous mansion.

More interior photos, page 240

Mar-a-Lago's grand living room makes the perfect setting for a grand entrance, and Donald J. Trump works the scene perfectly: 'This is great, right?' he asked, arms outstretched, as he and wife Melania greeted guests for a pre-Easter dinner at the private Mar-a-Lago Club in 2009 (right).

Of Palm Beach's largest 1920s estates, Mar-a-Lago is the only one that remains with its property intact. Trump saved the 128-room gem from demolition in 1985 by buying the national landmark for $10 million. 'The first check I wrote for Mar-a-Lago was $10,000 to cancel the demolition contract,' he says. 'It was just two weeks away from demolition.'

7. Mar-a-Lago

Post cereal heiress Marjorie Merriweather Post was Mrs. E.F. Hutton when she reportedly hacked her way through beach jungle to find an appropriate setting for the castle she planned to build.

She commissioned architect Marion Sims Wyeth to construct a 58-bedroom, Spanish-Moorish-Portuguese-Venetian palace on the 17 acres she purchased between the ocean and Lake Worth (the Intracoastal). By the time it was finished in 1927, Joseph Urban, a Viennese architect and theater designer, had provided much of the ornamentation.

Six hundred workers labored for more than three years to build this mansion, using boatloads of Italian stone and approximately 36,000 antique Spanish and Portuguese tiles, as well as old marble floors and roof tiles from Cuba. The living room's 30-foot-tall, gold-leafed ceiling is a copy of the famous "Thousand-Wing Ceiling" in the Accademia gallery museum in Venice — only with secular rather than ecclesiastical motifs.

For decades, the estate's 75-foot tower has been a navigational aid for local boaters.

Marjorie Merriweather Post, then married to Joseph E. Davies, aboard Sea Cloud in 1948. It was the largest private luxury yacht in the world. The ship still sails.

Historical Society of Palm Beach County

Facing page photo:
Richard Graulich
The Palm Beach Post

When she died in 1973, Post gave Mar-a-Lago ("Ocean to Lake" in Spanish) to the U.S. government for a presidential retreat. But the government balked at its $1million-a-year maintenance cost and its site under Palm Beach International Airport's flight path.

In 1985, Donald Trump paid $10 million for the estate, which contained 33 bathrooms, three bomb shelters and a nine-hole golf course. Ten years later, he converted it to a private club with a spa, tennis and croquet courts, a new ballroom and a beach club. Current initiation fees are $200,000.

Of the largest 1920s Palm Beach estates, Mar-a-Lago is the only one to survive nearly intact through the decades.

Mrs. Post's bathroom and dressing room, so large that it also served as her office. In the mornings, Mrs. Post would meet here with her secretary and masseur, exercising, bathing, dressing, writing letters and compiling staff memoirs and making phone calls. The rare pink-and-gold marble lining the walls, accented with gold fixtures, is the same stone used in Sea Cloud, Mrs. Post's yacht.

1993, The Palm Beach Post

What does Trump like most about Mar-a-Lago? 'It's a work of art,' he says. And despite its size, it's a very warm place. It's comfortable.'

And one more thing: 'Of all of Palm Beach's great homes, this is the greatest.'

1993, The Palm Beach Post

< THEN: Architect Joseph Urban said he copied Mar-a-Lago's 30-by-50 foot dining room from a mid-17th century room in the Chigi Palace in Rome, used in the 1920s by Benito Mussolini.

The "pietre dure" table, which weighs 4,000 pounds and seats 34, took 17 artists a full year to complete. Post once said, "this table was probably the most important thing in the entire house." Her will stipulated it be moved to Hillwood, her estate outside Washington, D.C.

> NOW: The dining room of The Mar-a-lago Club contains small tables for more intimate dining.

Mar-a-Lago

Photos from the Historical Society of Palm Beach County

8. Casa Apava

This property was once part of the historic Blossom-Bingham Estate, dating to 1894. In 1918, architect Abram Garfield, the son of President James Garfield, built the house on a ridge of original beach hammock for Chester Bolton, a Cleveland congressman; and his wife, Frances, a member of the Bingham family. She served out her husband's term after his death and was re-elected for nearly 30 years.

The estate's palm garden was so thick that a 1970s architectural survey of the property reported that sunlight did not reach the ground.

Ron Perelman, the Revlon boss, owned the seven-bedroom, 18-bath home in the early 2000s while married to actress Ellen Barkin. He sold it in 2004 to Virginia home builder Dwight Schar for $70 million, at that time the highest price ever paid for residential real estate in the U.S.

Early photos show the rear of the house (above). Frances Payne Bingham and Julia Raymond (left) in Palm Beach, Christmas 1898. Frances later built Casa Apava and became a member of Congress.

Casa Apava today (left), stretches along nearly 300 feet of oceanfront. A salvaged portion of the estate's original tiled wall was moved to Pan's Garden in Palm Beach.

Richard Graulich/The Palm Beach Post

9. Il Palmetto

In 1930, it cost $2.5 million and took 450 workers eight months to build this 60,000-square-foot home for Joseph Widener, a Philadelphia industrialist, horseman and the founder of Hialeah Race Track. Maurice Fatio's design for the Italian Renaissance estate included a 50-foot-long living room and a 16th-century carved ceiling. Today, the home's site, south of Southern Boulevard where Ocean Boulevard curves sharply east, is known as "Widener's Curve."

In 1951, when the big estates had gone out of style, Il Palmetto sold for $97,000. Twenty years later, Jan Annenberg Hooker, one of publisher Moses Annenberg's seven daughters, bought it for $975,000. Il Palmetto was in poor condition when Netscape co-founder James Clark purchased it for $11 million in 1999. He since has completed a major renovation.

Richard Graulich/The Palm Beach Post

Il Palmetto, one of the grandest homes Maurice Fatio built, as it looks today, after a complete renovation.

'Our lives revolved around the Vanderbilts and their guests'

My parents, Anna and Alex, worked for Harold Stirling Vanderbilt and his wife, Gertrude, from around 1936 until 1978. My father was the superintendent of Vanderbilt's Manalapan estate, and my mother was a personal maid for Mrs. V as well as the housekeeper.

The Vanderbilts took a real interest in our lives. When I was born in 1943, my parents and I lived in Mrs. V's bedroom until they built a home for us on the estate in 1948.

Everyone called the Vanderbilts "madam" or "sir," and I had to curtsy when I shook hands with them.

Living at the estate gave me a chance to experience a totally different world, not just a different way of life. In summer, I could invite my friends to go roller skating in the basement, which had a long hallway.

There were three laundresses to wash and iron, three chambermaids (one to clean the help's quarters and set the help's dining room, the other two for cleaning — dusting, polishing the silver, arranging flowers and pulling down the beds during dinner) — plus,

Alexandra (Sandy) Scavnicky on the lawn of Harold Vanderbilt's estate, 1969.

The caretaker's home on the Vanderbilt estate.

the houseboy, the butler, the valet and the chauffeur, who dusted the five cars every day.

Our lives revolved around the Vanderbilts and their guests:

7:30 a.m.: Mother would bring breakfast and help Mrs. V. with her morning "ablutions." Daddy would go to the farm for flowers and vegetables.

Noon: Mother would help Mrs. V get ready for lunch or an afternoon outing. Then she would be off from about 1:30 until 5:30. During that

time she went shopping for Mrs. V's needs. Daddy would take a nap.

5:30 p.m.: Mother would help Mrs. V dress for dinner. By 8 p.m. Mother's workday would be done.

At the end of the winter season, every piece of furniture and the rugs were covered with a layer of tissue paper, then mothballs and then sealed in brown paper.

— ALEXANDRA (SANDY) SCAVNICKY, *who now lives in West Palm Beach*

Harold S. Vanderbilt was a sore loser.

Throughout the 1920s, the scion of one of America's oldest and wealthiest families had tried to persuade the Town of Palm Beach to close South Ocean Boulevard in front of his Addison Mizner mansion, called El Salano (much later, owned briefly by John Lennon and Yoko Ono). After all, the town had already removed hurricane-damaged North Ocean Boulevard from the front yards of the Phippses, the Stotesburys and other millionaire "snowbirds."

When the town refused to budge, Vanderbilt took his money and the Vanderbilt penchant for building palatial homes and headed south in 1929. He was soon followed by his sister and his aunt.

At the time, Manalapan was a long ribbon of undeveloped beach and Hypoluxo Island still a jungle when this Vanderbilt trio put them both on high society's map. Harold and his sister — Consuelo Vanderbilt Balsan (the former Duchess of Marlborough) — built grand estate houses, designed by aristocratic architect Maurice Fatio. At the same time, their aunt, Lila Vanderbilt Webb, designed her own oceanfront house a short distance down the beach in Gulf Stream, with Fatio's advice.

And all because a Vanderbilt was in a snit.

GRAND VISION: Harold S. Vanderbilt put Manalapan on the high-society map.

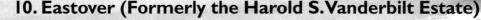

Lantana Rd.
Lantana Ocean Ave.

Eastover, former Harold Vanderbilt Estate
1100 S. Ocean Blvd.

MAP AREA

MARTIN
Lake O.
PALM BEACH COUNTY
HENDRY
BROWARD

Hypoluxo Island

Atlantic Ocean

Manalapan

Lake Worth Lagoon

A1A   N

THE KING OF HIS (SAND) CASTLE: Harold S. Vanderbilt's mansion sprang from Manalapan's beach wilderness (top) while the Great Depression raged throughout the country.

10. Eastover (Formerly the Harold S. Vanderbilt Estate)

Harold S. Vanderbilt was the great-grandson of "The Commodore," 19th-century industrialist Cornelius Vanderbilt, who created the family's vast railroad fortune. A two-time America's Cup winner and the developer of the scoring system for the game of contract bridge, Harold commissioned Maurice Fatio to design a 32,000-square-foot Italianate mansion.

Between 1929 and 1931, while the country was sinking into the Great Depression, Vanderbilt's sand castle went up on a long stretch of beach, with 52 rooms, a two-bedroom guest house and three-bedroom beach house, tennis courts, a pool and boat dock.

Palm Beach Life magazine wrote in 1933: "Transformation of a waste of rolling sand dunes into an estate of semi-tropical beauty was most notably achieved in the execution of the palatial residence and estate of Mr. Harold S. Vanderbilt."

In 1986, shopping-mall magnate Mel Simon and his wife, Bren, paid $6 million for the estate, where they hosted a party for President Bill Clinton and a dinner for Hillary Rodham Clinton's campaign for U.S. Senate. They renamed it Villa di Venezia.

In 2000, Veronica and Randolph Hearst purchased the mansion for $29.9 million — a local real-estate record at the time. Randolph, the father of kidnap victim Patty Hearst and the son of newspaper publisher William Randolph Hearst, died a few months later.

In an attempt to keep the estate, Veronica lopped off a wing of the house to sell an oceanfront lot, but it wasn't enough. By 2008, Villa di Venezia was in foreclosure and was sold on the Palm Beach County Courthouse steps to its creditors for $22 million.

New owners Franklin Haney, a Washington-based real-estate developer; and his wife, Emeline, are restoring the mansion, which they bought for $23.5 million in 2008.

1994, The Palm Beach Post

The upper level of Eastover's grand entrance hall, as it looked in 1994, when shopping-mall developer Mel Simon and his wife, Bren, owned it. They called the house "Villa di Venezia." At lower right is the Simon's living room.

On 5 acres, the 20,000-square-foot house has seven bedrooms, eight baths and staff quarters.

Richard Graulich/The Palm Beach Post

1994, The Palm Beach Post

Miradero
LILA VANDERBILT WEBB

In the early 1930s, 71-year-old Lila Vanderbilt Webb designed Miradero (Spanish for "Lookout") herself with a little help from architect Maurice Fatio, who had built her niece's and nephew's homes nearby. Lila was one of "The Commodore's" granddaughters who married Seward Webb, a doctor who became addicted to morphine. She spent only three winters in her oceanfront retreat before she died in 1936.

After her death, Miradero languished for years. Beginning in 1969, Robert M. Ganger and his son, Robert W. Ganger Jr., restored the house but sold the tower, which now belongs to another owner. A few years ago, Ganger Jr. wrote a book about Lila called *Miradero: Window on an Era.*

From Miradero: Window on an Era

Lila Vanderbilt Webb (left) with her husband, Dr. Seward Webb, in 1881. After his death, she busied herself building her dream beach house, which was completed in 1933.

Robert Ganger (below) in front of the restored Gulf Stream mansion in 2005.

Cydney Scott/The Palm Beach Post

Casa Alva   CONSUELO VANDERBILT BALSAN

Ray Graham/The Palm Beach Post

Consuelo Vanderbilt Balsan (right) hired Maurice Fatio to build her a pleasure palace in Hypoluxo Island's tropical jungle. Longtime Manalapan Mayor William Benjamin and his wife, Maura, (above, inside the estate) have owned the house since 1957. On nearly 5 acres, Casa Alva is for sale for $15.9 million.

Historical Society of Palm Beach County

In 1934, Consuelo Vanderbilt Balsan, the former Duchess of Marlborough, had finally found love, so she built a palace to contain it.

She hired Maurice Fatio to build her a house on tropical Hypoluxo Island, naming the house after her domineering mother, who had forced Consuelo into a loveless marriage with the Duke of Marlborough when she was 18. Yet by the time she built Casa Alva, Consuelo was divorced from the Duke; reconciled with her mother; and married to a man she loved, Jacques Balsan, a French aviation pioneer.

She decorated her wilderness mansion with the European taste acquired while living in Blenheim Palace, one of England's greatest estates. One winter, family friend Sir Winston Churchill visited and painted a portrait of the grounds.

In 1957, Consuelo sold her house and surrounding property to developer William Benjamin, who built a luxury gated subdivision called Point Manalapan.

THE GHOSTS OF PALM BEACH

LOST MANSIONS OF AN OPULENT AGE

If you think Palm Beachers live lavishly now, consider the era just after World War I.

Old money met new on the sands of Palm Beach. The millionaire's dream merchant was architect Addison Mizner.

In the 1920s, he constructed fantastical palaces on the island's high dune ridge, some large enough to entertain more than 1,000 people. The grounds of three of the largest — El Mirasol; Casa Bendita; and Playa Riente, the grandest of them all — covered dozens of acres, running from the Atlantic across the island to Lake Worth (the Intracoastal today).

But 40 years later, except for Mar-a-Lago, Palm Beach's biggest houses had been demolished, their owners broke or dead, their contents sold, and the vast gardens cut up into subdivisions.

Today, they're the ghosts of Palm Beach …

Playa Riente

El Mirasol

LIVING IN LUXURY: The homes that Addison Mizner built for Palm Beach's wealthy industrialists in the early 1920s looked as if they would survive for centuries. But 40 years later, most of the largest — including these three — were gone. Casa Bendita (below), built in 1922 for John S. Phipps, was dubbed "Phipps Castle" for its size and grandeur. After his death, the land was subdivided and sold, and the house demolished in 1961. Vast Playa Riente was built for an oil tycoon but purchased soon after by Anna Dodge, widow of the auto-maker. When the Town of Palm Beach refused to allow the mansion to become a private club or school, Dodge called in the wrecking crews in 1957. Decorative items from the house live on in several restaurants in Vero Beach. El Mirasol, built for Edward and Eva Stotesbury in 1919, started the craze for large, Mediterranean-style Mizner mansions. But the Stotesbury money was gone by the end of World War II, and El Mirasol was razed in 1958.

Casa Bendita

THE ISLAND'S OLD HAUNTS

In this 1920s aerial (below), El Mirasol, Casa Bendita and other large estates stretch across Palm Beach from the Atlantic to Lake Worth, and North Ocean Boulevard still runs along the estates' east side. After the 1928 Hurricane, the wealthy families persuaded the town to block the beach road on the south side of El Mirasol so that their ocean view would be unsullied. The landowners paid to have what is now North County Road (in the middle of the photo) widened through their properties.

NOW

Playa Riente

THEN

Note: Playa Riente, which was farther north, is not shown in this aerial.

Casa Bendita

At right, aerials of Palm Beach as it today. The red lines denote the approximate sites where Palm Beach's ghost mansions once stood, now cut up by roads and subdivisions. Within the 42-acre boundaries of El Mirasol (above), there are now more than 50 homes where once there was only one.

< PALM BEACH TODAY

El Mirasol

Aerials by Richard Graulich/The Palm Beach Post

It wasn't the biggest, but El Mirasol established the Mediterranean residential style that still defines Palm Beach. The exotic loggia (above) had a painted ceiling and tile murals. An entry arch probably designed by architect Maurice Fatio during later additions (facing page, left) and as it looks today (facing page, right) — the only publicly visible remnant of this Palm Beach ghost.

Historical Society of Palm Beach County

El Mirasol

This 40-room 1919 mansion cemented architect Addison Mizner's reputation — and elevated its owner, Eva Stotesbury, to social queen of the island resort. Before the Stotesburys built El Mirasol, most entertaining in the resort town took place in hotels. Eva changed all that by building a mansion large enough to entertain 1,200 people at a time.

Eva Stotesbury

Towering at the east end of 42 acres that spanned the island, El Mirasol ("Sunflower" in Spanish) required about 40 butlers, chambermaids, parlormaids, cooks, gardeners and housemen to keep it running. The gardens, filled with monkeys and aviaries of tropical birds, included groves of citrus trees and a Moorish tea house on the lake side.

Known for her ropes of natural pearls, Eva was once questioned by an acquaintance for wearing them during the day with a gingham dress.

"Yes, my dear," she reportedly said. "I used to feel that way too. But that was before I had the pearls."

In 1922, Eva's daughter, Louise Cromwell, married Gen. Douglas MacArthur in El Mirasol's living room. (Later, her son, James Cromwell, became Doris Duke's first husband.)

Such was the clout of the Stotesburys and their wealthy neighbors that, after the 1928 Hurricane, they helped persuade the town to reroute North Ocean Boulevard farther west to North County Road so that cars wouldn't disturb their ocean view.

But after World War II, Palm Beach's biggest palacios had become "white elephants," according to *All*

Florida magazine as early as 1954. Servants were in short supply. A new generation wanted to live less formally. The dozens of rooms maintained by an army of servants, the vast gardens, the lavish plutocratic lifestyles all belonged to an earlier age.

For Eva, the money ran out with the era. She had to sell her pearls. Everything else went after her death at an estate sale attended by 4,000 people, including the Duke and Duchess of Windsor.

El Mirasol wasn't yet 40 years old when the bulldozers rolled through the gates in 1958. The vast property that held one mansion became subdivisions that now contain more than 50 homes. All that remains is a fountain (on private property) and a tiled entrance arch visible from North County Road, between Via Los Incas and a street named El Mirasol.

Historical Society of Palm Beach County *Palm Beach Daily News*

Addison Mizner: Legacy of a dreamer

By ELIOT KLEINBERG | The Palm Beach Post

Addison Cairns Mizner kept his pet monkey, Johnnie Brown, on one shoulder and a bagful of dreams on the other. If Henry Flagler is Palm Beach County's godfather, Mizner is its Michelangelo.

He changed Palm Beach County's look from wood cottages and canary yellow to stucco castles and tropical pastels.

"When you get right down to it, Mizner is the first architect of significance to work primarily in Florida," Donald Curl, professor of history at Florida Atlantic University and author of *Mizner's Florida*, said in 2001, when Mizner entered the Florida Artists Hall of Fame.

Born to prominent Californians, Mizner went to college in Spain, mined gold in Alaska, saw Australia and Asia, and finally settled into architecture.

In 1918, the then-45-year-old was invited down to Palm Beach by Singer sewing-machine heir Paris Singer. Mizner was hooked.

Beginning with the Everglades Club on Worth Avenue, Mizner created a new world of mansions and homes from 1919 to 1932. The exact number isn't known, but it's around 100.

They were famed for their rough stucco walls, handmade barrel-tile roofs, archways and loggias, and rooms that opened to the ocean.

He created a home and workplace at Via Mizner, designing covered walkways filled with first-floor shops and topping them with his tower apartment.

Though his private romantic life was a mystery, the never-married Mizner enjoyed socializing and entertaining, though he sometimes played second fiddle to his salesman-playwright-raconteur brother Wilson, whose witticisms included, "Get the big snobs, and the little snobs will follow."

Eventually, Mizner the designer became Mizner the developer.

In the early 1920s, Boca Raton was a settlement of a few hundred. Mizner wanted a hotel to help lure land investors, so he built the $1.25 million Cloister Inn, the forerunner of the Boca Raton Resort & Club, and designed 29 homes in a neighborhood called Old Floresta.

At its peak, Mizner's enterprise was making $2 million — about $25 million in 2009 dollars — in sales every week. Then the bust hit, and by 1927, his company went bankrupt.

Mizner died of heart failure in 1933 at age 60.

But look around Palm Beach County and Mizner lives — in our distinctive "Palm Beach look."

Historical Society of Palm Beach County

Addison Mizner designed Via Mizner and the Everglades Club on Worth Avenue, as well as 100-something homes. His first design decree, aimed at Henry Flagler: "I'd build something that wasn't made of wood, and I wouldn't paint it yellow." Mizner's monkey, Johnnie Brown, shown on his shoulder, is buried in Via Mizner. Tourists can still spot the grave marker.

Playa Riente

Of all the stories of the Palm Beach ghost mansions, the tale of Playa Riente ("Laughing Beach") is the most haunting. It was Addison Mizner's masterpiece — massive, ornate and darkly Gothic — built for $2 million in 1923. Its owner was Joshua Cosden, a streetcar conductor who struck it rich in the oil fields of Oklahoma, married "the most beautiful girl in the state" and then built her a gargantuan mansion on 27 ocean-to-lake acres. To age its coquina stone walls, Mizner had the blocks sunk in the ocean for weeks.

Parts of the 70-room palace, built high on the dune line, seemed to hover over the Atlantic, whose waves lapped for 1,000 feet along the east end of the estate. The front door opened to an 80-foot entrance hall, which ended in a massive stone staircase. Marble steps led directly into the Atlantic. In addition to 15 master bedrooms, a "bachelor wing" allowed single male guests to come and go without disturbing the rest of the house.

But by 1926, Cosden had gambled away his fortune and sold Playa Riente to Anna Dodge, widow of auto-maker Horace Dodge. Three weeks later, she married her real estate agent, Hugh Dillman, director of The Society of the Four Arts and almost 20 years younger. The Dillmans became famous for their parties, and even introduced the Duke and Duchess of Windsor to Palm Beach society during one soirée in 1941. By 1947, the marriage — and the market for Palm Beach's grand sand castles — was over.

Anna Dodge (she resumed her earlier name) couldn't sell the mansion for $1 million in the early 1950s, not even when she threw in 24.7 acres of land for only another million. She then attempted to have the estate rezoned for use as a school or a private club, but the town council refused. Dodge sued the town and lost.

In a snit, she threw a lavish last par-

Photos from the Historical Society of Palm Beach County

In a town full of castles, Playa Riente was the palace. Built for an Oklahoma oilman who later gambled away his fortune, the 70-room mansion became the home of Anna Dodge Dillman, widow of auto-maker Horace Dodge. Murals made for a king of Spain decorated the music room (top), used for the Dillmans' famous parties, where they entertained the Rockefellers, the Hearsts, the Woolworths, impresario Flo Ziegfeld, and the Duke and Duchess of Windsor. When the Town of Palm Beach refused to allow her to turn Playa Riente into a private club or a school, Dodge had it demolished in 1957. Pieces of the house live on in several Vero Beach businesses, including parts of the Spanish bar at The Patio Restaurant.

ty, sold everything at an estate sale, and called in the wrecking crews in 1957. Of the legendary mansion, not even a street name remains in Palm Beach. To see remnants of Playa Riente — and El Mirasol — you have to drive 90 minutes north to Vero Beach.

In the 1940s and '50s, the late Indian River County pioneer and restaurateur Waldo Sexton bought bits and pieces of the grand old mansions as they were torn down. He installed the tile walls, carved-wood doors, statues and Moorish lanterns in his restaurants, which are still open today. Playa Riente's tiled Spanish bar is still used in The Patio Restaurant. The Driftwood Resort, Ocean Grill and Szechuan Palace restaurants are all decorated with what little is left of the grandest of Palm Beach's ghost mansions.

UNHAPPILY EVER AFTER: A few weeks after purchasing Playa Riente in 1926, Anna Dodge married the much-younger Hugh Dillman (above), a former actor who was her real-estate agent. The couple entertained lavishly at Playa Riente until divorcing in 1947.

Casa Bendita

In 1922, Addison Mizner built this mansion on 28 acres, part of a much larger parcel Henry Phipps had purchased for his three children in 1912. At one time, the Phipps family owned much of Palm Beach and West Palm Beach, including about 25 miles of South Florida oceanfront property.

(Phipps South Ocean Park in Palm Beach and Phipps Park in West Palm Beach are former family holdings.)

Casa Bendita was John S. "Jay" Phipps' winter home, named for his wife, Margarita, known as "Dita." During construction, it was dubbed "Phipps Castle" by one newspaper writer, awed at its size.

Perched on one of the highest points along the old dune line, Casa Bendita had a four-story octagonal tower, a large courtyard on three sides, and a romantic covered pool framed by arched columns.

Phipps, who founded the original Palm Beach Polo Club in Gulf Stream, kept the house until his death in 1958. Afterward, his heirs razed the mansion and subdivided the land.

In the 1990s, the Phipps estate became Phipps Estates when part of its former grounds became Palm Beach's only planned development. One 6-acre lot remains in the center of the island,

Susie Phipps Cochran

owned by Susie Phipps Cochran and her husband, Bob Eigelberger, who playfully dubbed their house "Casa Phippsberger."

All that's left of Casa Bendita are the bits of walls, statuary and fountains that the couple used to build picturesque ruin walls on their own estate, which contains one of South Florida's most spectacular private gardens.

Photos from the Historical Society of Palm Beach County

The Phipps family did everything in a big way. In the 1920s, they owned about one-third of Palm Beach, as well as huge chunks of land between Stuart and Miami. When John S. "Jay" Phipps built Casa Bendita, he did it on a scale that prompted a reporter to dub the house "Phipps Castle." Arched colonnades surround the covered pool (left). Also noteworthy was the drawing room (above).

Lannis Waters/The Palm Beach Post

Beginning in the early 1990s, developer Bob Eigelberger created a garden of more than 10,000 rare tropical plants on the last remnant of the legendary Phipps Estate, where he lives with his wife, Susie Phipps Cochran.

Perched on one of the highest points along the old dune line, Casa Bendita had a four-story octagonal tower, a large courtyard on three sides, and a romantic covered pool framed by arched columns

They don't make houses like this anymore.
And that's just one lure of Palm Beach County's historic neighborhoods.

'You just won't find this house in the suburbs.
Plus, a lot of people move here not just for the homes but for the neighborhood.'

— Linda Cullen, a real-estate agent who has lived in West Palm Beach's historic Flamingo Park neighborhood since 1985.

HISTORIC NEIGHBORHOODS

From Cozy Bungalows to Classic Colonials

AT HOME WITH HISTORY

By BARBARA MARSHALL | The Palm Beach Post

The past is still present in the county's historic neighborhoods, where houses with heavy stucco walls and arched windows tell a tale of Jazz Age glamour. And where simple wood-frame cottages are testament to a hard-working family's pursuit of a simpler Florida dream.

In the late 1980s, these heavily shaded streets drew new residents who began restoring the old homes and petitioning to have their neighborhoods declared historic districts. Today, there are 26 historic residential neighborhoods in Palm Beach County.

One of Palm Beach County's 26 historic districts is El Cid, in West Palm Beach. The home pictured is on Medina Way in El Cid.

Allen Eyestone/The Palm Beach Post

LOOKS LIKE HOME

Six common architectural styles found in Palm Beach County

Lannis Waters/The Palm Beach Post

Eliza Gutierrez/The Palm Beach Post

Meghan McCarthy/The Palm Beach Post

Frame Vernacular 1895-1919

These were the homes of the tradesmen and professionals who built Palm Beach County's first cities and towns. As plain and basic as their owners, they emphasized practicality over beauty. Perched on brick piers for circulation, they had front porches and steeply pitched roofs with overhangs to shed rain and to shade windows. Front porches were critical as the "air conditioners" of the time. This home is on Vallette Way in West Palm Beach's Mango Promenade neighborhood.

Bungalow 1919-1924

By the late teens, Palm Beach County's growing cities required new neighborhoods. The first homes built in these new "suburban" neighborhoods were often simple, low-slung bungalows — a style that originated in India. Constructed with tapering brick or concrete piers supporting a substantial veranda, bungalows, such as this one on North Palmway in Lake Worth, were lauded for their adaptability to a hot and humid climate.

Mission 1922-1930

To the dreamers and schemers who poured into Florida during the 1920s, "Spanish" homes were exotic, tropical antidotes to the lives they left up north. Stucco-clad, with flat roofs behind parapet walls, these inexpensive Mission Revival houses were built by the dozens in the neighborhoods spreading north and south from the county's downtowns. Mission-style houses, like this one on Claremore Drive in West Palm Beach's historic Flamingo Park neighborhood, were the most popular housing style of the county's boom era.

Ray Graham/The Palm Beach Post

Taylor Jones/The Palm Beach Post

The Palm Beach Post

Mediterranean Revival 1922-1930

As ornamental as wedding cakes, Mediterranean Revival homes mimicked the sand castles of the Palm Beach swells, though on a much smaller scale. These glamorous homes, built for the area's newly prosperous professionals, captured the extravagance and optimism of the county's Jazz Age, with cast-stone ornamentation and romantic echoes of Italy, Morocco, Spain and Venice. This home on 32nd Street is one of five built by famed architect John Volk in West Palm Beach's Old Northwood neighborhood.

Traditional 1930s-1940s

Starting in the 1930s, during the Great Depression, and extending through the war years, ostentation was out; simplicity was in. Homeowners wanted traditional homes as a bolster against uncertain times. Colonial Revival, Monterey/Bermuda and Minimal Traditional are some of the "resort cottage" styles built by winter visitors and residents who could afford new homes. This 1934 house in the Nassau Square neighborhood in Delray Beach is an example of one of these "snowbird" cottages.

Mid-century Ranch 1950s-1970s

After World War II, tourism and returning GIs created a demand for inexpensive, easy-to-maintain family homes that left plenty of time for leisure activities. Land was cheap, so builders constructed sprawling one-story "ranches" on large lots. In the days before air conditioning, jalousie windows directed the sea breezes through the "Florida room," an indoor/outdoor space that helped to tame the subtropical environment. This house on Almeria Road at Flagler Drive is typical of homes built in the 1950s.

By BARBARA MARSHALL | The Palm Beach Post

This section includes Palm Beach County's historic neighborhoods as of May 2009.
It does not include historic districts that are primarily commercial.

Compiled by Richard A. Marconi, Historical Society of Palm Beach County

WEST PALM BEACH

J.D. Vivian/The Palm Beach Post

Due to its proximity to the water, most of the original homes in Northwood Harbor were built as vacation homes before World War II. After the war, permanent residents moved into the small cottages and newer ranch-style homes.

This home is at 415 54th St.

1. Northwood Harbor

Became local historic district in 2006

Beginnings: From 1925-1955, residences were built as vacation homes and for local businessmen and artisans.

Architectural styles: Mission Revival and Vernacular; examples of post-World War II architecture include Minimal Traditional, Modern, Ranch, Art Moderne and Bungalow.

Notable details: The private Flotilla Club, established before World War II, was converted into a Coast Guard station during the war. The Coast Guard insignia is still visible on the building.

2. Northboro Park

Became local historic district in 1992; named to National Register of Historic Places in 2000

Beginnings: Developed from 1923-1940, Northboro Park is a Traditional neighborhood with alleys at the backs of the lots.

Architectural styles: Mediterranean Revival, Mission, Frame Vernacular.

Notable homes: The first house in the neighborhood was constructed in 1923 and is at 418 36th St. The 1925 Northboro Elementary School, built by DaCamara and Chace, is at the corner of 36th Street and Spruce Avenue.

3. West Northwood

Became local historic district in 1993

Beginnings: Platted in 1925 as part of a 400-acre parcel owned by Pinewood Development Co., this neighborhood was developed for the upper-middle class.

Architectural styles: Mediterranean and Mission Revival, with a couple of Frame Vernacular homes.

4. Northwood Hills

Became local historic district in 2003

Beginnings: In the boom of the 1920s, Northwood Hills' first lots were sold from tents every two weeks. Because the development was on a coastal ridge at least 50 feet high, some buyers purchased lots with views of Lake Mangonia, Lake Worth and the ocean.

Architecture styles: Mediterranean Revival, Mission Revival, Vernacular, and post-World War II styles.

Notable homes: Some were designed by prominent architect Maurice Fatio. It's said that pirates and rum-runners built "castle homes" on the hilltops of Northwood Hills so that they could have a clear view of the Intracoastal Waterway and the Atlantic Ocean.

2002, The Palm Beach Post

The Hurst home at 3509 Eastview Ave. in Northwood Hills is one of the neighborhood's famous "castle" homes. Its spectacular living room is shown at left. Local lore says the "castles" were built high on a hill by Prohibition rum-runners so they could see their boats, but the stories are probably just legends. What is true is that the neighborhood has one of the highest elevations in the county.

James Ponce, longtime resident of Northwood Hills, outside his home. Ponce is a well-known local historian who leads walking tours of Palm Beach.

2003, The Palm Beach Post

Greg Lovett/ The Palm Beach Post
4000 Westview Drive, Northwood HIlls

Chris Matula/ The Palm Beach Post
964 39th Court, Northwood Hills

Chris Matula/ The Palm Beach Post
957 39th Court, Northwood Hills

5. Old Northwood

Became local historic district in 1991; named to National Register of Historic Places in 1994

Beginnings: A 1920s Land Boom development.

Architectural styles: Mediterranean Revival, Mission, Frame Vernacular, Neoclassical Revival, American Foursquare, Dutch-Colonial Revival, Minimal Traditional, Ranch, Bungalow, Art Moderne.

Notable homes: Probably the most historic is the Frame Vernacular home at 401 29th St. Pioneer Elbridge Gale arrived here in the 1880s and constructed a log cabin that used to sit at what is now the intersection of 29th Street and Poinsettia Avenue.

Gale homesteaded much of Old Northwood, and his log cabin is said to have been incorporated into the house. It was relocated when Dixie Highway was constructed.

In 1916, local contractor W.O. Newlon purchased the house. David Dunkle, a local attorney and mayor of West Palm Beach from 1920-21, built the 1922 Frame Vernacular house at 501 30th St. Dunkle was a partner in the Pinewood Development Co., which developed Old Northwood. The house is now the Hibiscus House Bed & Breakfast.

Prominent architects John Volk, William Manley King and Henry Stephen Harvey designed some of the houses in Old Northwood. Volk designed the homes at 440, 505, 511, 512 and 561 32nd St.

Brandon Kruse/The Palm Beach Post

Taylor Jones/The Palm Beach Post

Ray Graham/The Palm Beach Post

Raleigh Hill and Colin Raynor became neighborhood activists in the 1980s after buying former Mayor David Dunkle's 1922 house at 501 30th St. in Old Northwood. While fighting crime and the city's neglect, the two men helped usher in the historic-preservation movement in West Palm Beach. Along the way, they created the Hibiscus House B&B.

Arches let in light and air on the sleeping porch of Villa Mimosa, one of five Mediterranean Revival homes in Old Northwood designed by Palm Beach architect John Volk.

The Hisbiscus House pool (above) and detail of fountain (left).

Colin Raynor and Raleigh Hill have decorated their home with antiques to give guests a feeling for what West Palm Beach was like in the early 1920s.

The living room of Villa Mimosa, which owner Terry Marince has left almost exactly as it was when Volk designed the house in 1926.

A baronial front door with barred window is one of Villa Mimosa's treasures. Twisted cast-stone columns flank the front door, near the original courtyard fountain.

The exterior of Terry Marince's home, Villa Mimosa.

Richard Graulich/The Palm Beach Post

Retired teacher Alice Moore stands in front of her 1917 historic home on Fourth Street. Moore is the adopted daughter of Dr. Alice Frederick Mickens, a West Palm Beach civil-rights leader.

Brandon Kruse/The Palm Beach Post

724 N St., a 1909 Dutch Colonial in Grandview Heights.

Lannis Waters/The Palm Beach Post

The main streets of the Mango Promenade district are actually sidewalks. Garages are in the rear, along alleys.

6. Northwest

Named to National Register of Historic Places in 1992; became local historic district in 1993

Beginnings: One of the first areas settled by black residents, Northwest was segregated from the 1920s to the 1960s.

Architectural styles: American Foursquare, Bahamian Vernacular, Shotgun, Mission, American Bungalow.

Notable homes: The house built in 1917 at 801 Fourth St. was owned by Dr. Alice Mickens, a philanthropist and educator. West Palm Beach's first black architect, Hazel Augustus, designed the 1924 Payne Chapel African Methodist Episcopal Church at 801 Ninth St. At the corner of Eighth Street and Division Avenue is another 1920s church, Tabernacle Missionary Baptist, founded in 1893 in Palm Beach.

7. Grandview Heights

Became local historic district in 1995; named to National Register of Historic Places in 1999

Beginnings: Established in 1910 because of its high elevation, Grandview Heights is one of West Palm Beach's oldest neighborhoods. Developed for the middle class, most of the homes were constructed from 1914-1947. Many were demolished in 1989 for the development of CityPlace.

Architectural styles: Craftsman/Bungalow, Vernacular, American Foursquare, and Mediterranean and Mission Revival.

Notable homes: West Palm Beach architect and Mayor Henry Stephen Harvey built the house and garage at 733 New York Ave.

8. Mango Promenade

Became local historic district in 1995; named to National Register of Historic Places in 1999

Beginnings: Developed from 1915-1940, Mango Promenade was one of the first neighborhoods established south of downtown.

Architectural styles: Craftsman/Bungalow, Colonial Revival, American Foursquare, Mediterranean Revival, Mission Revival, Monterey, Queen Anne, Prairie, Dutch Colonial, Vernacular.

Notable details: This neighborhood features two pedestrian zones: Orange Court, which runs east from Olive Avenue; and Mango Promenade, which links Dixie Highway to Olive Avenue.

Just south of downtown West Palm Beach, 296 Vallette Way is one of the Wood-Frame Vernacular homes built in Mango Promenade shortly after the turn of the 20th century. Today, many homes house students from Palm Beach Atlantic University.

Lannis Waters/The Palm Beach Post

Linda Cullen, a neighborhood activist and longtime member of the Flamingo Park Neighborhood Association, is only the second owner of her 1925 Flamingo Park home.

Damon Higgins
The Palm
Beach Post

Taylor Jones/The Palm Beach Post

The house at 701 Flamingo Drive (above, left) was designed by Harvey and Clarke architects for Alfred Comeau, who also commissioned the firm to design the Comeau Building, West Palm Beach's first "skyscraper." Red tiles line the roof of Katherine Kress' Flamingo Park house (above, center). Greg and Rebecca Weiss stand outside their historic 1924 home in Flamingo Park (right).

Richard Graulich/The Palm Beach Post

9. Flamingo Park

Became local historic district in 1994; named to National Register of Historic Places in 2000

Beginnings: Flamingo Park's original name was High Ridge Park because of the sand ridge running through the middle of the area. In 1891, the Florida Pineapple Co. bought the property but failed.

The area then went to the Model Land Co. in 1907 and finally was sold to M.E. Gruber for $240,000 in 1921. Gruber sold the land to the Royal Palm Realty Co. for $360,000.

When the boom went bust, Farmers Bank and Trust and Gruber repossessed the subdivision. With only 16 houses built, Gruber continued the development, adding 79 homes in the mid-1920s. More homes were added in the 1950s and '60s.

Architectural styles: Mediterranean Revival, Mission.

Notable homes: Alfred Comeau, financier of the 10-story Comeau Building on Clematis Street, lived in the 1924 Mediterranean-style house (designed by Harvey and Clarke) at 701 Flamingo Drive.

10. El Cid

Became local historic district in 1993; named to National Register of Historic Places in 1995

Beginnings: Before being developed during the Land Boom of the 1920s, El Cid was devoted to pineapple farming. The Phipps family developed the El Cid subdivision.

Architectural styles: Mediterranean and Mission Revival, Monterey, Colonial Revival, Art Moderne, Vernacular, Bungalow.

Notable homes: Some El Cid homes were designed by the county's top architects, such as Maurice Fatio, William Manley King, Henry Stephen Harvey and Louis Phipps Clarke, and Belford Shoumate.

One of West Palm Beach's early attorneys, Charles C. Chillingworth, lived in the Mediterranean-style house at 257 Granada Road. His 26-year-old son, Curtis E. Chillingworth, the youngest judge to be appointed in 1922, lived at 221 Dyer Road.

(On orders from Municipal Judge Joseph Peel, Curtis Chillingworth and his wife, Marjorie, were murdered in 1955.)

Ralph Norton, founder of the Norton Museum of Art, and his wife, Ann, lived in a Mediterranean-style home at 253 Barcelona Road. Architect Marion Syms Wyeth redesigned it into a Monterey style.

The 1925 Mediterranean-style home at 245 Valencia Road was used in 1989 for Burt Reynolds' television series *B.L. Stryker*. Jerome Wideman, a Palm Beach County attorney and judge, owned the house.

Uma Sanghvi/The Palm Beach Post

A Flagler, an astronaut and, apparently, a Florida panther all spent time in Joyce and John (left) Raymond's El Cid house. It was built in 1924 around an atrium (above). In the late 1950s the house was owned by Jean Flagler Matthews, Henry Flagler's granddaughter. Later, former astronaut Scott Macleod owned it — and may have had something to do with the big cat, possibly a Florida panther, seen lapping up pool water in an undated videotape found in the house.

The garden behind 265 Granada Road, one of El Cid's loveliest Mediterranean Revival homes. The historic home is known as "Double Dog" for the dog statues flanking the front gate.

Lauren Llacera (left), outside her El Cid home, which a Chicago magazine in 1928 declared was architecturally perfect. Little has changed inside since that time, including the two-story living room.

11. Prospect Park/Southland Park

Became local historic district in 1993

Beginnings: Originally part of a four-subdivision plat that included Prospect Park, Southland Park, Monceaux and El Cid Court, this area was developed from the 1920s-1940s for affluent Northerners and businessmen. It features medium to large lots and mostly two-story homes.

Architectural styles: Mediterranean Revival, International, Tudor Revival, Dutch Colonial, Neoclassical, Colonial Revival, Prairie, Art Moderne, Craftsman/Bungalow, Monterey, American Foursquare.

Notable details: The north end has an unusual design of street patterns, similar to Prospect Park in Brooklyn, with a public park with a fountain at the center of the neighborhood.

Photos by J.D. Vivian/The Palm Beach Post

This Colonial-Revival house is at 229 Edgewood Drive in Prospect Park/Southland Park.

12. Vedado-Hillcrest

Became local historic district in 2007

Beginnings: The 50-acre Vedado-Hillcrest subdivision was developed during the 1920s (only a few survive from the '20s) and during the post-World War II era.

Architectural styles: Mission, Spanish Colonial, Mediterranean Revival, Minimal Traditional, Minimal Ranch, Split-Level, Contemporary.

Notable details: This district includes three blocks of the Hillcrest subdivision. In the 1980s, most Hillcrest homes were moved or demolished for expansion of Palm Beach International Airport.

This Mission-Revival house is at 926 Paseo Andorra in the Vedado-Hillcrest Historic District. This home was built in 1925.

13. Central Park

Became local historic district in 1993

Beginnings: Once known as the Estates of South Palm Beach, Central Park was developed in 1919 as an exclusive neighborhood with sidewalks and a dock on Lake Worth at what is now Southern Boulevard.

The history of the district dates to the 1880s, when James W. Copp paid more than $300 for the land with money he borrowed from a friend.

Architectural styles: Central Park is a mix of mostly Mission-Revival and Frame Vernacular homes, with two small business areas, on Southern Boulevard and Dixie Highway.

This Mission-Revival house is at 217 Walton Blvd. in the Central Park Historic District.

14. Belair

Became local historic district in 1993

Beginnings: Started as an 1890s pineapple plantation, Belair became a residential community in the 1920s. Richard Hone owned the plantation and built a Frame Vernacular house (211 Plymouth Road) in 1895. In 1902, Hone was murdered by an unknown assailant who fired through a window.

Hone's wife sold the property to George Currie, who sold it to William Ohlaber, who platted the subdivision and built a house at 205 Pilgrim Road.

Architectural styles: Mediterranean Revival, Mission Revival, and Frame and Masonry Vernacular.

Notable homes: The Hone house was bought by Max Brombacher in 1947 and is still owned by the family.

This Mission-Revival house is at 244 Pilgrim Road in the Belair Historic District.

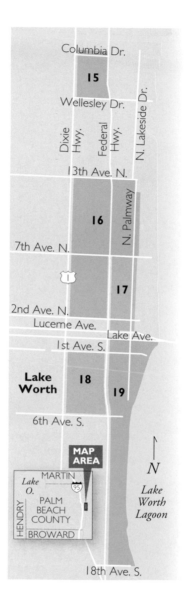

Gary Coronado/The Palm Beach Post

Scott Eller with Boo Boo in front of their home at 322 Cornell Drive in College Park.

15. College Park

Became local historic district in 1999; named to National Register of Historic Places in 2001

Beginnings: Platted in 1924 by the Edgeworth Realty Co., the College Park neighborhood became a development for the middle to upper class. It grew in two stages: first during the 1920s Land Boom, then during the post-World War II era.

Architectural styles: The earliest architecture in College Park is the Mediterranean-Revival and Mission styles of the Land Boom era. Construction stopped after the boom and resumed after the war. Post-war styles include Minimal Traditional, Masonry Vernacular and Ranch.

Notable details: Developers laid out narrow lots so that homeowners had to buy two lots to have enough land to construct homes. Streets are named after colleges and universities.

16. Northeast Lucerne

Became local historic district in 2002

Beginnings: Developed mainly from the 1920s Land Boom through the post-World War II years.

Architectural styles: Frame Vernacular.

Scored plaster walls give this home at 232 N. M St. a charmingly eccentric appeal.

Eliza Gutierrez/The Palm Beach Post

A restored Craftsman-style bungalow at 222 North Palmway in the Old Lucerne Historic District.

230 North Lakeside (left) and 226 North O Street, both in Old Lucerne, are examples of the city's quaint cottages, often built for winter visitors but now home to permanent residents.

Photos by Eliza Gutierrez/The Palm Beach Post

17. Old Lucerne

Became local historic district in 1999; named to National Register of Historic Places in 2001

Beginnings: Former slaves and early pioneers Samuel and Fannie James homesteaded this area in the late 19th century. The Palm Beach Farms Co. purchased the property and subdivided it for sale. Homes date from 1913-1949.

Architectural styles: Frame and Masonry Vernacular, Mission, Mediterranean Revival, Craftsman, Art Moderne, Colonial Revival, Tudor Revival, Ranch, Neoclassical.

18. Southeast Lucerne

Became local historic district in 2002

Beginnings: Developed mainly from the 1920s Land Boom through the post-World War II years.

Architectural styles: Small, Frame Vernacular homes.

Notable detail: The urban look of some of the streets comes from development in the 1920s-1930s.

1999, The Palm Beach Post

Some historians believe this home at 315 S. L St. is where Lake Worth's first settlers, Samuel James and his wife, Fannie, are buried. James may have been a freed slave, although accounts differ.

1999, The Palm Beach Post

2007, Palm Beach Post

The 1925 Gulfstream Hotel is a downtown Lake Worth landmark. Now closed, it was bought in 2005 by Ceebraid-Signal Corp., the owner of Palm Beach's Brazilian Court hotel.

Designed by one of Addison Mizner's draftsmen, this 1925 house was originally called "La Florentia." But ever since a previous owner gave it to his wife on her birthday in 1954, it's been known as "The Birthday Cake Castle."

19. South Palm Park   *Became local historic district in 2000*

Beginnings: After the Palm Beach Farms Co. bought this land from early pioneer settlers Samuel and Fannie James, it was platted by 1913 for speculative development.

Architectural styles: Frame and Masonry Vernacular, Mission, Mediterranean Revival, Craftsman, Colonial Revival, Art Moderne, Minimal Traditional, Monterey, Ranch.

Notable details: The historic Gulfstream Hotel, at the east end of Lake Avenue just before the bridge, is a Boom-era six-story Mediterranean-Revival structure.

The architectural firm of G. Lloyd Preacher and Co. in Atlanta designed the hotel, which overlooks the Intracoastal Waterway. The Gulfstream was added to the National Register of Historic Places in 1983.

DELRAY
BEACH

Photos by Taylor Jones/The Palm Beach Post

Classic wooden cottages painted bright colors, like this one (above) near the Del-Ida Park district; and 1114 Vista del Mar (above, right), reflect Delray Beach's history as a beach resort. During the 1930s and 40s, artists and writers rented many of the small homes, creating a winter arts colony.

20. Del-Ida Park

Became local historic district in 1988

Beginnings: The planned residential community of Del-Ida Park was platted in 1923 and built from the 1920s-1940s.

Architectural styles: Mediterranean and Mission Revival, Bungalow, Minimal Traditional, Frame Vernacular.

Notable details: Distinctive for its odd layout: Streets are arranged diagonally with some triangular lots; others have curved corners.

2004, The Palm Beach Post

118 Dixie Blvd. in the Del-Ida Park Historic District.

Taylor Jones/The Palm Beach Post

J.D. Vivian/The Palm Beach Post

OLD SCHOOL SQUARE: The Hunt House, now owned by the Delray Beach Historical Society, was built on Northeast Fifth Avenue for farmers Horace and Rae Hunt. Horace also started the city's first commercial fishing business. Originally built in 1908 as a vernacular farmhouse, it was later "modernized" into the Bungalow style. In 2007, the house was moved to 111 N. Swinton Ave. in the Old School Square neighborhood.

MARINA HISTORIC DISTRICT: 60 Palm Square is an example of the dazzling number of architectural styles on display in the Marina Historic District, which began as part of the city's winter resort colony. The neighborhood's shaded street are the result of a former plant nursery on the site.

J.D. Vivian/The Palm Beach Post

WEST SETTLERS: During segregation, the former La France Hotel at 140 N.W. Fourth Ave. was the only place African Americans could stay in Delray Beach. Now it's housing for senior citizens.

J.D. Vivian/The Palm Beach Post

WEST SETTLERS: The West Settlers neighborhood was home to many of the city's African-American pioneers. This Mission Revival-style home at 170 N.W. Fifth Ave. was home to educator Solomon D. Spady, the first principal of George Washington Carver High School. It's now the home of the Spady Cultural Heritage Museum.

J.D. Vivian/The Palm Beach Post

NASSAU PARK HISTORIC DISTRICT: Built between 1932 and 1964, the clapboard winter cottages in the Nassau Park Historic District evoke the seaside idyll that Delray Beach visitors enjoyed in the years surrounding World War II. Homes such as 1120 Nassau St. (above, left) and 1104 Nassau Street (right) reflect an era when Colonial Revival styles of architecture were in vogue.

21. Old School Square

Became local historic district in 1988; named to National Register of Historic Places in 1988

Beginnings: The area covers about 15 blocks of the original center of the city, and 101 of 176 buildings are 50 years or older. This historic district is named for the downtown area's Old School Square complex, which consists of Delray Beach's first school, a Masonry Vernacular building (1913); the Mediterranean-Revival high school building (1926); and its Mediterranean-Revival gymnasium (1926).

Architectural styles: Frame and Masonry Vernacular, Bungalow, Mission, Mediterranean Revival.

Notable home: The 1902 John Sundy House, 106 Swinton Ave., is a Frame Vernacular structure that was home to Delray's first mayor and was added to the National Register of Historic Places in 1992. It is now a restaurant and inn.

22. West Settlers

Became local historic district in 1995

Beginnings: First settled by black pioneers in 1894, the area originally was nicknamed "The Sands" because of the sandy soil. From 1895-1920, residents established a school, several churches and a Masonic lodge.

Architectural styles: Frame Vernacular dating back to 1905. In the 1920s, Bungalow and Mission-Revival architecture were added.

Notable homes: The 1926 Mission Revival-style house at 170 N.W. Fifth Ave. belonged to notable leader and educator Solomon D. Spady, who served as the first principal of George Washington Carver High School in Delray Beach. His home now houses the Spady Cultural Heritage Museum.

The two-story, 16-room La France Hotel at 140 N.W. Fourth Ave. was built in 1949 for owner Charles Patrick Jr. For years during segregation, the hotel was the only one serving African Americans. In 2007, the structure was converted into housing for senior citizens.

This 1902 frame farmhouse at 106 S. Swinton Ave. was built for John Sundy, Delray's first mayor, who served seven terms. This photo was taken beween 1910 and 1919.

Florida Photographic Collection

23. Marina

Became local historic district in 1988

Beginnings: Along the Intracoastal Waterway, this neighborhood was mostly developed from 1922-1943.

Architectural styles: Mediterranean, Mission, Colonial Revival, Monterey, Frame Vernacular, Art Moderne.

Notable details: Several buildings were designed by some of Palm Beach County's most distinguished architects, include Samuel Ogren Sr. (who also created designs for Nassau Park), John Volk and Gustav Maass.

24. Nassau Park

Became local historic district in 1988

Beginnings: On the barrier island, the quaint Nassau Park neighborhood was platted in 1935 and was Delray Beach's first planned residential area south of Atlantic Avenue.

Architectural styles: Minimal Traditional — to complement the island resorts on South Ocean Boulevard.

Notable detail: Developer R.C. MacNeil hired architect Samuel Ogren Sr. to design the first house in 1935 in the two-block neighborhood, which is centered on Jo-Jo Avenue (renamed Nassau Street by MacNeil).

*Damon Higgins
The Palm Beach Post*

Now on the National Register of Historic Places, Sundy House is a renowned restaurant and inn famous for its tropical gardens.

25. Pearl City

Became local historic district in 2002

Beginnings: Platted in 1915 for black workers, the neighborhood's name might have come from the street name Pearl, the name of the first child born there; or from a type of pineapple grown on nearby farms: the Hawaiian pearl. Alex Hughes, a community leader, bought one of the first lots.

Architectural styles: Frame and Masonry Vernacular.

Notable details: When the neighborhood was laid out, the streets were named Ruby, Pearl and Sapphire. Ebenezer Baptist Church is part of Pearl City. Of Pearl City's 32 structures, 18 were constructed from 1920-1965.

A clapboard home at 156 Pearl St. in the Pearl City Historic District.

Ebenezer Baptist Church, (left) 200 Ruby St., in the Pearl City Historic District, Boca Raton.

*J.D. Vivian
The Palm
Beach Post*

26. Old Floresta

Became local historic district in 1990

Beginnings: In the mid-1920s, architect Addison Mizner began building a small neighborhood with Spanish-named streets such as El Cid and Via Fernando for employees of the Cloister Inn. Mizner completed 29 homes and then went bankrupt.

Herman V. von Holst and a group of investors bought the subdivision and named it Old Floresta, which translates as "pleasant woods, groves or forest" or "delightful rural place." Boca Raton's first subdivision is only six blocks square.

Architectural styles: Spanish Mediterranean.

Notable homes: Mizner's brother, the Rev. Henry Mizner, lived in "Acacia," at 888 Oleander St.

Herman V. von Holst lived at 875 Alamanda St., which he named "The Lavender House." He later served on the Boca Raton Town Council from 1934-1948 and on the planning board from 1940-1953. In 1995, "The Lavender House" was listed on the National Register of Historic Places.

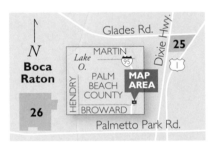

The 1926 Mediterranean-style residence at 801 Hibiscus St. (named to the National Register of Historic Places in 1992) was built for Fred Aiken, a prominent film producer and mayor of Boca Raton from 1929-1938.

Other notables who lived in Old Floresta include author Theodore Pratt; Philip "Don" Estridge, head of the team that developed IBM's personal computer; Thomas J. Fleming Jr., founder of First National Bank and Trust and Florida Atlantic University; and Nathaniel Weyl, a noted author who wrote *Red Star Over Cuba*.

The beautiful district originally had street names such as El Cid, Via Fernando, Aviz, Alvarado and Gonzalo. After von Holst and his group took over the property, the street names were changed.

In 1990, the City of Boca Raton designated Old Floresta as its first historic district.

J.D. Vivian/The Palm Beach Post

Architect Addison Mizner gave Old Floresta homes plain facades, saying simplicity was "...always dominant in the best of Spanish architecture." 875 Alamanda St. demonstrates how elegant simple rough stucco walls, wrought-iron balconies and red-tile roofs can be. Named "The Lavender House" by former owner Herman V. von Holst, who once owned the entire neighborhood, the house is on the National Register of Historic Places.

Addison Mizner's Old Floresta homes were originally quite small – in fact, some had dining alcoves instead of formal dining rooms. While many owners have built additions over the years, they have remained true to the homes' architectural roots. This home at 888 Oleander St., was once home to Mizner's brother.

Looking today much as it did in the 1920s (see house at upper left in real estate ad, right), 801 Hibiscus St. was the home of film producer, Fred Aiken, Boca Raton's mayor from 1929-1938. It's also on the National Register of Historic Places.

Fred and his wife, Lottie, share a smooch in front of their home.

Many of the homes at Boca Raton will make no claim to pretentiousness but in such houses as these the luxury of comfort, convenience and Florida's glorious climate, may be enjoyed at less cost than popular conception attaches to the acquisition of a home in Florida.

A 1920s real estate ad for Old Floresta. Another ad from the same era read "...I am the dream of a genius, the materialization of a magical mirage, I am the sun porch of America, I am Boca Raton in 1927."

Richard Graulich/The Palm Beach Post

As stately as a 1930s ocean liner, the Wagner House in West Palm Beach reflects the formal side of Streamline Moderne, a late version of Art Deco style. Porthole windows and an entry designed to look like stylized breaking waves reflect its original waterfront site, before Flagler Drive was constructed between the house and the Intracoastal Waterway.

A look at ART DECO

By BARBARA MARSHALL | The Palm Beach Post

Not all historical architecture looks to the past. Even seventy years after they were built, Art Deco buildings still seem modern, even futuristic.

Most of Palm Beach County's Art Deco homes and commercial structures were built between the stock market crash of 1929 and World War II, during the Streamline Moderne phase of the style. Built to resemble ships, machines, Mayan temples or geometry homework, they were a Depression-era expression of hope for the future.

Art Deco Society of the Palm Beaches

Original photographs of the Wagner home's interior show spacious rooms, decorated with furniture as streamlined as the architecture, set on polished terrazzo floors.

Wagner House
West Palm Beach

2631 South Flagler Drive is the largest Art Deco home in Palm Beach County, designed in 1937 by Belford Shoumate for Ralph and Edna Wagner. Shoumate was the area's best-known modernist architect, who designed everything from bus stations to Palm Beach mansions.

In 1999, current owners, Cheryl and Homer Marshman, added a guest house in the same formal Art Deco style.

Lake Worth

This is one of pair of identical houses built in 1939 on South Lakeside Drive in Lake Worth. Architect Edgar S. Wortman designed the waterfront Nautical Moderne homes with large porthole windows made of blue Depression glass.

Taylor Jones/The Palm Beach Post

The Wenger House, this hand-made 1940s Art Deco house near Boynton Beach, was the county's first to be placed on the National Register of Historic Places. Note the heart-shaped breakfast nook, part of its wonderfully wacky charm (below).

Wenger House *Boynton Beach*

Ruth and Ray Wenger must have been one wild and crazy couple.

The zany house they built themselves in an unincorporated pocket of Boynton Beach, finishing in 1948, is a math lesson in lines and circles, planes and angles – not to mention hearts, a symbol of their love.

It was also the first house in Palm Beach County to be placed on the National Register of Historic Places, thanks to lobbying by Linda Stabile, a retired college professor, who owns the house with her husband, Calvin Zimmer. With help from an artist friend, they painted the abstract forms with nine different colors of paint.

Taylor Jones
The Palm Beach Post

Brandon Kruse/The Palm Beach Post

Lake Theatre
Lake Worth

The Lake Theatre opened at 601 Lake Avenue in Lake Worth in 1939, designed by Roy A. Benjamin of Jacksonville. In the 1980s, the late Palm Beach art collector, J. Patrick Lannan, turned it into a gallery for his collection. After his death, philanthropists Bob and Mary Montgomery bought the building, creating the Palm Beach Institute of Contemporary Art, which closed in 2005.

Armory Art Center *West Palm Beach*

In 1939, architect William Manly King designed the National Guard Armory, built with Works Progress Adminstration funds which created jobs during the Great Depression. In addition to housing soldiers, it was at times a farmer's market, dance hall, and during the Cuban Mariel boatlift in the early 1980s, a temporary home to Cuban refugees.

It's now the home of the Robert and Mary Montgomery Armory Art Center gallery and school.

With research help from Sharon Koskoff of the Art Deco Society of the Palm Beaches and author of Art Deco of the Palm Beaches.

A ticket for a ride on Africa U.S.A's Jungle Train

2009
Florida East Coast Railway Station

1910

Lofthus 1898

2009 Lofthus underwater

Lofthus shipwreck

VOID

ADULT

432

VOID

AFRICA - U.S.A.
BOCA RATON - FLORIDA
JUNGLE TRAIN TO
Fare $1.09   Fed. Tax .16
TOTAL . . . . . $1.
● THIS TICKET VOID WHEN PUNC

LOFTHUS
Built in England in 1868, this 222-foot, three-masted barque originally was christened Cashmere. Acquired by a Norwegian firm and renamed, Lofthus was sailing with a cargo of lumber from Pensacola when she wrecked in 1898. The crew was saved, but the vessel was a total loss.

STATE UNDERWATER
ARCHAEOLOGICAL PRESERVE

A FLORIDA HERITAGE SITE

What's left of the Africa U.S.A.'s Watusi Geyser, Camino Gardens, Boca Raton

2009

1960
Africa U.S.A.'s Watusi Geyser

BOYNTON WOMAN'S CLUB

The Boynton Woman's Club was designed in the Mediterranean Revival style by the famous Palm Beach architect Addison C. Mizner. The Woman's Club is significant for both its architectural merit and contributions to the cultural development of Boynton Beach. The Club was built in 1925 as a memorial to the founder of the town, Major Nathan S. Boynton. Along with providing a social and civic community, it served as the town's

Boynton Woman's Club 2009

From 1951 until 1955, Palm Beach Junior College students went to school at Lake Park Town Hall (left). Built in 1927 when Lake Park was called Kelsey City, the Mediterranean Revival building retains its 1927 charm today (below).

Top photo from the Historical Society of Palm Beach County

A MAGICAL HISTORY TOUR

PALM BEACH COUNTY'S HISTORIC LANDMARKS

Landmarks as of April 1, 2009
Compiled by Richard A. Marconi, Historical Society of Palm Beach County
Photos by J.D. Vivian, The Palm Beach Post

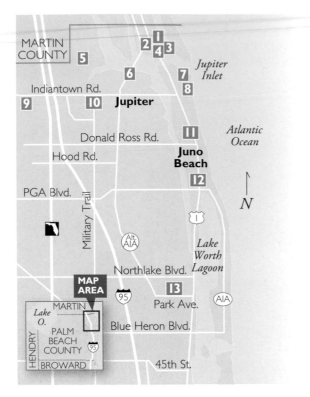

JUPITER

1. Jupiter Lighthouse

Marker is on the grounds of the lighthouse at the U.S. Coast Guard Station at Lighthouse Park, 500 Capt. Armour's Way

EXCERPT OF INSCRIPTION: Designed by George G. Meade, who served as the federal commander at Gettysburg. First lighted on July 10, 1860. It was dark during the War Between the States — its mechanism hidden by Southern sympathizers.

Jupiter Lighthouse was relighted on June 28, 1866. It has not missed a night in more than 100 years. One of seven early lighthouse keepers was James A. Armour. It has been operated by the U.S. Coast Guard since 1939.

2. Fort Jupiter and Jupiter Lighthouse

Marker is on the west side of U.S. 1, in front of the Northern Palm Beach County Chamber of Commerce, 800 N. U.S. 1

EXCERPT OF INSCRIPTION: Fort Jupiter was three miles west of here, along the Loxahatchee River. The fort was erected in January 1838 by troops establishing a base for operations during the Seminole Indian Wars.

3. "Dive Into History" (Año 1659)

Marker is on the grounds of Lighthouse Park, 500 Capt. Armour's Way

EXCERPT OF INSCRIPTION: These shipwrecked iron cannons and anchor were uncovered in July 1987, east of here, in 10 feet of water, off Jupiter Inlet. Archives and research link these maritime remains to the Spanish ship San Miguel de Archangel, bound for Spain; its last port was Havana, Cuba.

In December 1659, the San Miguel foundered and wrecked. The 33 surviving sailors lived with local Jeaga Native Americans until rescued by a vessel dispatched out of St. Augustine.

4. World War II U.S. Naval Housing Building

Marker is on the east side of the barracks building, which now houses the Loxahatchee River Historical Society and Museum, in Lighthouse Park, 500 Capt. Armour's Way

EXCERPT OF INSCRIPTION: The U.S. Navy constructed this building around 1939. Built as married men's quarters, the two-story wood-frame building had six two-bedroom apartments and a continuous screened first-floor porch facing the inlet. During World War II, Navy personnel lived in this building. One of their missions: to locate the German submarines torpedoing ships off Florida's coast. Most of the wood-frame structures were demolished, starting in 1958.

5. Tennessee Volunteers and Militia Camp

Marker is on the site of the Tennessee Volunteers and Militia Camp, Second Seminole War, next to 6264 Winding Lake Drive

EXCERPT OF INSCRIPTION: After the Second Battle of the Loxahatchee River, fought Jan. 24, 1838, the Tennessee Volunteers and Militia camped on this site.

"DIVE INTO HISTORY": These two cannons and the anchor date to 1659, when a Spanish ship foundered off Jupiter Inlet.

6. Sawfish Bay

Marker is in Sawfish Bay Park, 1133 N. Alternate A1A, about 25 yards north of the park's south end

EXCERPT OF INSCRIPTION: The waterfront location of today's Sawfish Bay Park played a major role in the prehistoric and historic settlement of the Jupiter area. First inhabited 5,000 years ago, this site provided access to an intricate transportation system within the Everglades. Marine life sustained these early peoples until contact with European diseases devastated the local population in the 1700s.

The earliest historic written record of human activity on the site was the Cabot Home, built by Frederick M. Cabot II in 1892. By 1894, this site had become the center of commerce when a railroad spur, which is still evident, connected the river community of Jupiter to the Northeastern United States.

The wharves, businesses, post office and warehouses that followed shifted the town west from the southern banks of Jupiter Inlet. The large "Cabot Oak" tree on the property is more than 200 years old.

7. Jupiter Inlet Midden I

Marker is in front of the DuBois House, in DuBois Park, 19075 DuBois Road

EXCERPT OF INSCRIPTION: Jupiter Inlet Midden I is an ancient shell mound built by Jeaga Indians. This shell mound is the site of the village of Hobe, where Jonathan Dickinson and his fellow shipwreck survivors were held captive by the Jeaga Indians in 1696.

8. U.S. Jupiter Life-Saving Station

Marker is on the west side of State Road A1A, next to the wooden fence, in Carlin Park, 400 S.R. A1A

EXCERPT OF INSCRIPTION: Marks the location of the U.S. Jupiter Life-Saving Station, 1886-1896. Some of the men who staffed the station remained and started families here, including John R. Carlin, Harry DuBois and Daniel Ross.

9. Powell's Battle

Marker is at the entrance to Riverbend Park, 9060 Indiantown Road

EXCERPT OF INSCRIPTION: On Jan. 15, 1838, during the Second Seminole War, the Seminoles met and defeated U.S. forces in the First Battle of the Loxahatchee River.

Trying to end the war, Maj. Gen. Thomas Jesup had brought troops to South Florida, including the Water-borne Everglades Expeditionary Unit, commanded by Navy Lt. Levin Powell. Powell's unit entered the southwest fork of the Loxahatchee River in small boats. They were led by a captured Seminole woman.

SAWFISH BAY: The "Cabot Oak" is more than 200 years old.

Loxahatchee River Historical Society

Then: JUPITER INLET MIDDEN I: The DuBois House sits atop an ancient shell mound. Harry DuBois built the house for his bride, Susan, who wanted to live on the inlet so she could watch boats pass.

Now: Built in 1898 of pine and cypress, the historic DuBois House still looks much the same as in the earlier, undated photo above. The home was recently renovated. Shown in both photos is the home's south side.

Marching west, they were suddenly met by musket fire from Seminole warriors. Powell's small group, overpowered by a much larger force of Seminole swamp fighters, suffered severe casualties but escaped.

10. Military Trail

Marker is about 20 feet north of the intersection of Military Trail and Indiantown Road

EXCERPT OF INSCRIPTION: After the second Battle of the Loxahatchee, fought on Jan. 24, 1838, during the Second Seminole War (1835-1842), Maj. Gen. Thomas S. Jesup directed Maj. William Lauderdale, commander of the Tennessee Battalion of Volunteers, to cut a trail south from Fort Jupiter to Fort Dallas (in present-day Miami). Lauderdale's mission: to capture Seminoles who had escaped the Loxahatchee battle.

Lauderdale, with about 200 Tennessee Volunteers and the U.S. Third Artillery Regiment, marched south, following the Seminoles. To avoid swamps and lagoons, they kept to the higher coastal pine ridge that extended from Fort Jupiter to the New River.

Lauderdale built a fort (in present-day Fort Lauderdale) and moved on to Fort Dallas. Because Lauderdale and his troops had blazed a trail covering 63 miles through overgrown terrain in only four days, the route was designated "Lauderdale's Trail." It was used for military operations through the end of the Third Seminole War, in 1858, and became known as "Military Trail." It is now a major commercial thoroughfare.

JUNO BEACH

11. Celestial Railroad

Marker is on the west side of Ocean Drive, along the seagrape hedge, on the east side of Loggerhead Park

EXCERPT OF INSCRIPTION: Erected as a memorial to the pioneers of this section of Florida. On this spot, the Celestial Railroad, which once connected Jupiter with Juno, is crossed by Federal Highway.

PALM BEACH GARDENS

12. Old Dade County Courthouse

Marker is about two-10ths of a mile north of the intersection of PGA Boulevard and U.S. 1, on the east side of the road, along the sidewalk

EXCERPT OF INSCRIPTION: About 300 feet east of this marker stood the Dade County Courthouse, in Juno, the county seat from 1890-1900. Juno — since abandoned — was the southern terminus of the Celestial Railroad, which ran from Jupiter to Juno; and was the northern terminus of the boat and connecting stage-coach line to Miami.

LAKE PARK

13. Lake Park Town Hall

Marker is in front of the town hall, 535 Park Ave.

EXCERPT OF INSCRIPTION: Boston entrepreneur Harry S. Kelsey founded Kelsey City in 1921. He envisioned his town as a winter retreat for wealthy Northerners. The town hall was built of stuccoed brick and clay tile, in Mediterranean Revival style.

In 1939, the town changed its name to the Town of Lake Park.

MILITARY TRAIL: In 1838, U.S. troops searching for Seminole warriors hacked a 63-mile trail through overgrown terrain — in four days.

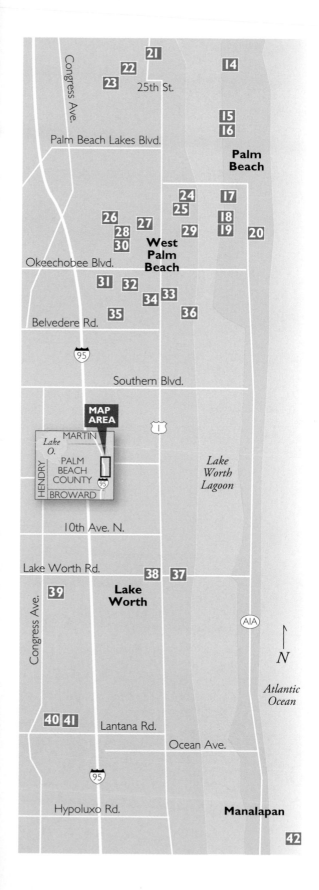

Meghan McCarthy/The Palm Beach Post

DUCK'S NEST: The oldest standing house in Palm Beach is Duck's Nest, built in 1891. Some parts were assembled in New York, then delivered by barge to the site.

PALM BEACH

14. First Post Office in Palm Beach

Marker was on North Lake Trail, north of Plantation Road; marker has been missing since the hurricanes of 2004 or 2005

EXCERPT OF INSCRIPTION: Just to the east is the site of the first post office between Fort Jupiter and Miami. It was in the home of the first postmaster, Valorus O. Spencer, appointed in 1880.

15. Duck's Nest

Marker is at 545 N. Lake Trail; the house is next door to the old Bethesda-by-the-Sea Episcopal Church

EXCERPT OF INSCRIPTION: This is the oldest standing house in Palm Beach, built in 1891 by Henry Maddock as his home. Parts of the house were assembled in New York and delivered by barge to Palm Beach, as this was the only means of transportation.

16. Old Bethesda-by-the-Sea Episcopal Church

This was the second Episcopal church and is now a private residence; marker is on North Lake Trail, about 175 yards north of Tangier Avenue

EXCERPT OF INSCRIPTION: East of this marker is the Episcopal Church of Bethesda-by-the-Sea, built in 1894. The last service was held Easter Sunday, April 12, 1925. Most worshippers came by boat, as there was no roadway.

17. Royal Poinciana Hotel

Marker is on Cocoanut Row, south of the Flagler Memorial Bridge

EXCERPT OF INSCRIPTION: The Royal Poinciana Hotel, built by Henry Flagler, opened Feb. 11, 1894. One of the

OLD BETHESDA-BY-THE-SEA EPISCOPAL CHURCH: Built in 1894 and now a private home, this was the second Episcopal church in Palm Beach. Most worshipers arrived by boat. The last service was held on Easter Sunday, April 12, 1925.

Historical Society of Palm Beach County

SEA GULL COTTAGE: Henry Flagler's first winter home.

largest wooden structures in the world at the time, the six-story hotel cost more than $1 million, accommodated 2,000 guests and faced Lake Worth. It was demolished in 1936.

18. Sea Gull Cottage — Palm Beach's Oldest House

Marker is next to the Royal Poinciana Chapel, 58 Cocoanut Row

EXCERPT OF INSCRIPTION: Built in 1886 by R.R. McCormick, a Denver railroad developer, Sea Gull Cottage was bought by Henry Flagler in 1893 and became Flagler's first winter residence in Palm Beach. The Royal Poinciana, Flagler's first resort hotel in Palm Beach, was next to Sea Gull Cottage. In 1984, the cottage was moved and is now the Parish House of the Royal Poinciana Chapel

19. Royal Poinciana Chapel

Marker is on the north side of the chapel, 60 Cocoanut Row

EXCERPT OF INSCRIPTION: This interdenominational chapel was created in 1884 under the auspices of the Home Missionary Society of

EPISCOPAL CHURCH OF BETHESDA-BY-THE-SEA: The bell tower of the church, built in 1926.

the Congregational Church by the Rev. A.B. Dilley. The current church building, erected on a site donated by Henry M. Flagler and later enlarged, opened in December 1895.

20. Episcopal Church of Bethesda-by-the-Sea

Marker is on the church grounds

at Barton Avenue and North County Road

EXCERPT OF INSCRIPTION: The original church, built in 1889 on the eastern shore of Lake Worth, was the first Protestant church building in Southeast Florida. The current edifice was erected in 1926.

WEST PALM BEACH

21. Old Northwood Historic District

Marker is in front of the house at 3510 Spruce Ave.

EXCERPT OF INSCRIPTION: In 1884, the Rev. Elbridge Gale retired to the area that became Old Northwood. He was the first to build a cabin on the west side of Lake Worth. Gale grew mango trees, one of which provided the seeds for what became the well-known Haden mango.

During the Florida Land Boom of the 1920s, the Pinewood Development Co., led by David F. Dunkle, purchased 400 acres, and 173 structures were built between 1921 and 1929 for upper-middle-class families. Notable architects included John Volk. One of the district's most unusual features is its network of alleys that allow access to garages and utilities.

22. Evergreen Cemetery

Located at 2825 N. Rosemary Ave., just north of 25th Street; marker is attached to the right side of the arched entry wall

EXCERPT OF INSCRIPTION: Evergreen Cemetery is the final resting place of some of the city's most influential African-American citizens — and of many lesser-known African-Americans who contributed to the development of West Palm Beach. In 1916, the Evergreen Cemetery Association was formed, with M.J. Gildersleeve as president.

Prior to the creation of this cemetery, African-Americans had been buried in what was identified only as "Colored Cemetery" on South Dixie Highway. African-Americans were denied burial in Woodlawn Cemetery, West Palm Beach's municipal cemetery, until 1966.

Those buried in Evergreen Cemetery include Dr. T. Leroy Jefferson, the city's first black physician; J.W. Mickens, an early educator; Henry Speed, a real estate investor; and Dr. J.R. Vickers, a physician.

The City of West Palm Beach assumed responsibility for Evergreen Cemetery in 1987.

23. Hurricane of 1928 Mass Burial Site

Site and marker are at the intersection of 25th Street and Tamarind Avenue

EXCERPT OF INSCRIPTION: On Sept. 16, 1928, a hurricane roared ashore near Jupiter Lighthouse and traveled west to Lake Okeechobee, destroying hundreds of buildings and causing millions of dollars in property damage. The storm also killed 1,800 to 3,000 people when the Lake Okeechobee dike collapsed, flooding the populated south side of the lake.

EVERGREEN CEMETERY: The wife of T. Leroy Jefferson is among those buried in this cemetery, now operated by the City of West Palm Beach. He was the city's first black physician.

About 1,600 victims were buried in a mass grave in Martin County. In West Palm Beach, 60 white victims were placed in a mass grave in Woodlawn Cemetery; 674 black victims were buried in a mass grave in the city's pauper's burial field at Tamarind Avenue and 25th Street.

24. Dade County State Bank Building (1893)

Marker and building (now the Palm Beach High School Museum) are at the corner of Flagler Drive and Fourth Street

EXCERPT OF INSCRIPTION: Dade County State Bank, 1893, donated to the City of West Palm Beach through the West Palm Beach Bicentennial Committee in 1976 by Mrs. Crystal Eggert in memory of her late husband Johnny.

DADE COUNTY STATE BANK BUILDING (1893): The building now houses the Palm Beach High School Museum.

25. Old St. Ann's Church

Marker is on a concrete base between the St. Ann Parish Office and St. Ann Catholic Church, 310 N. Olive Ave.; across the street from the Palm Beach County Governmental Center

EXCERPT OF INSCRIPTION: Dedicated March 15, 1898, on the southeast corner of Rosemary Avenue and Datura Street, St. Ann Church was moved to this site, donated by Henry Flagler, in 1902. It served the Catholic community until 1913, when the new church was dedicated. The old church was then used as the forerunner of what became St. Ann School, built in 1925. St. Ann Catholic Church is the oldest Catholic church and parish in the Diocese of Palm Beach.

26. Seaboard Air Line Railway Station

Marker is in the station courtyard, 203 S. Tamarind Ave.

EXCERPT OF INSCRIPTION: The Seaboard Air Line Railway Station has played an important role in the history of West Palm Beach and Palm Beach County. It is an example of early 20th-century railroad architecture in the Mediterranean Revival style. Harvey & Clarke, the largest architectural firm in Palm Beach County in the 1920s, designed the facility.

The station opened with the arrival of the Orange Blossom Special on Jan. 25, 1925. It was the flagship station of the entire Seaboard line, which ran from

Coleman to Homestead. Amtrak began passenger service here in May 1971, and the Tri-County Commuter Rail Authority began passenger service from here to Miami in January 1989. After being renovated, the station was rededicated in 1991.

27. Clematis Street Commercial Historic District

Marker is in front of 521 Clematis St., west of Dixie Highway

EXCERPT OF INSCRIPTION: For more than 100 years, Clematis Street (named after the clematis flower) has been the primary retail street in West Palm Beach. The eastern end of Clematis Street developed first, but by 1916, the business district began to expand west. During the real estate boom of the 1920s, new buildings were erected in the 500 block of Clematis Street — which boasts the highest concentration of historic buildings in the downtown retail area.

28. Palm Beach Junior College (now Palm Beach Community College)

Marker is on the southwest side of 812 Gardenia St., on the grounds of Dreyfoos School of the Arts

EXCERPT OF INSCRIPTION: This building housed Palm Beach Junior College, Florida's first public community college, when it was established here in 1933. William Manly King, a West Palm Beach architect, designed this building in the Mediterranean Revival style. Three students were in the first graduating class, in 1936.

The college outgrew these facilities and moved in 1948 to Morrison Field, a U.S. Army Air Base, renovated to accommodate the influx of students during peacetime. In 1955, the college moved to its current site at 4200 Congress Ave. in Lake Worth. It is now called Palm Beach Community College. The historical marker was dedicated in 1993 to commemorate the 60th anniversary of PBCC.

PALM BEACH JUNIOR COLLEGE: When, in 1933, PBJC was established, classes were held here. Only three students were in its first graduating class, in 1936.

29. Flagler Park

Marker is in Centennial Square, at the intersection of Clematis Street and Narcissus Avenue

EXCERPT OF INSCRIPTION: Flagler Park, formerly known as City Park, has been an important public space in West Palm Beach since the founding of the community. West Palm Beach was laid out in 1893 as a grid pattern of streets running north-south and east-west. The only variation was at the eastern end of Clematis Street, where two angled, short streets branched off to create a triangular, public common area.

30. Central Schools — Palm Beach High School

Marker is on the arch in front of the Dreyfoos School of the Arts at Sapodilla Street and Hibiscus Avenue, just west of CityPlace.

EXCERPT OF INSCRIPTION: In 1886, the first settlers on the island of Palm Beach built a one-room school, which still stands on the island, in Phipps Ocean Park, as the oldest school in Southeast Florida. Students were transported by boat until the school closed in 1901 and was relocated to West Palm Beach.

Other one-room schools also had

been built along the shores of Lake Worth. As the number of first- through 12th-grade students increased, so did the need for a central school that also had a high school. In 1901, Palm Beach High School opened on Dixie Highway between Clematis and Datura streets. The schools were moved to this site in 1908 and were known as the "School on the Hill."

After the last graduating class in 1970, the school was renamed Twin Lakes High School. The buildings were restored in 1997. The school is now called the Alexander W. Dreyfoos Jr. School of the Arts.

31. Stub Canal Turning Basin

Marker was in Howard Park on Parker Avenue, south of Okeechobee Boulevard; marker has been missing since the hurricanes of 2004 or 2005

EXCERPT OF INSCRIPTION: The Stub Canal Turning Basin represented an important link between West Palm Beach and the agricultural communities around Lake Okeechobee. In the late 19th century, Florida began draining the Everglades and the Lake Okeechobee basin to provide water transportation routes and to create farmland from swamps.

In 1905, when the Board of Drainage Commissioners authorized

Historical Society of Palm Beach County

Then: CENTRAL SCHOOLS: This 1917 postcard shows the so-called "Central Schools." The new schools were needed due to rapid population growth.

Now: DREYFOOS SCHOOL OF THE ARTS: The campus, restored in 1997, is an arts high school.

construction of a canal network, a connection to West Palm Beach was not included. In 1911, local businessman George Currie petitioned Gov. Albert Waller Gilchrist for a canal from Lake Okeechobee to Lake Worth.

Known as the West Palm Beach Canal, the 40-mile channel was completed in 1917. By 1918, an extension, or stub, was constructed to bring the canal directly into the West Palm Beach business district. The city built shipping facilities and this turning basin. Until 1925, the stub canal served as a dependable route for passenger travel and for the shipment of produce from, and provisions to, the western agricultural communities.

32. Grandview Heights Historic District

Marker is in the median at the intersection of Florida Avenue and Palm Street

EXCERPT OF INSCRIPTION: In response to the heavy influx of new residents into South Florida at the turn of the century — and the introduction of the automobile — local developers and real estate agents purchased less-expensive land outside the West Palm Beach downtown area and developed the first speculative suburbs.

Platted during the 1910s and 1920s as three subdivisions for working-class families, Grandview Heights is one of the earliest attempts at southwestern expansion of the city. Originally stretching from Okeechobee Boulevard to Park Place, the property was chosen because of its relatively steep topography (for South Florida). It was considered a desirable place to live because it was less than a mile from downtown and provided a view of the Everglades.

The neighborhood consists primarily of Bungalow-type homes that reflect mainly the Craftsman and Mission styles, both popular during the 1920s Florida Land Boom.

33. Pioneer Memorial Park

Marker is at Jefferson Road and Dixie Highway, just north of the Norton Museum of Art. A marble monument just north of the marker has a plaque containing the names of male pioneers who settled on the shores of Lake Worth from 1873 to 1893.

EXCERPT OF INSCRIPTION: The Lakeside Cemetery Association (LCA) was formed in 1891 by a group of pioneer families. In 1895, the LCA bought this site to use as a private cemetery. From 1895 until about 1920, pioneer families buried their dead in this cemetery. More than 200 of the earliest and most prominent citizens of what is now Palm Beach

FIRST SCHOOLHOUSE: Lake Worth's City Hall Annex stands on the site of the first schoolhouse in the city. Built in 1912, the wood-frame school measured 24 by 36 feet. The initial enrollment: 24 pupils.

County were buried here.

Initially, African-Americans as well as white pioneers were buried here — very unusual for that time. In 1902, the LCA purchased 2 acres located two blocks to the south to serve as a separate cemetery for African-Americans.

In 1914, Henry M. Flagler donated, to the City of West Palm Beach, the land immediately to the west of this site, on which Woodlawn Cemetery was created as West Palm Beach's municipal cemetery.

Most of the pioneers buried on this site were exhumed and re-interred in Woodlawn Cemetery. However, as many as 40 were not removed and remain buried on this site today.

34. Flamingo Park

Marker is at Park Place and Dixie Highway

EXCERPT OF INSCRIPTION: This site was originally the southeast corner of an 80-acre parcel bought by George L. Marsteller for $100 in 1884.

Two blocks north, between South Dixie Highway and South Olive Avenue, the Lakeside Cemetery Association platted Lakeside Cemetery in 1893. It operated as a racially integrated facility — unusual for the time.

In 1902, the association bought 2 acres from West Palm Beach to serve as a separate cemetery for African-Americans. The association platted 190 lots and, by 1913, had interred about 100 people. Maps of the era called it "Colored Cemetery."

By 1921, unable to maintain the cemetery, the Lakeside Cemetery Association donated it to the city, which converted it to a public park.

35. Flamingo Park Historic District

Marker is in the traffic circle at the intersection of Georgia Avenue and Flamingo Drive

EXCERPT OF INSCRIPTION: Built on the highest coastal ridge between downtown West Palm Beach and Miami, Flamingo Park was platted on May 17, 1921, and soon became home to many prominent citizens.

Almost 80 building permits were issued in 1923. The Alfred Comeau House, 701 Flamingo Drive, was built in 1924. Comeau was a prominent businessman who also built one of the first West Palm Beach skyscrapers, in 1925.

The Florida Land Boom era is represented here in a concentration of architecturally significant homes, built from 1921 to the mid-1930s, in a variety of styles, including Mission, Mediterranean Revival, Art Moderne and Craftsman/Bungalow.

36. El Cid Neighborhood

Marker is at the intersection of Pershing Way and Flagler Drive

EXCERPT OF INSCRIPTION: In 1876, Benjamin Lanehart homesteaded land that is now the north end of El Cid. Lanehart started the first commercial pineapple operation in the area, but by the turn of the 20th century, competition and plant diseases had ruined the pineapple business.

The El Cid neighborhood was a product of the 1920s Florida Land Boom. Beginning in 1921, Pittsburgh socialite John Phipps, the son of Andrew Carnegie's partner in U.S. Steel, began developing the former pineapple fields. He named his development El Cid after the medieval Spanish hero

Rodrigo Diaz de Vivar, whose Moorish enemies called him "Cid," an Arabic word meaning "lord."

LAKE WORTH

37. First Schoolhouse

Marker is at 414 Lake Ave. at City Hall Annex (the Museum of the City of Lake Worth is in this building)

EXCERPT OF INSCRIPTION: This is the site of the first schoolhouse erected in the Town of Lake Worth, in 1912 — a wood-frame building of 24 by 36 feet. Initial enrollment was 24 pupils. In February 1916, the building was replaced by one made of concrete. It is now the City Hall Annex.

38. First Town Hall

Marker is at Lake Worth City Hall, 7 N. Dixie Highway

EXCERPT OF INSCRIPTION: This is the site of a building erected in 1915 as the first town hall of Lake Worth, which was chartered in 1913. Civic and social affairs before 1915 had been conducted in a wooden building nearby. J.W. Means was serving as mayor in 1913; on May 2, 1914, James M. Love became the first elected mayor.

39. Palm Beach Junior College (now Palm Beach Community College)

Marker is in front of the Administration Building, PBCC, 4200 Congress Ave.

EXCERPT OF INSCRIPTION: The first public junior college was instituted by the Palm Beach County School Board during the Great Depression to make higher education available to local high school graduates unable to meet the expenses of attending school away from home.

Palm Beach Junior College admitted its first students in 1933. Its goal: to provide the first two years of college studies. Soon it also offered career and vocational education, as well as adult-education programs. In 1947, Palm Beach Junior College began to receive state assistance under new legislation. Beginning in the 1950s, the junior-college program in Florida began to expand.

The educational goals of Palm Beach Junior College served as a model for Florida's developing community-college program.

LANTANA

40. Coastal Patrol Base No. 3, Civil Air Patrol (1942-1943)

Marker is at the entrance to Palm Beach County Air Park (Lantana Airport), 2633 Lantana Road

EXCERPT OF INSCRIPTION: Coastal Patrol Base No. 3 at Lantana Airport was one of three experimental bases established on the East Coast of the United States to assist with anti-submarine patrols. Civilian aviators flew missions up to 60 miles out to sea between Palm Beach and Cape Canaveral in search of German U-boats.

In May 1942, near Cape Canaveral, Lantana Civil Air Patrol members Marshall E. Rinker and Tom Manning found a U-boat stranded on a sand bar and called for a military bomber. But the U-boat freed itself and escaped before the plane arrived.

The incident led to the arming of the small civilian planes that CAP used. The experimental units were so successful that 18 more were established in the U.S., with four more bases in Florida.

During the unit's term of service (in August 1943, anti-submarine patrols were transferred to the military), its members flew 18,712 hours; 1,546,500 miles; and made 14 attacks, dropping 20 bombs on suspected U-boats.

The patrols also saved the lives of numerous mariners by attacking and driving off U-boats and by directing rescue boats to burning and sinking ships. In 1948, 53 members of the unit received the U.S. Army's Air Medal.

41. Owen H. Gassaway Jr. Airfield

Marker is on the ground, next to the tall clock, north of the entrance to Palm Beach County Air Park (Lantana Airport), 2633 Lantana Road

EXCERPT OF INSCRIPTION: As a boy in the 1930s, Owen H. Gassaway flew model airplanes at Morrison Field, now Palm Beach International Airport. During World War II, he served with Gen. Patton's Third Army as a tank mechanic.

Owen H. Gassaway Jr., as depicted on a marker at Lantana Airport. He served during World War II as a tank mechanic.

Lantana Airport, built in the 1940s, was home to Lantana Flying Service, under the leadership of Owen, who had earned a "pilot" rating in many aircraft. He later established Florida Airmotive Inc., a charter service.

Gassaway encouraged and supported young people's interest in aviation, donating his time and funds. His involvement with the Civil Air Patrol became legendary. Lantana Airport — of which Owen H. Gassaway Jr. Airfield is a part — has played a crucial role in aviation history in South Florida.

MANALAPAN

42. Lofthus (a shipwreck)

Marker is underwater, on the site of the wreck, about 175 yards offshore of Manalapan and about a mile north of Boynton Inlet, in 15 to 20 feet of water

EXCERPT OF INSCRIPTION: Built in England in 1868, this 222-foot, three-masted barque originally was named Cashmere. Acquired by a Norwegian firm and renamed, Lofthus was sailing with a cargo of lumber from Pensacola when she wrecked in 1898. The crew members were saved.

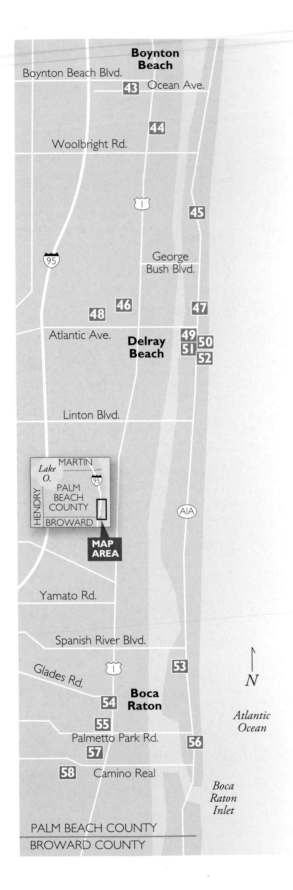

BOYNTON BEACH

43. 1913 Boynton Elementary School

Marker is in front of the Schoolhouse Children's Museum, 129 E. Ocean Ave.

EXCERPT OF INSCRIPTION: Boynton Elementary School/Boynton School's original staircase and floors were built with Florida pine. On Sept. 8, 1913, it opened; it was Boynton's only school for 14 years. The school housed 12 grades and had indoor plumbing; electricity was installed in the 1920s. It was used as a public school and for community activities until 1989.

During 1998 and 1999, the building underwent a $14 million restoration. On Nov. 29, 2001, it opened to the public as the Schoolhouse Children's Museum. Its mission: to encourage families to learn the history of Boynton Beach and Palm Beach County through interactive exhibitions and programs.

Boynton Beach Historical Society

Then: 1913: Boynton School housed all 12 grades.

Now: After a $14 million renovation, the former school reopened as a children's museum.

44. Boynton Woman's Club

The building and marker are at 1010 S. Federal Highway (U.S. 1)

EXCERPT OF INSCRIPTION: Designed in Mediterranean Revival style by Palm Beach architect Addison Mizner, the Boynton Woman's Club is significant for its architectural merit and its contributions to the cultural development of Boynton Beach. The club was built in 1925 as a memorial to town founder Maj. Nathan S. Boynton.

In addition to providing a social and civic center for the community, the club served as the town's first public library and as the first meeting place for several churches and service organizations. The second floor features a grand ballroom and a stage.

GULF STREAM

45. North Ocean Boulevard

Two markers are on North Ocean Boulevard. The southern marker is on the east side of State Road A1A, about one-10th of a mile north of George Bush Boulevard; the northern marker is on the west side of S.R. A1A about 20 yards south of Sea Road

EXCERPT OF INSCRIPTION: In 1992, North Ocean Boulevard (State Road A1A) in the Town of Gulf Stream was designated as a State Historic Scenic Highway in order to preserve the last remaining Australian-pine canopy and the original character and beauty of the 1920s-era S.R. A1A.

S.R. A1A through Gulf Stream, one of the earliest and most scenic highways in Palm Beach County, officially opened in 1916. In the 1920s, fast-growing Australian pines were planted on both sides of the road in South Florida to act as a windbreak. Soon, a canopy over S.R. A1A developed, adding greatly to the beauty, charm and character of the area. The canopy has been destroyed, with the exception of that remaining in Gulf Stream.

DELRAY BEACH

46. Florida East Coast Railway Station

Building and marker are at 200 N.E. First St.

EXCERPT OF INSCRIPTION: This 40-foot freight section is all that remains of the old railroad station constructed in 1896 by the Florida East Coast Railway Co. The station originally stood on the east side of the tracks, one block south of Atlantic Avenue.

The original 100-foot-long Stick-style building (characterized by flat board banding and other ornamentation, applied in geometric patterns to the exterior) contained ground-level waiting rooms and a raised freight area. The

Then: BOYNTON WOMAN'S CLUB: The club was designed by Palm Beach architect Addison Mizner, shown on-site.

Now: The club today (below).

Boca Raton Historical Society

Bob Shanley/The Palm Beach Post

NORTH OCEAN BOULEVARD: Scenic State Road A1A through Gulf Stream has the last remaining Australian-pine canopy. In the 1920s, the trees were planted along S.R. A1A in South Florida as a windbreak.

station was expanded in the 1920s; another addition was constructed in the 1940s. Passenger service was discontinued in the 1960s.

The passenger area was razed, but public outcry to save the station stopped its total destruction. In 1968, the remaining freight section was split in two and moved. The 1920s portion was destroyed by fire in 1984, but the original 40-foot area of the 1896 station was moved west of the city and used as an office and for storage.

In 1994, this surviving section of the historic station was purchased by the Delray Beach Historical Society, which had the building moved to its current location and restored.

47. Orange Grove House of Refuge No. 3 (1876-1927)

Marker is on State Road A1A, north of Atlantic Avenue, across from Berkshire by the Sea, 126 S.R. A1A

EXCERPT OF INSCRIPTION: One of several houses of refuge built by the U.S. Treasury Department between Cape Canaveral and Cape Florida for rescue and sustenance of the shipwrecked. Named for a wild sour-orange grove nearby.

H.D. Pierce, the first keeper, arrived with his family in May 1876. Here, on Aug. 15, 1876, was born the first white girl between Jupiter and Miami: (Mrs.) Lillie Pierce Voss. The area's first post office was located in the house from 1888 to 1892; Mrs. Annie E. Andrews served as postmaster. The house burned on March 2, 1927.

48. B.F. James and Frances Jane Bright Park

Delray Beach Historic Sites

Marker is on the east side of Northwest Fifth Avenue, about 100 yards north of Atlantic Avenue; it dedicates five historic sites in the Delray Beach area

EXCERPT OF INSCRIPTION: The City Commission of Delray Beach, in recognition of these organizations' contributions to the city's cultural development, designated these

FIRST PRESBYTERIAN CHURCH FELLOWSHIP HALL: This building housed Gibson Memorial Baptist Church from 1924-28. It now serves as the church's Fellowship Hall. The white cross to the left was on the roof until blown down by Hurricane Frances in 2004.

locations as historic sites on April 11, 1989.

1895: School No. 4, Delray Colored, located at this site (Fifth Avenue Northwest)

1896: Greater Mt. Olive Missionary Baptist Church, 40 N.W. Fourth Ave.

1897: St. Paul African Methodist Episcopal Church, 119 N.W. Fifth Ave.

1898: Free and Accepted Masons, Lodge 275, 85 N.W. Fifth Ave.

1911: St. Matthew Episcopal Church, 404 S.W. Third St.

Late in the 19th century, a group of black settlers established a community in this area, which became part of the Town of Linton and, later, the City of Delray Beach. These hardy pioneers established the cultural organizations necessary to foster education, fellowship and spiritual needs, despite the difficult environmental conditions and isolation.

49. First Presbyterian Church Fellowship Hall

Marker is in front of the church, 33 Gleason St.

EXCERPT OF INSCRIPTION: An orange grove, once on this site, played a role in the early development of Delray Beach. Until 1876, a sour-orange grove was the only distinguishable characteristic within 60 miles of a sparsely inhabited subtropical wilderness between Lake Worth and Biscayne Bay.

Settlers around 1894-95 who saw the grove — partly surrounded by a rock wall — speculated that the trees had been planted by Seminoles, Minorcan immigrants or Spaniards. But its origin remains unknown.

The grove became the site of this Mediterranean Revival-style building, the Gibson Memorial Baptist Church, in 1924. After the real estate crash of 1926 and the hurricanes that followed, the congregation ran into financial difficulties. After the 1928 hurricane, Presbyterians rented the church and later bought it.

After a new sanctuary was built in 1977, the original church became the Fellowship Hall for First Presbyterian Church.

Bob Shanley/The Palm Beach Post

J.B. EVANS HOUSE: Now a nature center, this is one of the few remaining Resort Colonial Revival-style homes on Delray's beach.

AFRICA U.S.A.: Giraffes and camels were only a few of the unusual offerings at this popular Boca Raton attraction.

Life magazine

SOCIABLE SAFARI at Africa U.S.A. in Boca Raton, Fla. is surrounded by friendly giraffes and camels coming up to greet Jeep-loads of young sightseers and forage for food. Visitors usually tour park on small train. Africa U.S.A. opened six years ago with one giraffe, now has 13, the biggest herd in the U.S.

50. Beach Donation

Marker is along sidewalk on the east side of South Ocean Boulevard (State Road A1A) at the intersection of South Ocean Boulevard and Bay Street

EXCERPT OF INSCRIPTION: Sarah Gleason, Belle G. Dimick Reese and Ella M. Dimick Potter dedicated this beach to the public in 1899.

51. J.B. Evans House, also known as the Sandoway House Nature Center

Marker is in front of the Sandoway House Nature Center, 142 S. Ocean Blvd. (State Road A1A)

EXCERPT OF INSCRIPTION: The Sandoway House Nature Center was designed as a home by Samuel Ogren Sr. in 1936 for Delray Beach winter resident J.B. Evans, a retired produce broker. It is one of the last remaining Resort Colonial Revival-style houses in Delray Beach.

Significant architectural elements include board-and-batten siding, the open second-story porch and the original double-hung windows. Built during the Great Depression, the only

ostentation is the cathedral window on the south side. The dune garden and native plantings surrounding the house retain the oceanfront setting that was typical of the neighborhood in the 1930s.

In 1998, the house opened to the public as a nature center.

52. Delray Wreck

Marker is next to the sidewalk, at the beach, on State Road A1A, just north of Casuarina Road

EXCERPT OF INSCRIPTION: The old shipwreck known as the Delray Wreck rests at the bottom of the ocean in 25 feet of water about 150 yards offshore of the south end of Delray Beach's municipal beach. The wreck, which is broken and scattered into five sections, has long been one of the most popular diving spots in South Florida.

The S.S. Inchulva was grounded by a hurricane on Sept. 11, 1903. The 386-foot steel-hull British steamship was bound for Newport News, Va., from Galveston, Texas, carrying wheat, cotton, lumber and a crew of 28 men. The storm struck at about 5 p.m.,

tossing the ship and causing the cargo to shift. Steering became impossible, so the captain put out both anchors, but to no avail.

The anchors parted, and the Inchulva grounded. At dawn, the battered crew members saw that land and a town were just a short distance away.

By noon, all the remaining men except Capt. G.W. Davis and two mates had landed on shore in a hastily built raft. They found hot food and coffee at Chapman House, a local hotel, where many of Delray's residents had taken shelter during the storm.

BOCA RATON

53. Barefoot Mailmen

Marker is on the west side of State Road A1A in Spanish River Park, at the entrance to the south tunnel

EXCERPT OF INSCRIPTION: Along this beach in the 1880s and early 1890s walked U.S. mailmen on their 66-mile journey between Palm Beach and Miami. The trip required three

Boca Raton Historical Society

Then: (OLD) BOCA RATON TOWN HALL: The men of the Boca Raton Fire Department (*circa* 1926).

Now: The building is home to the Boca Raton Historical Society.

days each way; they passed this spot the second day. They walked barefoot at the wet surf line, the hardest surface, with their mail bags and shoes over their shoulders. One of them, James E. Hamilton, drowned trying to cross Hillsboro Inlet.

54. Pearl City Historic District (1915)

Four bronze plaques for Pearl City are west of Federal Highway, along the north side of Ruby Street (Northeast 12th Street)

EXCERPT OF ONE INSCRIPTION: In April 1915, an auction was held to sell lots on the land that became Pearl City. The 15-acre parcel was advertised as "a brand-new colored city." The origin of the name Pearl City is uncertain.

Various explanations include: It was named after the first black child born in the community; or for the community's major street; or for the Hawaiian pearl pineapple, processed in a shed on the site.

55. (Old) Boca Raton Town Hall

Building and marker are at 71 N. Federal Highway; the Boca Raton Historical Society is now located here

EXCERPT OF INSCRIPTION: Designed in Mediterranean Revival style by architect Addison Mizner and completed by architect William E. Alysmeyer, Boca Raton Town Hall opened in April 1927 as the city's first municipal building, fire station and police department.

In 1976, the Boca Raton Historical Society opened its office here. Several municipal offices occupied the building until 1983. In 1984, the old town hall was restored to its original architectural design by the Boca Raton Historical Society for use as a local-history museum and archives.

56. Sanborn Wall

Marker is on the south side of Sanborn Wall, on the south side of The Beresford condominium, 350 S. Ocean Blvd.; marker is next to the sidewalk on the east side of State Road A1A

EXCERPT OF INSCRIPTION: On this spot in June 1942, spies from German U-boats landed and occupied Dr. William Sanborn's home, built in 1937. The submarines, deployed during World War II as part of Hitler's Operation Drumbeat, torpedoed tankers and freighters traveling the East Coast shipping lanes and carrying supplies to the United States and to England. Twenty-four ships were sunk

off the coast of Florida — 16 between Cape Canaveral and Boca Raton.

57. Florida East Coast Railway Depot

Marker is on the north side of the railway depot, 747 S. Dixie Highway

EXCERPT OF INSCRIPTION: Henry Flagler's Florida East Coast Railway reached, in 1895, what later became Boca Raton, providing an essential link in the extension of the system south to Miami and the Florida Keys and fostering tourism and agricultural development in the area.

The railway depot was built in 1930 by Clarence A. Geist, a utilities magnate from Philadelphia, who wanted to carry out Addison Mizner's vision in Boca Raton.

Geist's plans included building a passenger depot on the FEC Railway line to provide service for guests of the Boca Raton Club, the crown jewel of Mizner's plans for Boca; and to serve as a gracious entrance to the community.

To ensure that the station would be designed in a style to complement the Boca Raton Club, Geist donated the land and rights to the FEC Railway. FEC architect Chester Henninger designed the depot in Mediterranean Revival style, with a gently pitched gable roof, stucco walls, and arched loggias with delicate spiral columns. The FEC Railway passenger station operated until 1968. The station was restored in 1989.

58. Africa U.S.A.
Marker is on the ground, in a park on the south side of the street in the Camino Gardens community, 400 Camino Gardens Blvd.

EXCERPT OF INSCRIPTION: On this site in 1953, John D. Pedersen and his family established Africa U.S.A., a major Boca Raton tourist attraction for nearly a decade.

The 350-acre site drew 2,000 visitors daily to view the park's camels, giraffes, elephants, and other exotic animals and plants.

The Watusi Geyser erupted hourly from the rock, still visible in the lake, throwing — each minute — 1,000 gallons of water 160 feet into the air. Dedicated by the Camino Gardens Association in March 2003 to commemorate the 50th anniversary of Africa U.S.A.

LANDMARKS:WEST

CANAL POINT

59. Conners' Toll Highway
Marker is on the west side of U.S. Highway 441/U.S. Highway 98, just north of Third Street

EXCERPT OF INSCRIPTION: Before 1923, travel into or out of the Lake Okeechobee area was accomplished only by boat or canoe. In the early 1920s, W.J. Conners, a New York winter visitor, bought 4,000 acres of undeveloped muck land near this site. Developing the land required building a road.

After obtaining approval from both houses of the Florida Legislature, he set about building Conners Highway, using dredges and a temporary railroad. Work began in October 1924 and was completed in June 1925. Cost of the 52-mile road: $1.8 million. The road was hailed as an engineering marvel and contributed greatly to the growth of the area.

Though the toll was only 3 cents a mile, the average daily amount collected was $2,000. Conners died on Oct. 5, 1929. The road eventually was sold to the State of Florida for $660,000.

BELLE GLADE

60. Everglades Research
Marker is at the Everglades Research and Education Center, 3200 Palm Beach Road (County Road 880)

EXCERPT OF INSCRIPTION: The Everglades Experiment Station was established on this site in 1921 to help pioneering families deal with the challenges of living and working in the area. Soil-nutrient deficiencies and two major hurricanes, in 1926 and 1928, hindered early research. Nevertheless, University of Florida faculty in agronomy, horticulture, soil science and animal science began to develop solutions that made Everglades agriculture possible. That research continues.

EVERGLADES RESEARCH: In 1924, the "subsidence post" was driven down 9 feet to bedrock; its top was level with the soil surface. More than 6 feet of soil has been lost since. Shown is Norman Harrison, information-technology specialist at the Everglades Research and Education Center.

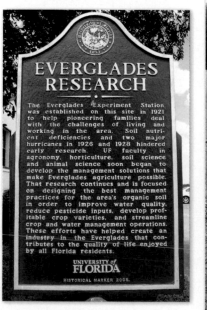

The start of the fifth annual Marathon of the Palm Beaches, in December 2008, on Flagler Drive in West Palm Beach. The Chamber of Commerce of the Palm Beaches founded the race. The inaugural event in 2004 — it included a 26.2-mile marathon, a half-marathon and a relay — drew 3,600 contestants. The 2008 event attracted 7,104.

Photo by Greg Lovett
The Palm Beach Post

This section of the 30-foot-high, 143-mile-long Herbert Hoover Dike (far left) protects the City of Pahokee. The original earthen dike, built around 1915, failed during hurricanes in 1926 and 1928 — killing thousands and flooding towns and farmland in the Glades. Construction on a new, stronger system of levees began in 1930. The dike was dedicated on Jan. 12, 1961, by former President Hoover himself.

Greg Lovett
The Palm Beach Post

An aerial view of RiverWalk (left), a DiVosta development north of Okeechobee Boulevard in West Palm Beach. During the past 40 years, the company founded by Buzz DiVosta has built about 40,000 homes in Florida, from the quaint houses at Abacoa in Jupiter to the suburban spreads in RiverWalk and Wellington's VillageWalk.

Richard Graulich
The Palm Beach Post

All roads to the FUTURE ...

The Scripps Research Institute's Jupiter facility is adjacent to Florida Atlantic University's campus. The La Jolla, Calif.-based Scripps is the world's largest private — and nonprofit — biomedical-research facility. What will Palm Beach County taxpayers, who supported Scripps Florida with about $200 million, derive from its presence? Jobs, prestige — and a jump-start on our second century. Scripps now employs about 280 people. By December 2013, according to its agreement with the state, Scripps' payroll must reach a minimum of 545.

Richard Graulich
The Palm Beach Post

... begin with bold steps in the PAST >

The Lake Worth High School Class of 1924 had 16 students, including Signie Hagg (back row, fourth from left); Harold Emerine (front row, fifth from left, wearing "LWHi" sweater); and Pete Garnett (far right). In those days, buildings lacked air conditioning and heat. When temperatures dropped during the winter, teachers often took their classes to the roof so that the sun and black tar would warm them. If the temp dropped below 50, the school closed.

Take your place in the scrapbook

Ineria Hudnell Collection

This is Industrial High School's "first all-student football team," the 1930-31 Maroon Devils. Industrial High School for black students opened in 1917. "Its purpose was to teach African-Americans about vocations, agriculture and trades — industrial education," says Samuel Bruce McDonald, who graduated from the West Palm Beach school in 1946. "At Industrial, there was a nice sense of developing student leadership," adds McDonald, who lives in Lake Worth. He served as president of his senior class. In 1969, he became the county's first black principal at a predominantly white school, Boca Raton Junior High. McDonald retired in 1984 as superintendent of south county schools. Charles H. Stebbins Jr. taught social studies at Industrial High until, in 1941, he filed a lawsuit against the Palm Beach County school district asking for equal pay for black teachers. He was fired. Eventually, the courts ruled for equal pay.

# of Palm Beach County's first century ...

Soldiers — or, possibly, members of the National Guard — on the steps of the Palm Beach County Courthouse in 1917. No one, including the dog (front row, third from right), is identified. On Nov. 11, 1993 — Veterans Day — Palm Beach County had 36 surviving World War I vets. When Al Ross, 101, died on April 30, 2003, something else died with him: Barracks 507, a WW I veterans group based in West Palm Beach. Al had been its last member.

Historical Society of Palm Beach County

OUR HISTORY, OUR HOME ... discover it for yourself

AT THE PALM BEACH COUNTY HISTORY MUSEUM

The oldest artifact: This coral spearhead, which dates to 1000 B.C., is the oldest object in the museum. It was found, along with other Native American artifacts, in fall 2007 when levels in Lake Okeechobee dropped to historic lows.

Nothing screams Palm Beach County history like ...

A GIANT MOSQUITO!

A buzzing, looming, 3-foot-wide fiberglass mosquito!

If you think that the supersize skeeter flying above exhibits inside the Richard and Pat Johnson Palm Beach County History Museum exists just to get your attention, take note: Mosquitoes were so thick back in Palm Beach County's pioneer days that swarms of the critters could kill cows.

Our paradise was once a treacherous wilderness, and one of America's last frontiers.

To learn more, visit the history museum, housed inside the restored 1916 courthouse. The museum opened in March 2008 after the historic courthouse was painstakingly restored for $18.9 million.

< The historic courtroom looks like it's from a scene in 'To Kill a Mockingbird': It features dark wood floors and a mezzanine (where blacks had to sit during the years before integration). No photographs could be found of Palm Beach County's original courtroom, so REG Architects created a design based on other courtrooms from the same time period. The DeSoto County Courthouse in Arcadia best represents our courthouse and courtroom.

The eagle watches all: No close-up photos could be found of the original eagle that presided over the entry of the 1916 courthouse, so sculptors re-created an imposing eagle. It was hand-carved from five pieces of limestone and weighs 8 tons (left, middle).

The benefactors: Richard and Pat Johnson (left, bottom), both from prominent West Palm Beach families, donated $1.25 million toward the history museum.

"Having the courthouse restored to its original condition, and having the yard so that you can sit there, admiring it in its glory around the modern buildings, gives all of us a sense of stability," said Dick Johnson.

His father, Richard Green Johnson Jr., worked for Palm Beach County Tax Collector Stetson Sproul and ran a family farm in Pahokee. Pat Johnson's father, Clyde Seaton, was a prominent insurance man.

What: Richard and Pat Johnson Palm Beach County History Museum   **Where:** 300 N. Dixie Highway, West Palm Beach   **Admission:** Free

ACKNOWLEDGMENTS

Harvey E. Oyer III speaks at the grand-opening ceremony for the restored 1916 courthouse in March 2008. Oyer's great-great-grandfather, H.D. Pierce, arrived here in 1872, making the area's second homestead claim. He was assistant keeper of the Jupiter Lighthouse and among the settlers who named the area "Palm Beach."

Lannis Waters/The Palm Beach Post

First, credit for this book goes to Harvey E. Oyer III, past chairman of the Historical Society of Palm Beach County.

He's a fifth-generation Palm Beach Countian who puts his energy where his roots are.

Without Harvey's passion for our past, it's safe to say that the 1916 courthouse would not have been restored; the Richard and Pat Johnson Palm Beach County History Museum would not be a local attraction; and even the fourth-grade curriculum about Palm Beach County history would not exist.

Harvey became an early proponent for this book, getting Michael Bornstein of the county's Centennial Commission onboard.

Bornstein is Lantana's town manager — and such a history buff he dresses up as the "barefoot mailman" at least once a year. (Bornstein even draped himself in silicone so a sculptor could create a "barefoot mailman" mannequin for the history museum.)

The Centennial Commission — with encouragement from County Commission Chairman Jeff Koons and Commissioner Karen Marcus, who grew up in North Palm Beach — sanctioned *Palm Beach County at 100: Our History, Our Home* as the county's official centennial book.

Oyer also got the historical society's team of researchers onboard — plus former CEO Loren A. Mintz, current Chairman Mark B. Elhilow and the wonderful and creative Kae Jonsons, director of development, who helped us shape and sell our vision.

Our thanks go, too, to the staff of *The Palm Beach Post*, whose names appear here and throughout the book. Special thanks to former Vice President of Marketing and Community Relations Gale Howden, who was instrumental in the launch of this book and our two previous history books — *Our Century* in 2000 and *Pioneers in Paradise: West Palm Beach, the First 100 Years*, in 1994.

We also owe a debt of gratitude

to several longtime supporters of the community, including Dame Celia Lipton Farris, one of our generous centennial sponsors, and the curators and archivists at the county's local historical societies, who were generous with their wisdom and photographs. Nobody knows the fascinating and quirky details of our diverse communities like these historians, who prize local photo albums and other treasures more than gold.

We also thank Tony Ellison of Ellison Graphics for his patience and beautiful printing work, and his customer service manager Gina O'Brien for reading every page. Gina's excitement kept us energized.

Finally, we thank the thousands of *Palm Beach Post* readers who shared their memories with us. Hundreds of you will find your names and photos in these pages. All of you have our gratitude — and our shared devotion to our history and our home.

— *Jan Tuckwood, Editor*
Palm Beach County at 100: Our History, Our Home

THE PALM BEACH POST

Publishing coordinator:
Lynn Kalber

Researchers:
Niels Heimeriks
Michelle Quigley

Photo assistant:
Gwyn Surface

Design assistants:
Jenna Lehtola
Jessica Jordan

Palm Beach Life:
Joyce Reingold
Yolanda Cernicky

Promotion and marketing:
Laura Cunningham
Scott Velozo
Jeanne Martin

Ferne Morgan
Charlee Nolan

Sales and advertising:
Judy Green
Jackie Cesaretti
Sami Forzano
Peggy Mazza
Donna Taylor
Dori Foster
Jorge Gomez
Kelly Dryden
Gloria Hirjak
Marta Abreu

Printing coordinator:
Christy Davis

Production:
Rob Fersko
Sandy Fink
Christopher Huhn

HISTORICAL SOCIETY OF PALM BEACH COUNTY

Harvey E. Oyer III
Past Chairman

Mark B. Elhilow
Chairman of the Board

Loren Mintz
President and CEO (retired)

Debi Murray
Director of Research and Archives

Richard A. (Tony) Marconi
Curator of Education

Steven Erdmann
Curator of Collections and Exhibits

Kae Jonsons
Director of Development

INDEX
Ever A. Olano

LOCAL HISTORIANS

- Susan Gillis, Boca Raton Historical Society
- Dottie Patterson, Delray Beach Historical Society
- Robert Ganger, Delray Beach Historical Society
- Vera Farrington and Daisy Fulton, Spady Museum
- Janet DeVries, Boynton Beach City Library
- Beverly Mustaine, Museum of the City of Lake Worth
- Ineria Hudnell
- Everee Jimerson Clarke
- Bill Williams
- Karen Davis, author of *Public Faces — Private Lives: Women in South Florida, 1870s-1910s*
- Donald Curl
- Babe Davidoff
- Linda Corley
- Pat Crowley
- Norman Harrison, information-technology specialist for the University of Florida's Everglades Research and Education Center, Belle Glade
- The late Dr. Joseph Orsenigo, curator of the Lawrence E. Will Museum, Belle Glade

FROM THE PALM BEACH POST: The staff of *Palm Beach County at 100: Our History, Our Home*. From left: Book designer Rebecca Vaughan, timeline writer Eliot Kleinberg, editor Jan Tuckwood, copy editor J.D. Vivian.

Photos by Damon Higgins/The Palm Beach Post

FROM THE HISTORICAL SOCIETY OF PALM BEACH COUNTY: Richard A. Marconi and Debi Murray pose inside the Richard and Pat Johnson Palm Beach County History Museum. They are major contributors to this book and to the Historical Society's ongoing connection to the community.

Index

'It was a Garden of Eden,
where the sky was bluer, the water clearer,
the flowers sweeter, the song of birds more musical
than anywhere else on the continent.
Could mortal woman ask for more?
...We did not.'

— MARION GEER, *in an 1896 journal.*
Mrs. Geer was among a group of pioneers who arrived on Palm Beach in 1876.
Then, this land was part of Dade County, which stretched from Jupiter to Miami
and had about 250 residents.
Palm Beach County was carved from Dade County in 1909.